TAINE'S WORKS.

Uniform Library Edition. 12mo, Green Cloth,
$2.50 per volume.

ENGLISH LITERATURE. 2 vols.

ITALY, ROME, AND NAPLES.

ITALY, FLORENCE, AND VENICE.

ON INTELLIGENCE. 2 vols.

LECTURES ON ART. First Series. Containing The Philosophy of Art ; The Ideal in Art.

LECTURES ON ART. Second Series. Containing The Philosophy of Art in Italy ; The Philosophy of Art in the Netherlands ; The Philosophy of Art in Greece.

NOTES ON ENGLAND. With Portrait.

NOTES ON PARIS.

A TOUR THROUGH THE PYRENEES.

(THE SAME. Illustrated by Gustave Doré. 8vo, cloth, $10.00 ; full morocco, $20.00.)

THE ANCIENT RÉGIME.

THE FRENCH REVOLUTION. 3 vols.

THE MODERN RÉGIME. Vol. I.

THE MODERN RÉGIME. Vol. II.

JOURNEYS THROUGH FRANCE.

ENGLISH LITERATURE. *With 28 portraits.* 4 vols. in box. *Cheaper Edition.* 8vo. $6.00.

ENGLISH LITERATURE. Condensed by John Fiske. One vol. 8vo, $1.40 net.

HENRY HOLT & CO., Publishers,

NEW YORK.

Notes on England

BY

H. TAINE

D.C.L. OXON., ETC.

TRANSLATED, WITH AN INTRODUCTORY CHAPTER, BY

W. F. RAE

Author of "Westward by Rail."

WITH A PORTRAIT OF THE AUTHOR.

NEW YORK
HENRY HOLT AND COMPANY
1885

DA
533
T313
1885

1024337

CONTENTS.

	PAGE
INTRODUCTORY CHAPTER, CONTAINING—	
1. A SKETCH OF M. TAINE'S LIFE AND CAREER	ix
2. AN OUTLINE OF HIS METHOD OF CRITICISM	xxx
3. COMMENTS UPON HIS OPINIONS AND WRITINGS	liv

CHAPTER		PAGE
I.	BOULOGNE TO LONDON BRIDGE	1
II.	SUNDAY IN LONDON. THE STREETS AND PARKS	9
III.	ST. JAMES'S PARK, RICHMOND, THE DOCKS, AND EAST-END	25
IV.	VISIT TO EPSOM AND TO CREMORNE GARDENS	37
V.	TYPICAL ENGLISH MEN AND WOMEN	47
VI.	ENGLISH GIRLS AND AUTHORESSES	82
VII.	ENGLISH MARRIAGES AND MARRIED WOMEN	94
VIII.	ENGLISH HOUSEHOLDS	109
IX.	ENGLISH SCHOOL BOYS AND SCHOOL LIFE	120
X.	LIFE AT THE UNIVERSITY	137
XI.	VILLAGES AND FARMHOUSES	153
XII.	LANDED PROPRIETORS AND ENGLISH GENTLEMEN	166
XIII.	MANSIONS, PARKS, AND GARDENS	177
XIV.	THE CLERGY	190
XV.	THE GOVERNING CLASSES AND THE GOVERNMENT	196
XVI.	RAGGED SCHOOLS, HOSPITALS, WORKHOUSES, AND THE VOLUNTEERS	205
XVII.	THE CONSTITUTION, THE HOUSES OF PARLIAMENT	218
XVIII.	THE CLUBS, THE BRITISH MUSEUM, THE CRYSTAL PALACE	229

CONTENTS.

CHAPTER	PAGE
XIX. STREET PREACHERS AND RELIGIOUS SENTIMENTS	234
XX. ARISTOCRATIC ASCENDENCY	240
XXI. SOCIETY AS DEPICTED BY "PUNCH"	244
XXII. SPORTING, POLITICAL, AND SOCIAL CARICATURES IN "PUNCH"	252
XXIII. INNS OF COURT, BARRISTERS, AND JUDGES	261
XXIV. THE THEATRES. LIVING IN LONDON	266
XXV. MANUFACTURES AND ARTISANS	272
XXVI. MANCHESTER AND LIVERPOOL	279
XXVII. ENGLISH WORKING MEN	286
XXVIII. SCENES IN MANCHESTER	300
XXIX. CHARACTERISTICS OF THE ENGLISH MIND	306
XXX. FRENCH WIT AND ENGLISH HUMOUR	320
XXXI. ENGLISH PAINTINGS AND ENGLISH PAINTERS	328
XXXII. MODERN PAINTERS AND RUSKIN'S CRITICISMS	335
XXXIII. ENGLISH POETRY AND RELIGION	344
XXXIV. A TRIP THROUGH SCOTLAND	356
XXXV. RETURN HOME. FRENCHMEN AND ENGLISHMEN	369

INTRODUCTORY CHAPTER.

LAST summer the University of Oxford resolved to confer upon Dr. Döllinger the honorary degree of Doctor of Civil Law. It was considered fitting that a famous and an accomplished Frenchman should be associated in the exceptional mark of respect paid to an erudite and illustrious German. Out of the numerous Frenchmen of eminence and renown who might with propriety have been chosen, M. Taine was unanimously selected.

Shortly afterwards, the publication of a series of papers, entitled "Notes on England," was begun in the columns of the Paris *Temps*. Wherever French newspapers circulate and the French language is read, these "Notes" attracted attention. They were quoted, commented on, praised, and criticised. Almost contemporaneously, a selection from them, translated into English, appeared in the columns of *The Daily News*. Wherever English is read, these translations furnished matter for talk and discussion; extracts from them were published by the Press of the United Kingdom, of the United States, of India, of Canada, of Australia; they were made the themes of leading articles; they were employed to point morals and to clench arguments. Again and again was the question put, "Who is M. Taine, what is his history, how has he learned to treat English topics with so much intelligence and effect?" The more enlightened and critical reader, whose acquaintance with current literature embraces what has been written in the *Athenæum*, the *Saturday Review*, the *Spectator*, the *Examiner*, the New York *Nation*, the *Edinburgh* and *Westminster Reviews*, could have been at no loss in returning an answer to this inquiry, and in stating with considerable precision the rank of M. Taine as a writer, and his general character as a critic and a philosopher. Yet every newspaper reader is neither perfectly well informed nor personally laborious in adding to his defective stock of accurate information. Nor, as far as M. Taine is concerned, would a natural or acquired thirst for useful instruction be speedily and completely slaked by taking the recognised short cut to the fountain of knowledge, and turning to a dictionary of contemporary biography. The best modern biographical dictionary contains very meagre and unsatisfactory details about the doings and life of M. Taine. It is my present intention to supply the more interesting and important particulars which are lacking. By weaving them into a brief sketch of M. Taine's career, and by furnishing an outline of his literary achievements and aims, I hope to supply such an introduction to this volume as may prove serviceable to all who, before or after they shall have perused it, may feel specially desirous of forming a closer personal intimacy with its author.

I.

At Vouziers, a small town on the frontier of Champagne and Ardennes, Hyppolite-Adolphe Taine was born on the 21st of April, 1828. His family belonged to the French middle class; to that superior class which has no exact equivalent in this country, which is composed of those who belong to Nature's aristocracy by virtue of intellect and education, who, though never formally ennobled by a monarch, are fully as much respected in France as the lineal descendants of the Crusaders, and the undisputed possessors of the oldest and most renowned historic titles. His father was a solicitor; his uncles and his cousins were notaries, merchants, civil engineers. His grandfather was sub-prefect at Rocroi during the first Bourbon restoration of an hundred days; several of his relations, on his father's and his mother's side, held posts of influence and distinction, were deputies in the Lower House of the Legislature during the reign of Louis Philippe, and in the Assembly during the Republic of 1848. They were well-to-do but not wealthy people. His father, who was a man of studious habits and considerable learning, taught him Latin. An uncle, who had resided in America for some time, taught him English. One of his early pleasures was reading English books, more especially the classical works of fiction of the last century. To him, as to other French schoolboys, light literature was forbidden fruit. Yet he was permitted to read any English book he pleased, the perusal of works in a foreign tongue being regarded as a species of study which it was right to encourage and commend. To the advantage he took of his opportunities in early youth, is attributable much of the familiar acquaintance which he displayed in after years with the immortal works of the best English writers.

When he was thirteen years old, his father died. His mother took him to Paris at the age of fourteen. For one year he was a boarder in a first-class private school, then he became a pupil at the College of Bourbon, an important public school, which, like many other institutions in France, changes its name when the government changes its form, and was consequently known during the monarchy as the College of Bourbon, during the Republic of 1848 as the Fourcroy Lyceum, during the Second Empire as the Bonaparte Lyceum, and is at present called the Condorcet Lyceum. He had two sisters, whose training and happiness were the objects of his mother's special care and forethought. Nevertheless, she was naturally unremitting in promoting her only son's welfare and advancement, watching over his studies with tender solicitude, rejoicing in his triumphs as if they were her own, encouraging him amid his difficulties and mortifications, nursing him during long illnesses, keeping house for him in his riper years, and only relinquishing her assiduous maternal cares when he finally obtained a not less devoted and affectionate companion in the person of a wife.

When M. Taine was studying at the College of Bourbon, other youths, who afterwards became famous, were pupils also; but none eclipsed him, either in mental precocity, or in successful rivalry for distinction. At the general competition in 1847, he carried off the first prize for the Latin essay in rhetoric, and in 1848 he obtained the two second prizes for philosophy. His attainments warranted him in becoming a candidate, in the latter year, for admission to the Normal School. This is a seminary of learning into which none are admitted except those who succeed in passing a severe examination, and in which the pupils qualify themselves for enrolment among the higher class of teachers in connection with the University, and under the control of the Minister of Public Instruction. Many, however, make use of it as a stepping-stone to a purely literary career. Several Frenchmen of note in the world of letters passed through the Normal School at the same time as M. Taine, acted for a short time as Professors, as he did, and then, severing their connection with the department of education, devoted themselves exclusively to cultivating the field of literature. Four of these men were his comrades and competitors. They were the late M. Prevost-Paradol, M. Edmond About, M. Francisque Sarcey, M. J. J. Weiss. The first was junior to him by one year, the second and third were his own age, the fourth was one year his senior.

Of the four, M. Prevost-Paradol was in many respects the most remarkable. The son of a celebrated actress, he, too, was educated at the College of Bourbon, and distinguished himself there. After passing through the Normal School, he spent some years in private study, prepared a work to which the French Academy awarded the prize for eloquence, took his degree of Doctor of Letters, and then accepted the post of Professor of French Literature in the college at Aix. He filled this chair for one year only. Tempting offers to enter the ranks of journalism made him not only resign this post, but also withdraw his name from the list of those who desired employment as University instructors. He was first engaged upon the staff of the *Journal des Débats*. To this journal, as well as to others, and to the *Revue des Deux Mondes*, he contributed articles, which excited notice for the delicacy, the point, the polish, the incisiveness of their style. He was a French Junius. He resembled the great unknown English pamphleteer in being a literary irreconcilable, differing from him, however, in wielding a sharp, glittering rapier, instead of a heavy, crushing club. He attacked the Second Empire by his epigrams and allusions with quite as great effect as Junius did when he warred against the policy of George III. and the friends of that monarch by scathing sarcasm and unmeasured denunciation. The *Courier du Dimanche*, to which he was the principal contributor, became a thorn in the side of the Imperial Government. Even more annoying than his effective yet indirect onslaughts upon Imperialism, was the cleverness with which he avoided a direct breach of the laws prohibiting freedom of discussion. M. Prevost-Paradol's art consisted in saying what he pleased, in such a way as to give the maximum of pain to his opponents, without affording them a legitimate opportunity for putting their fingers upon the passage which rankled in their minds, and stating, with good reason, that the incriminated passage was discourteous, in bad taste, contrary to fact, and a disgrace to the writer. Nothing was left them but to put themselves wholly in the wrong, by exercising arbitrary repression. As the *Courier du Dimanche* could neither be legally prosecuted nor conclusively answered, it was summarily suppressed. A pamphlet which M. Prevost-Paradol wrote on the "Old Parties" was interpreted by subservient judges as inciting to the overthrow of the Imperial dynasty, and for this hypothetical offence he was fined £40 and imprisoned for a month. The injustice and persecution of which, in common with the late Count Montalembert, he was the victim, recoiled upon its instigators and perpetrators.

M. Prevost-Paradol became popular in all independent circles, and enjoyed the esteem of all unbiassed critics. His admirers were nearly as numerous in this country as in his own. Indeed, an English reader could hardly help thinking favourably of the French writer who constantly held up constitutional government in England as a pattern deserving ungrudging praise and careful study. To his political attitude, rather than to the intrinsic value of his writings, he owed it that, at the early age of thirty-seven, he was elected a member of the French Academy, a body which usually refuses to open its ranks to young men, however promising, who have merely produced a few ephemeral works, unless their authors are Ministers of State, or Archbishops. His highest ambition was now gratified.

About this time he received the remarkable and gratifying distinction of being asked to contribute to *The Times*, letters on French topics of the day. In common with his brother Academicians, he enjoyed by his position, and irrespective of his personal achievements, the reputation of being a master of his incomparable mother-tongue. Many of them doubtless spoke English without hesitation, read it with pleasure and understanding. But how many among them would have ventured upon undergoing the ordeal of satisfying the critical readers of the great English journal? His own wonderful success, the fluency, ease, grace, and vigour with which he expressed himself in English, formed an additional claim to the admiration and respect of Englishmen. For his own part, he assured his English friends that, never till he had become a contributor to *The Times*, had he learned the real value of his pen. Despite the liberality with which he was remunerated, he found the support of his family a heavy burden. He had no private means; he had accumulated little, and he was weary of writing at all and still more weary of writing for gain. Then it was that by him, as by many other patriotic and eminent Frenchmen, the prospect of the establishment of constitutional and parliamentary government was hailed with delight. He unquestionably preferred ordered liberty with the Empire, to the almost inevitable alternative of a revolution accompanied with bloodshed and followed by anarchy. To refuse to give fair play to the new order of things, to reject the repentance of the eleventh hour which promised to be all the more sincere inasmuch as it was based upon irresistible expediency, appeared to him worse than a blunder. He accepted the apparent transformation, and did so in good faith. Everything appeared going smoothly and satisfactorily when the astute and unscrupulous M. Rouher ceased to be the first minister of Napoleon III. M. Ollivier, who succeeded him, was known to be vain and ambitious; but he was supposed to be honest, and was believed to be competent. Along with others who had been in opposition during the evil days, M. Prevost-Paradol became reconciled to the Imperial Government when a happier and brighter era seemed to have dawned upon France. He gave a visible hostage of his confidence and expectations by accepting the honourable and coveted post of Minister at Washington. Hardly had he entered upon the duties of his office than he learned that France had challenged Prussia to mortal combat. What his feelings were can be easily surmised. During the year 1867 he discussed in *La France Nouvelle* the contingency of a war between France and Prussia, adding the following significant and memorable reflections: "On the supposition that Prussia were victorious, it is easy to see that such an occurrence would be the death of the greatness of France, though the nation would not be destroyed. . . . . Some rectification of our frontier to the advantage of Prussia—the sad prelude to still greater—would be the immediate effect of our reverses. . . . . Germanic unity, hastened and pushed forward by the force and prestige of Prussian victories, would be instantly consummated. Yes, France is destined to pay in any event; with the blood of her sons if she conquers; with her greatness, and, perhaps, with her national existence, if she succumbs." Despairing of his country should she prove the victor, or be vanquished, he died by his own hand. More courageous, or more desponding than the members of the dynasty which had duped him, he surrendered his life as a sacrifice to the intrigues and deceptions of a crooked and baneful Imperialism.

M. Edmond About has shown himself, on the whole, a very different man from M. Prevost-Paradol. M. About has made money by his writings, and he has not yet been made an ambassador. He has dabbled in politics, and left it an open question whether he has any permanent and rational political convictions. He has written novels, pamphlets, plays; his writings have all been successful, but his plays have not all been applauded. His great distinction is his style; his great success consists in putting things. When he left the Normal

School, he obtained admission into the School at Athens, maintained by the French Government with a view to perpetuate and advance the study of Grecian archæology. He wrote one lively treatise on an archæological topic, and then published his work on "Contemporary Greece," a work which charmed the reading public everywhere save in Greece, and of which the success determined his vocation. Since then he has been a prolific author, and become a conspicuous notability in literature. The adaptability of his character is as marked as the elasticity of his style. He can write well on any subject; he imparts freshness to whatever he touches, and he upholds with extreme fervour and with an air of conviction the side which he espouses. If the Germans could be terrified by phrases, he would have put them to flight. His letters as a War Correspondent, at the opening of the campaign, produced a very different impression in this country from that produced by "Tolla" and the "Roman Question." In them he exhibited himself as a fire-eater of the most ferocious type. His reputation in France, however, has apparently suffered no abatement. He has narrowly failed being elected a member of the Academy. That he will become an Academician, at least, is hardly doubtful. That he is one of the cleverest writers of the day cannot be denied.

M. Taine's other two comrades soon abandoned the profession of teaching the young for that of directing the adult through the columns of the public press. M. Sarcey was constantly squabbling with the authorities during the seven years that he acted as Professor. Indeed, those who had been the most brilliant pupils of the Normal School, immediately before the advent of the Second Empire, found it impossible to maintain harmonious relations with the Imperial administrators. Much of the bitterness which they manifested as journalists was due to the independent principles they had imbibed at school, coupled with the vexatious and inquisitorial conduct of their superiors, who expected that they would become meek and ready tools for the maintenance and glorification of the dynasty which had betrayed and strangled the Republic. As a contributor to popular Parisian journals, M. Sarcey is noted for his effective and sparkling articles. He remained in Paris whilst it was besieged by the Germans; and his account of what occurred is one of the best narratives of the siege that has been produced. M. Weiss continued to act as a Professor rather longer than any of the others. He filled with great success the chair of French literature, which M. Prevost-Paradol had occupied and adorned. His lectures were exceedingly able. Since he definitively entered the ranks of journalism, he has become one of its acknowledged ornaments.

During the regular term of three years that M. Taine was a pupil of the Normal School, the method of instruction which prevailed was well fitted to promote and stimulate intellectual activity. Personally, he required no special incentive to work hard and to excel.

He was able, by his marvellous quickness and industry, to condense an immense amount of study into a brief space of time. Sometimes, he performed the tasks of a month in the course of a week. Thus he gained three clear weeks during which to follow his own devices; and he utilized the time by studying theology and philosophy, reading all the authors of note in both departments, and discussing the questions which arose with congenial spirits of his own standing. All his fellow-pupils were subjected by him to a personal examination. To use his own phrase he loved to "read" (*feuilleter*) them; in other words, to probe their minds and scrutinize their thoughts. Although a Roman Catholic by early training, yet he was no implicit believer in Roman Catholic dogmas. With some pupils who were ardently attached to the Church of Rome, as well as with others who partially sympathised with him, he entered into discussions, in which theological doctrines were treated with entire freedom, tried by the touchstone of reason, and subjected to keen logical investigation. Indeed, the school was a theatre of controversy, the pupils openly arguing with each other, and the Professors sanctioning and encouraging the most thoroughgoing expression of individual and unfettered opinion. Trained in such an arena, it is no wonder that the pupils became imbued with a strong notion of individual independence, and were ill prepared to brook the slightest intellectual restraint or dictation.

Shortly before the three years' training of M. Taine

and his comrades was ended, the Director of the Normal School, M. Dubois, was constrained to resign the post he had adorned. M. Michelle, a less enlightened and able man, and a willing ally of the reactionary party, ruled in his stead. The times were unpropitious for liberty of thought. The Emperor Napoleon had attained the object of his life, and he had to pay the price which the priests claimed for their support. They had served him heart and soul; he furnished them, in return, with the arm of the flesh requisite for the maintenance of their spiritual pretensions. M. Taine was one of the sufferers from the new order of things. Those who pass a certain examination are appointed to the most easy and lucrative posts. He presented himself for examination, but was rejected on the avowed ground that his philosophical opinions were erroneous in themselves and mischievous in their tendency. This unfairness was resented by several men of eminence who had taken an interest in him, and who had been struck by his talents. Owing to the warm advocacy of M. Guizot, M. Saint Marc Girardin, and the Duc de Luynes, he hoped to procure a post which might compensate by its situation for its inferior character, and he requested, as a special favour, for his mother's sake rather than for his own, that he might be appointed to fill a vacancy in the North of France. The reply was a nomination to a post at Toulon, in the extreme South. Thence he was transferred to Nevers, and from Nevers to Poitiers, remaining four months only at each place. His salary for the first year was £66; a sum which, though a little in excess of that wherewith Goldsmith's good parson deemed himself passing rich, was considerably less than that upon which it was possible to live in comfort. However, he managed to exist by practising the most rigid economy.

His spare moments he spent in close study, occupying himself chiefly with the works of Hegel, and sketching out a comprehensive philosophical work. He was generally regarded as a suspicious character. It was no secret that his private opinions did not accord with those held and approved in official circles. Hence the partizans of the ruling powers were lynx-eyed and eager in detecting his failings. In France, nothing is easier than to circulate false reports, unless it be the ease in getting them accepted as authentic. Naturally, there was not the least difficulty in discrediting M. Taine by falsely representing that he had eulogised Danton in the presence of his pupils, and held up Paul de Kock to them as a model. This alleged grave sin of commission was followed by a still more heinous and perfectly incontestable sin of omission. The college chaplain preferred one of those requests which are equivalent to commands. He gave M. Taine the option of inditing, in honour of the Bishop of the diocese, either a Latin ode or a French dithyramb M. Taine declined to praise the Bishop either in prose or verse, either in ancient Latin or modern French. For this irreverent refusal, which was regarded as confirmatory of the darkest charges and the worst fears, he soon received a letter of censure from the Minister of Public Instruction. The official reprimand was coupled with a threat that, should he offend again, he would be instantly dismissed. Several months afterwards he was appointed to teach a class of little children at Besançon. This was a significant hint that he was regarded as a black sheep. He deemed it wise to give up a struggle in which he was certain to be checkmated at every turn. At his own request, he was placed upon the retired list.

Returning to Paris, he received an advantageous offer to act as Professor in a large private seminary. He closed with it, and recommenced teaching. But even here his sins soon found him out, or rather his enemies did. An order was issued forbidding those who were members of the University staff from giving lectures in private institutions. As a last resource he began to give lessons as a tutor, with the view both of earning his daily bread, and of being able to use his pen with entire independence. Moreover, he completed his own education, and enlarged the sphere of his attainments, by attending the courses of lectures at the School of Medicine, the Museum of Natural History, and some of the lectures at the Sorbonne and the Salpétrière. In 1853 he took the degree of Doctor of Letters. As is customary, he wrote two theses on this occasion, the one in Latin being "De Personis Platonicis," the other in French being an "Essai sur les Fables de Lafontaine." The latter was the reverse of an ordinary University essay. It was the formal enunciation of new critical doctrines; it was the gauntlet thrown down by a new aspirant for intellectual honours; it was the bold maintenance of a modern paradox, illustrated and enforced by examples drawn from Lafontaine. The novelty of the views advanced was matched by the freshness and vivacity, the vigour and variety of the language. By the public it was received with such favour that it speedily passed into a second edition.

The French Academy having offered a prize in 1854 for an essay upon Livy, considered as writer and historian, M. Taine entered the lists. Among the works sent in, his was admitted to be the best, yet the prize was not awarded to it on the ground that his essay "was deficient in gravity and in a proper degree of admiration for the splendid name and imposing genius of him whom he had to criticise." He recast his essay, and submitted it a second time to the judgment of the tribunal. It was now pronounced the best of those presented, and fully entitled to the prize. In reporting to the Academy the committee's decision, M. Villemain expressed their satisfaction in crowning a "solid and new work, wherein the sentiment of antiquity and the modern method were suitably blended, and which skilfully set forth all the questions concerning historic certitude, local truth, correct information, dramatic passion and taste to which the Annals of Livy had given rise. . . . . The young and clever man of learning, the victor in this competition, has had to produce a fragment of history as well as a piece of criticism." After intimating his disagreement with

M. Taine in matters of detail, M. Villemain concluded his report by saying, "Let us, however, congratulate M. Taine upon this noble and erudite first appearance in classical letters, and let us wish for similar candidates at our competitions, and similar instructors of youth in our schools." The Academicians smiled at this sarcastic reflection on the authorities for having refused to avail themselves of the teacher's services.

The prize essay was published with a short preface, which startled some members of the Academy, and made them desire to recall their praises and undo their acts. M. Taine wrote to the effect that, according to Spinoza, man's place in relation to nature, is not that of an empire within an empire, but of a part in a whole; that man's inner being is subject to laws in the same way as the external world; moreover, that there is a dominant principle, a ruling faculty, which regulates thought and imparts an irresistible and inevitable impulse to the human machine. Believing these things, M. Taine offered his "Essay on Livy" as an example of their truth. Upon this the cry was raised that to write in this way was to deny the freedom of the will, and to become the apostle of fatalism. A more cogent objection was the incongruity between the ideas represented by two such names as Spinoza and Livy, and the paradox implied in putting forward the writings of the Roman historian as confirmatory of the philosophical speculations of the Dutch Jew. Yet the general reader was gratified with the book. Its author's ability was indisputable. If he made few converts, he gained admirers.

A severe affection of the throat compelled him to quit Paris and to seek relief from the famous springs of the Pyrenees. After lasting two years, during which he lost the use of his voice, the malady finally succumbed to the curative action of the mineral waters. It is noteworthy that at this period his favourite book was Spenser's "Faerie Queene," a work which hardly any of his countrymen have read at all, and which few of mine have read through. To M. Taine's intimate knowledge of Spenser is due the splendid and discriminating eulogium passed upon the great Elizabethan poet in the "History of English Literature." His enforced sojourn among the mountains supplied him with fresh material for literary composition. This took the form of a "Journey to the Pyrenees," a work which became more popular than the "Essay on Livy." The habits of the people and of the tourists are depicted with much point, and the mountain scenery with great vividness; enough is said about botany, geology, natural history, to give pith to the whole, without wearying the reader who understands none of these things, or appearing commonplace to the reader who is perfectly conversant with them. An edition of this work, with illustrations by M. Gustave Doré, has since been published. The critic may be puzzled to decide whether the text or the illustrations ought to be singled out for special praise, but he cannot hesitate to pronounce the entire work a masterpiece

Another illness, of a still more threatening character, prostrated him at a later period. This was the result of over-work, and consisted in total incapacity for mental exertion. For a considerable time he could not concentrate his thoughts; could neither write nor read; even the perusal of a newspaper was beyond his power. Entire rest wrought a cure which, happily, was lasting as well as complete.

In addition to the works named above, he wrote numerous articles for the *Revue de l'Instruction Publique*, the *Journal des Débats*, the *Revue des Deux Mondes*. These articles have been collected and published in volumes. A volume which attracted much attention was partly composed of articles which had appeared in the first of these journals, and it bore the title of "French Philosophers of the Nineteenth Century." This work was an attack upon the official philosophy of the day, that rhetorical spiritualism which had the advantage, in the eyes of the authorities, of not giving umbrage to the priests, and the drawback, in the opinion of thinkers, of slurring over, or of evading the difficulties which it professed to explain and remove. Against M. Cousin, in particular, M. Taine opened a battery of censure and ridicule. The opponents of the former applauded the attack; his friends, like friends in general, doubtless relished it inwardly, while condemning it openly, for it was very clever and very telling; and M. Cousin himself regarded his adversary with more than a professional philosopher's antipathy

Meanwhile M. Taine was steadily labouring at his most ambitious historical work, "The History of English Literature." It was the fruit of six years' close study. In 1861, and subsequently, he visited England with a view of reading in the British Museum, and of seeing the country and people face to face. The "Notes" contained in this volume comprise the frequent observations of ten years. They were all revised after his last visit in 1871. Some are retained which would have appeared more applicable a few years ago than they do now, but in M. Taine's opinion, they are still substantially true, and represent permanent phases of our national life and character.

Upon the publication of the "History of English Literature," in 1863, its author's reputation was vastly increased, and his rank among modern writers acknowledged to be very lofty. The work was the event of the day, and the illustration of the year. That it should have been singled out by a committee of the French Academy, and unanimously recommended as worthy of a special prize, was perfectly natural. The value of this special prize, which is conferred on none but historical works of undoubted merit, is £160, a recompense which renders the honour a substantial as well as an enviable one. At a meeting of the Academy, where it was proposed to confirm the recommendation of the committee, Monseigneur Dupanloup, the Bishop of Orleans, rose and moved the non-confirmation of the report. He alleged as reasons for refusing to do honour to M. Taine's history, that the book was impious and immoral; that its author had alleged "virtue and vice to be products like sugar and vitriol;" that he had denied the freedom of the will; that he had advocated pure fatalism, had depreciated the ecclesiastics of the Middle Ages, had eulogized the Puritans, had pointedly commended the English Prayer-Book, had shown himself a sceptic in philosophy and a heretic in religion. M. Cousin thought the opportunity a favourable one both for showing how entirely he had become reconciled to the Church, and for taking his revenge on his youthful assailant. He seconded the Bishop's motion in a speech re-echoing the Bishop's charges. The success of these notable men was almost secured beforehand. Their hearers the more readily believed all they were told, because they had not read the work against which the attack was skilfully directed. The reporter of the Committee, who ought to have defended the Committee's choice, was only too ready to bow before the censure of the Bishop and the philosopher. Hence, this combined and ardent appeal to the worst prejudices of an assembly never distinguished for true tolerance and genuine liberality of sentiment, and of which the majority remembered with satisfaction how, during the previous year, M. Littré's candidature for admission into their midst had been rejected, proved altogether irresistible, and the motion was carried Since then the Academy has been materially changed in composition and spirit. M. Cousin has departed this life in the odour of sanctity. He atoned, long before his decease, for his youthful leaning towards intellectual freedom, by abjectly submitting to the most uncompromising dogmas of a powerful priesthood. His influence perished with him. He holds, and may continue to hold, a place among the literary idols of France, and will receive the more lip-worship because he is no longer believed in as an authority. The Bishop of Orleans has resigned his seat; M. Littré is a member of the Academy. Is it rash to predict that the illustrious body which, on hearsay and wholly insufficient evidence, refused to acknowledge the real merits of M. Taine's important work will one day regard his accession to a place among them as an addition to their collective strength and glory?

Little remains to be said about M. Taine's personal career. For some time he held the post of literary examiner in the military school of St. Cyr. Afterwards he was appointed professor of art and æsthetics in the Imperial Academy of the Fine Arts. He has travelled through Italy, and written an excellent account of his observations. He has published several works relating to art in Greece, Italy, and the Low Countries. One of his recent works is a philosophical one of note on "The Intelligence." The mere enumeration of these titles is a proof of his versatility. More rare still, is the circumstance that everything he has written is both readable and pregnant with matter for reflection. Indeed, all his writings have a flavour of their own which is very pleasant, a stamp of originality which is unmistakable. He always thinks for himself. He occupies a place apart among contemporary authors. Nor does he ever write at random, and without a special purpose. Every book or detached essay is designed to subserve the object of propagating his views respecting criticism, to expound and illustrate a method of discussing literary works which, if not discovered by him, he has made his own by systematic use and skilful adaptation.

II.

A critic is commonly supposed to be a man who, having carefully studied certain subjects, is specially qualified for giving an opinion upon the way in which these subjects have been treated by an author, a painter, an architect, an orator. The critic may either announce his decision after having applied to the matter in hand certain fixed rules or canons, or else he may enumerate his own rules and express an independent judgment. In any case the critique is a reasoned or arbitrary opinion, and nothing more. It may be disputed, if the standard to which the critic appeals has not been fairly and adequately applied. It may be disregarded, if the personal opinion appears to be merely an individual crotchet. To expect that the result could ever be accepted as universally and implicitly as the demonstrations of an authority in the natural sciences, of a botanist and a zoologist, is what no critic of eminence, with one conspicuous exception, has hitherto ventured to do.

That exception is M. Taine. He believes that he has succeeded in removing all ambiguity and fluctuation from critical judgments by following a particular method of procedure. He professes to have eliminated chance from ethical products, to have found a clue to the labyrinth of the mind. The ordinary saying that man is a creature of circumstances, he employs as a philosophical formula. The purport of his main contention and fundamental proposition is that man is the unconscious agent and manifestation of unseen forces. In his opinion, these forces may be measured, though they cannot be grasped; may be classified, though they cannot be directly controlled. He considers it practicable, by duly estimating and carefully determining their nature and effect, to explain why an author, artist, or architect produced a particular book, painting, or edifice; why an age was distinguished for a particular form of literature, art, or architecture; what was the mental history of past generations as exhibited in the writings or doings of individuals. In short, M. Taine deciphers the man in the age, and the age in the man, and becomes the historian of the human mind in depicting the events of a particular generation, and in exhibiting the share which the finished work of one era or race has had in moulding the work of the era which has succeeded, or the race which has displaced it. For him Raffaelle is no startling phenomenon, and Shakespeare no inscrutable mystery. Nor has he any difficulty in explaining the reason why the Middle Age was succeeded by the Revival, and the Revival by the Reformation; why England was transformed by the Revolution which destroyed Divine Right; why France was emancipated from the yoke of feudalism by the Revolution which replaced privilege by equality.

These are lofty pretensions. It is because all his writings have been designed to maintain and advocate them, that they have all merited special attention. On more than one occasion I have endeavoured to expound his method and weigh it in the balance.* Many French and English critics of note have pronounced their opinion upon it, and have pointed out what they regard as its imperfections or mistakes. The result has been to elicit from him an exposition of it, which he desires should be accepted as an authoritative and a binding statement of his views and intentions. It is prefixed to the second edition of his "Historical and Critical Essays." As this manifesto has not yet appeared in an English dress, and as it constitutes the case by which M. Taine would like to be judged by his readers and critics in England, as well as elsewhere, I shall proceed to translate it preparatory to offering any comments of my own upon his aims and performances:—

"Several critics have done me the honour sometimes to combat, sometimes to approve of what they are pleased to call my system. I am by no means so pre-

---

* See the following articles in the *Westminster Review*:—"The Critical Writings and Theory of H Taine," July, 1861; "Taine's History of English Literature," April, 1864; "Taine's History of English Literature: Contemporary Writers," January, 1865; "H Taine on Art and Italy," April, 1866.

tentious as to have a system; at most, I endeavour to follow a method. A system is an explanation of the whole, and indicates a work done; a method is a manner of working, and indicates a work to be done. My desire has been to labour in a certain sense and in a certain way—nothing more. The question is to learn whether this way is a good one. To do so it must be tried: if the reader will make the attempt, he will be able to judge for himself. In place of refuting refutations, I shall sketch the process in dispute; those who shall have repeated it will learn for themselves whether it conducts to truths.

"It is wholly comprised in this remark that moral matters, like physical things, have *dependencies and conditions.*

"I shall suppose that it is desired to verify this maxim, and measure its reach. Let the reader take for example some artist, learned man, or distinguished writer, a particular poet, novelist, and read his works, pen in hand. To read them properly, he will classify them in natural groups, and in each group he will distinguish the three distinct things called the personages or characters, the action or intrigue, the style or the manner of writing. Following the custom of every critic, he will note in each of these divisions, by a few brief and telling phrases, the salient particularities, the dominant traits, the qualities peculiar to the author. Arrived at the end of his first course, if he be somewhat practised in this work, he will see an involuntary phrase flow from his pen, one singularly powerful and significant, which will summarise all the operation, and will place before his eyes a certain kind of tact and of talent, a certain disposition of mind or of soul, a certain array of likes and dislikes, of faculties and of failings, in short, a certain *psychological state*, ruling and lasting, which is that of the author. Let him now repeat the same operation in the other portions of the same subject; let him afterwards compare the three or four summaries which each of these partial analyses have produced; let him add to the author's writings, his life, I mean his conduct towards men,—his philosophy, that is to say, his manner of regarding the world,—his ethical and æsthetical code, that is to say, his general views about the good and the beautiful; let him bring together all these small condensed phrases which are the concentrated essence of thousands of the remarks he has made, and of the hundreds of judgments he has passed. If these notations are precise, if he be accustomed to discern sentiments and faculties under the words which designate them, if the inner eye by which we sift and define in a moment the diversities of the moral being is sufficiently exercised and penetrating, he will observe that these seven or eight formulas *depend* the one upon the other, that the first being given, the others could not differ, that consequently the qualities they represent are interchained, that if one vary, the others vary proportionately, and that hence they compose a system like an organised body. Not only will he have the vague sentiment of this mutual accord which harmonizes the diverse faculties of a mind, but also he will have the distinct perception of it; he will be able to prove in logical fashion that a particular quality, violence or sobriety of imagination, oratorical or lyrical aptitude, ascertained as regards one point, must extend its ascendency over the rest. By continued reasoning, he will thus bind up the various inclinations of the man he examines under a small number of governing inclinations, whence they flow and by which they are explained, and he will provide for himself the spectacle of the admirable necessities which unite among each other, the innumerable, varied, entangled fibres of each human being.

"That is the simplest case. I shall now suppose that the reader wishes to make trial of this in a larger and more complex case, upon a large school, like that of the English or Spanish dramatists, the Florentine or Venetian painters, upon an entire civilisation like that of ancient Rome, upon a race like the Semitic, even upon a distinct group of races like that of the Aryan nations, and to take an example, upon a well-marked historic epoch, the age of Louis XIV. To do this it is necessary, in the first place, to have read and observed much; and probably, out of all the observations, some general impression has remained in the reader's mind; I mean to say, the vague sentiment of a badly-defined concordance between the heaps of works and of thoughts which have passed before his eyes. But I ask him to go farther, and by surer paths. In this, as in the preceding case and in every accurate search, it is necessary, in the first place, to classify the facts, and to consider each class of facts apart: firstly, the three great works of human intelligence, religion, art, philosophy; secondly, the two great works of human association, the family and the State; lastly, the three great material works of human labour, industry, commerce, and agriculture; and in each of these general groups the secondary groups into which they are subdivided. Take but one of them, philosophy; when the reader shall have studied the reigning doctrine from Descartes to Malebranche; when after having noted the method, the theory of extension and of thought, the definition of God, of morality, and the rest, he will clearly picture to himself the point of departure and the sort of spirit which have determined the entire work; when he shall have given precision to his idea by keeping in sight the imaginative and riotous philosophy of the preceding century, the distinctive and binding philosophy of contemporary England, the experimental and sceptical philosophy of the following century, he will arrive at sifting out from the French philosophy of the seventeenth century a certain distinct tendency whence proceed, as from a source, its submissiveness and its independence, its theological poverty and its logical lucidity, its moral nobleness and its speculative aridity, its leaning towards mathematics and its disdain of experience; on the one hand, that mixture of compromise and stiffness which foretells a race better fitted for pure reasoning than for general views; on the other hand, that mixture of elevation and calmness which foretells an age less enthusiastic than correct. Should a similar operation now be performed upon the other contemporary portions of human intelligence and action, should the summaries be compared together wherein in a handy and portable fashion the substance of the work observed has been similarly deposited; if, by that kind of chemistry which is termed psychological analysis, care be taken to recognise the ingredients of each extract, it will be discovered that elements of a like nature come together in the different phials; that the same faculties and the same wants which have produced philosophy have produced religion and art; that the man to whom this art, this philosophy, this religion address themselves was prepared by a monarchical society and drawing-room proprieties to taste and comprehend them; that the stage, conversation, goodness, family manners, the hierarchy of the State, the docility of the subject, the noble domesticity of the great, the humble domesticity of the low-born, all the details of private or public life, combined together to fortify the reigning sentiments and faculties, and that not only the diverse parts of this civilisation, so large and so complex, were united by common *dependencies*, but also that the cause of these dependencies was the universal presence of certain aptitudes and of certain inclinations, always the same, disseminated under diverse figures in the different compartments wherein the human metal was cast. Between an elm of Versailles, a philosophical and religious argument of Malebranche, one of Boileau's maxims in versification, one of Colbert's laws of hypothec, an anteroom compliment at Marly, a sentence of Bossuet on the royalty of God, the distance appears infinite and impassable; there is no apparent connection. The facts are so dissimilar that at first sight they are pronounced to be what they appear, that is to say, isolated and separated. But the *facts communicate between themselves by the definitions of the groups in which they are comprised*, like the waters in a basin by the summit of the heights whence they flow. Each of them is an act of that ideal and general man around whom are grouped all the inventions and all the peculiarities of the epoch; the cause of each is some aptitude or inclination of the reigning model. The various inclinations or aptitudes of the central personage balance, harmonise, temper each other under some liking, or dominant faculty, because it is the same spirit and the same heart which have thought, prayed, imagined, and acted; because it is the same general situation and the same innate nature which have fashioned and governed the separate and diverse works; because it is the same seal which is differently stamped on differing matters. None of these imprints can alter without leading to an alteration in the others, because if one change it is owing to a change in the seal.

"A step remains to be taken. Till now, the connection of contemporaneous things was in question; at present the connection between *successive* things must be considered. The reader has been able to prove that moral matters, like physical things, have their *dependencies;* at present he must prove that, like physical things, they have their *conditions*.

"You have sought and found the definition of a group; I mean that small, exact, and expressive phrase which encloses in its narrow compass the essential characters whence the others can be deduced. Let us here suppose that it designates those of our seventeenth century; compare it with those by which you have designated the preceding epoch and the others more ancient of the same history in the same country; search now whether the diverse terms of this series do not contain some common element. One is to be found, the character and spirit peculiar to the race, transmitted from generation to generation; the same through the changes of culture, the diversities of organisation, and the variety of products. This character and this spirit, once constituted, are found to be more or less disposed for discipline or personal independence; more or less fitted for nice reasoning or poetical emotion; more or less disposed to the religion of the conscience, or of logic, or of custom, or of the eyes. At a given moment, during a period, they produce a work; and their nature, joined to that of their work, is the *condition* of the work which follows; as in an organised body the primitive temperament, joined to the anterior state, is the condition of the succeeding state. Here, as in the physical world, the condition is sufficient and necessary; if it be present, the work cannot be wanting; if it be absent, the work cannot appear. From the English character and from the despotism bequeathed by the Tudors to the Stuarts proceeded the English Revolution. From the French character and from the aristocratic anarchy bequeathed by the civil wars to the Bourbons proceeded the monarchy of Louis XIV. To produce the superb flowering of the arts of design under Leo X. was required the precocious and picturesque Italian genius, with the prolonged reign of the energetic manners and the corporeal instincts of the Middle Ages. To produce in the first centuries of our era the astonishing growth of philosophies and mystical religions, the speculative aptitude of our Aryan races was required, at the same time as the crushing of the world, repressed under a despotism without outlet, and the enlargement of the mind, widened by the ruin of nationalities. Let the reader kindly make trial of this upon any one period; if he starts from the texts, if he reads and judges for himself, if he methodically exhausts his subject, if he rises by degrees from the characters which govern the smaller groups up to those which govern the larger groups, if he is careful in constantly rectifying and determining his summaries, if he is accustomed to see clearly the qualities and the general situations which extend their empire over centuries and entire nations, he will become convinced that they depend upon anterior qualities and situations as general as themselves; that the second being given the first must follow; that they play among them the great game of history; that they make or unmake civilisation by their disagreement or their harmony; that our little ephemeral life is but a wave upon their current, that in and by them we have action and being. At the end of a short time he will embrace with a look the whole which they govern; he will no longer see them as abstract formulas, but as living forces mingled with things, everywhere present, everywhere operating, veritable divinities of the human world, which hold out hands downward to other powers that are masters of matter as they are of mind, to form together the invisible choir of which the old poets speak, which moves across things, and through which throbs the eternal universe.

"It will be seen that what is in question here is a form of experiment similar to what scientific men perform in physiology or in chemistry. In the one as in the other case, a man says to you, 'Take that piece of matter, divide it such a way, practise upon it such and such operations, and in such an order; you will arrive at ascertaining certain dependencies, and at disengaging a certain principle. I have done this, in thirty or forty cases, while choosing different circumstances. A man's idea cannot be received or rejected till after counter-proof. It is no refutation to tell him, 'Your method is bad, for it renders style rigid and unpleasant.' He will reply aloud, 'So much the worse for me.' Nor is it any more a refutation to say, 'I reject your forms of procedure; for the doctrines to which they lead unsettle my moral convictions.' He will reply in a whisper, 'So much the worse for you.' Experience alone destroys experience; for theological or sentimental objections have no hold over a fact. Whether this fact be the formation of tissues observed through a microscope, an equivalent figure proved by a scale, a concordance of faculties and of sentiments proved by criticism, its value is the same; there is no other superior authority which can reject it at first sight and without previous control; one is obliged, in order to disprove him, to repeat the operation which he has obtained. When a physiologist tells you that the anatomical elements are formed by spontaneous generation in the living individual, and that the living individual is an aggregation of elementary individuals, each endowed with a personal and distinct life, do you think yourself entitled to protest in the name of the theological dogma of the creation or of the ethical dogma of the human personality? Objections of this sort which could be made during the Middle Ages cannot be made at the present day respecting any science, in history any more than in physiology and chemistry, since the right of regulating human consciences has wholly passed to the side of experience, and since precepts or doctrines, instead of authorising observation, receive from it all their credit. Besides, it is easy to see that objections of this species all proceed from a mistake, and that the adversary is unwittingly the dupe of phrases. He reproaches you with considering national characters and general situations as the sole great forces in history, and he starts from that to decide that you suppress the individual. He forgets that these great forces are but the sum of the tendencies and aptitudes of individuals, that our general terms are collective expressions which bring together under a single glance twenty or thirty millions of souls inclined and acting in the same direction, that when an hundred men move a wheel, the total force which displaces the wheel is but the sum of the forces of these hundred men, and that individuals exist and operate as well in a people, an age, or a race, as the component units in an addition of which the total figure is alone written down. In like manner again, he reproaches you with transforming man into a machine, making him the subject of some interior machinery, bringing him under the bondage of great surrounding pressure, denying to him independent and free personality, discouraging our efforts by informing us that we are constrained and led without and within by forces which we have not made and to which we must submit. He forgets what the individual soul is, as he forgot a moment since what an historical force was; he separates the word from the thing; he empties and puts it aside as a being efficacious and distinct. He ceases to see in the individual soul, as he did in the historical force, the elements which compose it, a moment since the individuals of which the historical force is but the sum, at present the faculties and tendencies of which the individual mind is but the whole. He does not observe that the fundamental aptitudes and tendencies of a mind pertain to it, that those it appropriates in the general situation or in the national character are, or become, personal to it in the foremost place, that when acting through them it is doing so by itself, with its own force, spontaneously, with complete initiative, with full responsibility, and that the artifice of analysis by means of which its principal motors are distinguished, the successive gearings and the distribution of its primitive movement, do not hinder the whole, which is itself, taking from it its impulse and its course—to wit, its energy and its effort. Nor does he observe that researches of this kind, very far from discouraging man by showing him his bondage, have the effect of increasing his hopes, by augmenting his power; that they terminate like the physical sciences in establishing the constant dependencies between facts; that the discovery of these dependencies in the physical sciences has furnished man with the means of foreseeing and modifying up to a certain point natural events; that an analogous discovery in ethical science ought to supply man with the means of foreseeing and modifying up to a certain point historical events. For we shall become all the more masters of our destiny when we shall discern more exactly the common ties of things. When we have arrived at knowing the sufficient and necessary condition of a fact, the condition of that condition, and so on, we shall have before our eyes a chain of data, in which to displace one link will suffice to displace those which follow; so that the last, though situated beyond the sphere of our action, will submit themselves by counter-effect as soon as one of the preceding ones comes within our reach. The whole secret of our practical progress, during three hundred years, is embraced therein;* we have separated and defined couples of facts so bound together that when the first appears the second never fails to follow, whence it occurs that in acting directly on the first we can act indirectly on the second. It is in this manner that accrued knowledge increases power, and the manifest consequence is that in ethical sciences, as in physical sciences, fruitful research is that which, discerning the couples—to wit, the *conditions* and the *dependencies*, sometimes permits the hand of man to interpose in the great mechanism, to shift or put right some small piece of machinery a piece light enough to be moved by

* See Mr. J. S. Mill's admirable "Logic," especially his theory of Induction.

man's hand, but so important that its displacement or smooth movement will lead to a mighty change in the working of the machine, and to employ it altogether, wherever it works, here in nature, there in history, to the profit of the intelligent insect by which the economy of its structure shall have been discovered.

" It is with this aim, and in this sense, that history is being transformed to day; it is by this sort of labour that from a simple narrative it can become a science, and determine laws after having set forth facts. Already we can perceive several of these laws, all very exact and very general, and corresponding to those which have been found in the sciences of living bodies. In that the philosophy of human history repeats, like a faithful image, the philosophy of natural history. Naturalists have observed that an animal's various organs depend the one upon the other—that, for example, the teeth, the stomach, the feet, the instincts, and many other given quantities, vary together according to a fixed connection, so much so that the transformation of one of them compels a corresponding transformation in the rest.* In the same way historians can observe that the various aptitudes and inclinations of an individual, of a race, of an epoch, are joined the one to the other in such a manner that the alteration of one of these given quantities, noticed in a neighbouring individual, in a group at hand, in a preceding or succeeding epoch, determines in them a proportional alteration of all the system. Naturalists have ascertained that the exaggerated development of an organ in an animal, like the kangaroo or the bat, leads to the impoverishment or the diminution of the correspond-

* The Connection of Characters, Cuvier's law. See the developments given by Richard Owen.

ing organs.* In like manner, historians can ascertain how the extraordinary developement of one faculty, like moral aptitude in Teutonic races, or the metaphysical and religious aptitude of the Hindoos, leads in these races to the weakening of the opposite faculties. Naturalists have proved that, among the characters of an animal or vegetable group, the one is subordinate, variable, sometimes weakened, sometimes absent; the others, on the contrary, like the structure or concentric layers of a plant, or the organisation around a chain of vertebræ in an animal, preponderate and determine all the plan of its economy. In like manner historians can prove that among the characters of a group, or of a human individual, the one is subordinate and necessary, the others like the preponderating presence of images or of ideas, or, better still, the greater or lesser aptitude for more or less general conceptions, dominate and fix beforehand the direction of his life and the nature of his inventions.† Naturalists show that in a class, or even a branch of the animal kingdom, the same plan of organisation is found in all the species; that the dog's paw, the horse's leg, the bat's wing, the man's arm, the whale's fin, are the same anatomical given quantity fitted by some contraction or partial extension to the different uses. By a similar method historians can show that as regards the same artist, in the same school, in the same age, of the same race, personages the most opposite as to condition, sex, education, character, all represent a common type—to wit, a nucleus of faculties and primitive aptitudes which, diversely contracted, combined, enlarged, supply the

---

* G. Saint-Hilaire's Law of Organic Counterbalances.
† Rule as to the subordination of characters, which is the principle of classifications in Botany and in Zoology.

xlvi   *INTRODUCTORY CHAPTER.*

innumerable diversities of the group.* Naturalists establish that in a living species the individuals which are the best developed and reproduce themselves the most surely, are those which a peculiarity of structure best adapts to ambient circumstances; that in the others inverse qualities produce inverse effects; that the natural course of things thus leads to incessant eliminations and gradual improvements; that this blind preference and dislike operate as a voluntary selection; that Nature thus chooses in each locality to give being and empire to the species best suited for the locality. By analogous observation and reasoning, historians can establish that, in any one human group, the individuals which attain the highest authority and the largest development are those whereof the aptitudes and the inclinations best correspond to those of their group; that the moral position, like the physical position, operates upon each individual by continuous excitations and repressions; that it renders the one abortive and makes the others bud in proportion to the concordance or disagreement which occurs between them and it; that this blind travail is a selection also, and that, by a series of imperceptible formations and deformations, the ascendency of the position brings on the scene of history artists, philosophers, religious reformers, politicians, capable of interpreting or accomplishing the thought of their age and of their race, as it brings on the scene of Nature species of animals and of plants, the best fitted for accommodating themselves to their climate and their soil.† Many other analogies between natural and human history might be enumerated. This is

* G. Saint-Hilaire's theory of analogues and unity of composition See the developments made by Richard Owen.
† Darwin's principle of Natural Selection.

because their two subjects are similar. In the one, and in the other, natural groups are operated on—to wit, individuals constructed after a common type, divisible in families, in kinds, and in species. In the one and in the other, the object is living—to wit, subjected to a spontaneous and continued transformation. In the one and in the other, the original form is hereditary, and the acquired form is transmitted in part and slowly by inheritance. In the one and in the other, the organised molecule is not developed save under the influence of its position. In the one and in the other, each state of the organised being has the twofold condition of the previous state and the general tendency of the type. By all these developments the human animal is a continuation of the brute; for the human faculties have their root in the life of the brain, as well the superior ones whereof man enjoys the privilege, as the inferior of which he has not the privilege; and by this hold the organic laws extend their empire even to the separate domain on the threshold of which natural sciences halt, to permit ethical sciences to rule. It follows from this that a career similar to that of the natural sciences is open to the ethical sciences; that history, the last comer, can discover laws like its elders; that it can, like them and within its province, govern the conceptions, and guide the efforts of men; that, by a train of well-conducted researches, it will end by determining the conditions of great human events—to wit, the circumstances essential to the appearance, to the duration, or the downfall of various forms of associations, of thought, and of action. Such is the field open to it; it has no limit; in a domain like that all the efforts of a single man can only bear it forward a pace or two; he observes one small corner, then another; from time to time he stops to point out the way he considers the shortest and the most certain. This is all I have endeavoured to do ; the keenest pleasure of a toiling spirit lies in the thought of the work which others will perform later."

Having permitted M. Taine to speak for himself, I may now offer an objection to his method which appears to me so serious as to be almost fatal. It relates to the fundamental difference between the positions occupied by the botanist and zoologist, and the critic and historian. The former have no personal and national bias in favour of the results of their observations. They may prefer, as a matter of taste, one plant or one animal to another, but this does not interfere in the slightest degree with the manner in which they classify and explain either. They do not care whether a group of plants, or of animals, exists in a particular country and under particular conditions. When a Frenchman examines a flower or dissects a bat, he thinks nothing about the spot on which the flower grew or the bat was produced. But when a Frenchman deals with an author or artist of a foreign nation, he does not forget, nor will he forget until the millennium shall arrive and human nature shall be transmogrified, that he is a Frenchman, and that the author or artist is a foreigner. Intentionally or unconsciously, he judges the eloquence, the style, the diction, the talent, and the works of the foreigner by a French standard and from a French point of view. M. Taine himself is a proof of this No foreigner has written more acutely and instructively about England and the English than he has done, yet, while the result is admired, the remark is made, either aloud or in a whisper: "Very wonderful, certainly, considering that M. Taine is a Frenchman." Language, that living expression of a nation's mind, is in its essence a sealed book to him who is not one of the nation. There is a flavour in words which a native of the land wherein they are current can alone detect and enjoy. No one but the native of an English-speaking country can ever enter into full communion with the spirit of Shakespeare; no one but a Frenchman can ever perfectly appreciate all that is grand in Corneille, pathetic in Racine, pointed in Pascal, graceful in Madame Sévigné, easy and neat in Voltaire; no one but an Italian can ever be adequately impressed by the might and mystery of Dante; no one but a Spaniard can heartily appreciate Cervantes; no one but a German can thoroughly explore and admire the masterpieces of Goethe. Even with all his mastery over our tongue, it is doubtful whether M. Taine can fully enjoy the English of Thackeray, simply as English, or detect the subtle grace and point which impart an inexpressible charm to the English of Hawthorne. We know that he rates English painting very low; he considers it false art, an appeal to the mind rather than to the eyes. But this opinion is merely due to his entertaining a particular view of art. When analysed, his decision amounts to this: "Your painting is not what I call art; it gives me no pleasure; consequently it is a failure." He says that Gainsborough's

INTRODUCTORY CHAPTER.

"'Blue Boy' already possesses the expressive and wholly modern physiognomy by which a work, falling within the painter's province, oversteps the limits of painting." He thinks it a fatal defect in the works of Hogarth, of Reynolds, of Sir Edwin Landseer, that they tell a story which the beholder is expected to appreciate quite as much as the colouring and the drawing. To tell a story in colours is surely no crime, even if it be treason to art; the natural reflection being, Then so much the worse for the art which can be so easily betrayed. When perusing his criticisms upon English painters, the wider applicability of what he says in defence of Raffaelle against the disparaging comments of Mr. Ruskin becomes apparent : "It is easy to condemn a painter, even a very great one, when something is required of him whereof he never dreamt" (p. 341). Hardly less curious than the sweeping charge brought against English painters, is the assumption that Mr. Ruskin is the accepted exponent of the true English theory of painting. For a time some young artists strove to give practical effect to Mr. Ruskin's theories; but the attempt had to be abandoned in despair, for the theories were so often altered, that, despite their author maintaining he was never more consistent than when, to all appearance, he enumerated contradictory propositions; no ordinary person could succeed in applying them in a uniform and rational manner. So far from Mr. Ruskin being the supreme authority in England on the subject of the great Masters, the objection which M. Taine offers to his strictures would find general acceptance among English artists and critics. The truth is, however, that M. Taine views art from a purely French point of view; he interprets it in accordance with French canons. I do not blame him for this. Indeed, he cannot act otherwise. But how can he note "psychological states," mark the "dependencies and conditions" which affect literary, artistic, or historical productions, if he starts with a set of foregone conclusions, which are alike personal and national, which have no universal sanction, and will not command universal respect? The case of a fauna or flora is so different, as to be palpable to the most superficial observer. The system which Linnæus applied to botany and Cuvier to natural history are systems of general applicability. They can be employed in the true scientific spirit, and made to yield genuine scientific results.

After examining the results of M. Taine's method, as applied by him to men of note in the world of art and letters, I do not find that these are so conclusive as to reflect glory upon the method itself. His volume about Lafontaine, which contains much exquisite writing, many shrewd remarks, and displays much dialectical skill, merely shows that Lafontaine was a poet. The "Essay on Livy" is designed to prove that Livy was an "oratorical historian." The explanation of Shakespeare is that he had "a complete imagination; all his genius lies in that phrase." This is quite as satisfactory as M. Victor Hugo's explanation that "Shakespeare was his intellectual twin brother;"

but it leaves the matter where it was, and is but M. Taine's way of saying, what other critics have said before him, that the great poet was a man of genius. Indeed, the words talent and genius when properly applied and suitably qualified, serve in reality as formulas like those which M. Taine educes by his method. For his particular method itself, M. Taine exhibits what appears to be a disproportionate affection. He acts with regard to it as Shelley said authors frequently do, resembling mothers in preferring "the children who have given them most trouble." Yet he is noteworthy as a writer not in consequence, but in spite, of his method. Strip off everything relating to it in his several works, and the works themselves will continue to attract and impress; they will still reflect the beauties of his own mind, and be radiant with the splendours of his brilliant style. Of the method itself, I may say what Condillac said of rules; like the parapet of a bridge, it may hinder a person from falling into the river, but will not help him on his way. M. Taine no more requires it to sustain him than Byron required bladders or corks, to buoy him up when he entered the water, after he had demonstrated his powers by swimming across the Hellespont.

The expectation which he has of ultimately using history for the purpose of framing laws, and so giving to it a place among the natural sciences, is an expectation which no one can entertain who disagrees with him as to first principles, who contemplates the universe in a different fashion, who puts a different interpretation upon the word cause. According to him a cause is a fact; in my opinion it is a figure of speech. He thinks that a fact can be found of such a kind that from it may be deduced the nature, the relations, and changes of other facts, and that this dominant and generative fact is the cause of the others; I regard the relations of cause and effect simply as sequences. All that we can know or note is that the one follows the other, and to call the one the cause of the other is merely another way of expressing this succession of continuity. Where he detects "dependencies and conditions," I merely perceive successions and appearances. Where he discerns laws, I perceive nothing but explanations, and explanations, too, of the case as put by him. With him I agree in thinking that the result of a closer observation and more careful estimate of facts will be to render both criticism and history more exact and trustworthy. But, after all, the individual critic and historian will announce his individual opinion. He will have no right to demand a hearing on any other ground than mastery of the subject and freedom from obvious and undue bias. He will, if endowed with M. Taine's industry, learning, skill in grouping facts, power in stating opinions, talent in manipulating words, be regarded, as M. Taine is deservedly regarded, as a master of his craft, as an authority in his sphere.

Yet, even if his philosophical views should be established beyond dispute, an insuperable difficulty will remain. To interpret the individual, or a course of historical events, after his fashion would require an investigator so entirely impersonal as to be almost superhuman. A man who had no national leanings or private sympathies might possibly deal with human beings and their literary, artistic, or historical concerns in the same scientific fashion that a physiologist deals with human crania, and a botanist with plants and flowers. So long, however, as it remains true that "there is a great deal of human nature in man," so long will the efforts of the profoundest thinkers and most brilliant writers fail to elevate and alter history and criticism to such an extent and in such a way as to make of them sciences fitted to rank in precision and universality with the recognised natural sciences.

III.

Inability to advocate all M. Taine's pretensions does not imply a want of admiration for what he has performed. He is greater than his method. His own personality is too marked to be concealed under any formula, however abstract; his powers are too rare to fail to extort the admiration of those who may differ the most from him on purely speculative points. His characteristic is a passion for facts; his excellence consists in the skill with which he can turn his facts to the best account. He has a keen appreciation of beauty in every form; he can convey his impressions to a reader in language of singular felicity. He requires the aid of no method to enunciate conclusions which are very plausible and often very just. His judgments are formed on so complete an array of evidence, and with such an unquestionable desire to be impartial, that they deserve to be treated with respect, even when they cannot be implicitly accepted.

In his "Notes on England," as in all his works, there is no lack of theories which may be called in question, of explanations which are sometimes partial and one-sided, of general views based upon insufficient data. He is emphatic in connecting drunkenness in this country with the English climate, and his theory of the race leads him to maintain that the English people, living in a murky air and beneath unkindly skies, must have an inordinate fondness for strong drinks. The truth is, the vice of drunkenness, which is one of the curses of the United Kingdom, is the curse also of the United States, of Canada, of Australia, where the sky is as bright as in France, where the air is as dry and exhilarating, where the temperature is never less agreeable, and is often more genial. But in these countries, as in ours till recently, strong drinks are cheap, and wine is dear; if wine were everywhere as cheap as it is in France, there might not be less drunkenness, but it would be of a less brutal type than that which shocked M. Taine. He made his first observations at a time when heavy duties imposed upon light wines gave to the artificially strengthened wines of Spain and Portugal the virtual monopoly of the market. He says: "Their common wines, port, sherry, very hot, very spirituous, are loaded with brandy in addition; this mixture deprives them of delicacy, yet if they were pure the English would consider them insipid; our Bordeaux wines, and even our Burgundies, are too light for them." (pp. 57, 58). Since this was written the tariff has been altered, the result being that, for one glass of light wine drunk then, a bottle is drunk now. Moreover, no better recommendation can be given to sherry at the present day than to affirm that it is a natural wine, and is wholly unfortified by brandy. The Custom-House returns prove the former assertion; the advertisements of wine-merchants uphold the latter.

More than once M. Taine gives as an explanation of the rich acting in a particular way, that they wish to escape *ennui*; this, he maintains, is one of the causes of the hospitality they dispense. However, neither the word nor the thing is known in this country. A person may be "bored," even "bored to death;" but this is very different. To be bored is to be oppressed by something of which there is a desire to get rid; to feel *ennui* is to restlessly long for something which cannot readily be procured. Indeed, I believe *ennui* to be simply a pestilent, yet imaginary disease, engendered by a word, which in France is commonly made the convenient excuse for ladies falling passionately in love with the wrong gentlemen and for gentlemen loving their neighbours' wives too well. It is as much a figment of the imagination as the "spleen," which the French insist is a malady peculiar to this country, but from which no English man, woman, or child has been known to suffer for a century, from which no native of Scotland was ever known to suffer at all, and which no native of Ireland can understand. The "spleen" departed from the southern part of the island along with its fashionable companion malady, "the vapours," but it seems to have destroyed its companion during the passage across the channel, and to have arrived in France alone.

Other matters of detail might be noticed and corrected. When it is said, for instance (p. 113), that the word "governor," as familiarly used by English boys, is a token of the position of authority which their father occupies in his house, this exemplifies one of those rapid generalisations which are due to an imperfect apprehension of the facts. Had M. Taine known that the word is a slang one borrowed from the poorer classes, that it has not been in use longer than thirty years, and that it is already becoming obsolete, he would hardly have cited it as confirmatory of his theory. Nor ought he to have chosen the case of a brutal parent whose consumptive son was afraid to return home to die without his father's permission, as being in any respect more typical of English family relations than the well-known instance of the red-haired chambermaid seen by a traveller at a hotel in France, as being indicative of the fact which he noted, that all the women of the country had red hair. Generally, however, when M. Taine records his own observations, he is alike acute and correct. Information given him by inexcusably ignorant persons appears to have misled him when he errs the most notably. Thus his informant who told him (p. 241) that medical men are not created peers because "no man who has held out his hands for guineas could take his place among peers of the realm," must have been strangely unacquainted with the fact known to every schoolboy that barristers not only take guineas, but accept them willingly, and that the more guineas they receive, owing to the increase of their practice, the better are their prospects of a seat on the woolsack and elevation to the peerage. Moreover, at least one member of the House of Lords entered it not many years ago solely because, as a banker, he had handled the money of his customers so judiciously as to have accumulated an enormous fortune. After all, however, these slips, and others which the well-informed reader will readily detect, are comparatively trivial blemishes. In estimating the work as a whole, it would be well to exchange, what Chateaubriand called the petty and meagre criticism of defects, for the comprehensive and prolific criticism of beauties. These "Notes on England" are really of first-rate quality; they form an admirable picture of what is truly distinctive and noteworthy. M. Taine approaches so closely to the ideal intelligent foreigner whose advent is so often proclaimed, but whose presence in the flesh we never enjoy; his general tone is so excellent and his endeavour to be fair so conspicuous; his qualifications are so exceptional and his actual achievements give him so clear a title to our esteem; he is so singularly free from the sins which beset his countrymen who retail their experience after having sojourned in this country; he is so sympathetic without stooping to flattery, and so candid without lapsing into discourtesy; he is, in short, such a model traveller, such an acute observer, such a graphic and an artistic narrator, that he merits, what he will doubtless receive, a cordial welcome from all who enjoy reading the opinions of a genial and capable foreign writer upon the social life, the domestic arrangements, the religious sentiments, and the political constitution of this country.

W. F. RAE.

L

BOULOGNE TO LONDON BRIDGE.

IT is eleven o'clock; Boulogne recedes, and lessens upon the horizon. The vessels in the harbour, the slender masts are first merged in the vague obscurity; presently the lights diminish, and soon appear nothing more on the verge of the sky than a heap of pale stars.

This is a strange and profound sensation; the sea is still, and a motionless mist broods over it. All has vanished; alone at the horizon a revolving light from time to time flings its reflection over the passing wave. It seems as if we were entering the kingdom of silence and of vacancy, the colourless and shapeless world of things which are not. Darkness, vast and vague, encompasseth us. The ship enters, and becomes lost in it. But a moment ago could still be descried, afar off, from the side of the stern, an uncertain fringe, the distant land; now, around the vessel, there is nothing but moving blackness. Thus engulfed, it still makes progress, with sure instinct, and opens up an entrance into the unseen. Like a laborious insect, it indefatigably moves its great iron limbs, and raises around its keel vague phosphorescent appearances. They shine with the changing reflection of opal and mother-of-pearl. One follows their long undulation, which keeps rising, falling, and developing its soft clearness. Variegated diamonds, bounding pearls turn in its hollows, and its fringe of foam makes a border of dead silver, a wrought, winding, waving frame to the nocturnal mirror.

The sun rose half an hour ago, but one does not see it; there is only a feeble brightening in the east; all the remainder is covered with clouds. Towards the east, the sea, as far as the eye can reach, streaks with its distinct line the clear and calm horizon. Right and left of the boat, a slight distant strip rises from the sea; it is land, and through the mist one begins to distinguish its greenish indentation. We advance; but in this enormous estuary, the land, so flat and small, appears but a mass of mud; humidity bathes the colours; all the tones are diluted, washed out; you would take it for a pale water-colour over which a child, with its finger, has drawn drops of water. Upon the right the coast approaches; this is now the real English landscape which I saw between Newhaven and London last year. Rising ground of a dull green, divided by hedges, strewn with isolated trees; one enclosed pasturage, then another, then another besides, and untended cattle, penned up permanently; a Belgium less flat and less uniform than the other, gleaming in the sun, but very dismal and very commonplace; the sky is showery, and this sky is frequently so. The river is enormous, but dirty, dotted with wan and false tints; turned back by the rising tide, it oscillates between mountains of mud, which in turn it covers and quits; under the pestiferous vapour its tiny waves have a lugubrious aspect: thus it rolls along, livid and muddy, but useful; it is a worker and porter unique of its kind. Ships now begin to move in bands along its back, the most of them laden, large, small, of every form and every size, and the sailors climbing in the rigging resemble busy spiders.

Conversation with an Englishman of the middle class, son of a merchant, I should suppose; he does not know French, German, or Italian; he is not altogether a gentleman. Twenty-five years of age; sneering, decided, incisive face; he has made, for his amusement and instruction, a trip lasting twelve months, and is returning from India and from Australia. Forty thousand miles in all. He says, "To understand the people, they must be seen." He is from Liverpool. A family that does not keep a carriage may live comfortably there upon three or four hundred pounds sterling. One must marry, that is a matter of course; he hopes to be married before two or three years are over. It is better, however, to remain a bachelor, if one does not meet the person with whom one desires to pass one's whole life. " But one always meets with her; the only thing is not to let the chance slip." He has met the proper person more than once when quite a young man; but then he was not rich enough; at present, being "independent," he will try again. A dowry is unnecessary. It is natural, and even pleasant, to undertake the charge of a portionless wife and of a family. " If your wife is good, and you love her, she is well worth that."

It is clear to me that their happiness consists in being at home at six in the evening, with a pleasing, attached wife, having four or five children on their knees, and respectful domestics. In the boat there is a family of four children, of whom the eldest is four and a half, and the mother twenty-three or twenty-four. At the sea-side, on the beach, I have often seen entire broods, the father of the family at their head; it is not rare to meet with children who mount in steps from the baby at the breast up to the girl of eighteen. The parents do not feel themselves either over-burdened or embarrassed. According to this Englishman, they owe nothing but education to their children; the daughters marry without a dowry, the sons shift for themselves. I know a solicitor who makes much money and spends it all, except £300 or £400 a year, with which he insures his life in the names of his children; at each new arrival, there is a fresh policy of £2,000, payable to the child at its father's death. In this way the child is provided for, and besides commerce, industry supplies him with a quantity of outlets which are denied to a young Frenchman.

Of all the countries this Englishman has seen, England is the most moral. Still, in his opinion, the national evil is "the absence of morality." In consequence he judges France after the English fashion. "The women are badly brought up there, do not read the Bible, are too fond of balls, occupy themselves wholly with dress. The men frequent cafés and keep mistresses, hence so many unfortunate households. This is the result not of race, but of education. French women in England, seriously brought up in English fashion, make very good wives here." "Is everything good in your country?" "No; the national and horrible vice is drunkenness. A man who earns 20s. a week drinks ten of them. Add to this improvidence, stoppage of work, and poverty." "But in cases of distress you have the poor-houses, the workhouses?" "They will not go to them, they prefer to fast, to die of hunger." "Why?" "For three reasons. Because they wish to drink at their ease. Because they hate being shut up. Because there are formalities; they must prove that they belong to the parish, but the most of them do not know where they were born, or find it too difficult to procure the necessary papers." He is a talkative fellow devoid of affected seriousness. Two other Englishmen with whom I conversed in the boat are like unto him. I have always found this disposition among the English; probably if they have the contrary reputation, it is because when in a foreign country and obliged to speak another language, they are silent through bashfulness, and keep watch in order not to commit themselves. Speak English imperfectly with a bad accent, they are no longer uneasy, they feel themselves your superiors. If you put a question to them politely, gently, or ask them to do you a small service, they are complying and even officious. I discovered this twenty times last year in London and everywhere else.

Other figures in the boat. Two young couples who remain on deck covered with wrappings under umbrellas. A long downpour has begun; they remain seated; in the end they were drenched like ducks. This was in order that husband and wife should not be separated by going below to the cabins. Another young wife suffered much from sea-sickness; her husband, who had the look of a merchant's clerk, took her in his arms, supported, tried to read to her, tended her with a freedom and expression of infinite tenderness. Two young girls of fifteen and sixteen, who speak German and French exceedingly well and without accent, large restless eyes, large white teeth; they chatter and laugh with perfect unconstraint, with admirable petulance of friendly gaiety; not the slightest trace of coquetry, none of our nice little tricks which have been learned and done on purpose; they never think about the onlookers. A lady of forty in spectacles beside her husband, in a worn-out dress, with relics of feminine ornaments, extraordinary teeth in the style of tusks, very serious and most ludicrous; a Frenchwoman, even middle-aged, never forgets to adjust herself—to arrange her dress. Patience and phlegm of a tall dry Englishman, who has not moved from the seat, has taken but a single turn, who has spoken to no one, who suffices to himself. As a contrast, three Frenchmen, who put random questions, make hap-hazard assertions, grow impatient, gesticulate, and make puns or something akin to them, appeared to me pleasant fellows.

Gradually the clouds have disappeared and the sky is radiant. Right and left we pass small country houses, pretty, clean, and freshly painted. Green grass is seen appearing at the horizon, here and there large trees well-placed and well-grouped. Gravesend on the left heaps its brown houses around a blueish steeple Vessels, warehouses, increase in number. One feels that one is approaching a great city. The small landing-stages project fifty paces into the river over the shining mud which the fallen tide leaves dry. Every quarter of an hour, the imprint and the presence of man, the power by which he has transformed nature, become more visible; docks, magazines, ship-building and caulking yards, stocks, habitable houses, prepared materials, accumulated merchandise; to the right is seen the skeleton of an iron church which is being prepared here for erection in India. Astonishment ends by turning into bewilderment. From Greenwich, the river is nothing but a street a mile broad and upwards, where ships ascend and descend between two rows of buildings, interminable rows of a dull red, in brick or tiles, bordered with great piles stuck in the mud for mooring vessels, which come here to unload or to load. Ever new magazines for copper, stone, coal, cordage, and the rest; bales are always being piled up, sacks being hoisted, barrels being rolled, cranes are creeking, capstans sounding. The sea reaches London by the river; it is an inland port; New York, Melbourne, Canton, Calcutta, are in direct connection with this place. But that which carries the impression to its height, is the sight of the canals through which the docks communicate with the sea; they form cross-streets, and they are streets for ships; one suddenly perceives a line of them which is endless; from Greenwich Park where I ascended last year, the horizon is bounded with masts and ropes. The incalculable indistinct rigging stretches a spiders'-web in a circle at the side of the sky. This is certainly one of the great spectacles of our planet; to see a similar conglomeration of erections, of men, of vessels, and of business, it would be necessary to go to China.

However, on the river to the west, rises an inextricable forest of yards, of masts, of rigging: these are the vessels which arrive, depart or anchor, in the first place in groups, then in long rows, then in a continuous heap, crowded together, massed against the chimneys of houses and the pulleys of warehouses, with all the tackle of incessant, regular, gigantic labour. A foggy smoke penetrated with light envelopes them; the sun there sifts its golden rain, and the brackish, tawny, half-green, half-violet water, balances in its undulations striking and strange reflections. It might be said this was the heavy and smoky air of a large hothouse. Nothing is natural here, everything is transformed, artificially wrought from the toil of man, up to the light and the air. But the hugeness of the conglomeration and of the human creation hinders us from thinking about this deformity and this artifice; for want of pure and healthy beauty, the swarming and grandiose life remains; the shimmering of embrowned waves, the scattering of the light imprisoned in vapour, the soft whitish or pink tints which cover these vastnesses, diffuse a sort of grace over the prodigious city, having the effect of a smile upon the face of a shaggy and blackened Cyclop.

II.

SUNDAY IN LONDON. THE STREETS AND PARKS.

SUNDAY in London in the rain: the shops are shut, the streets almost deserted; the aspect is that of an immense and a well-ordered cemetery. The few passers-by under their umbrellas, in the desert of squares and streets, have the look of uneasy spirits who have risen from their graves; it is appalling.

I had no conception of such a spectacle, which is said to be frequent in London. The rain is small, compact, pitiless; looking at it one can see no reason why it should not continue to the end of all things; one's feet churn water, there is water everywhere, filthy water impregnated with an odour of soot. A yellow, dense fog fills the air, sweeps down to the ground; at thirty paces a house, a steam-boat appear as spots upon blotting-paper. After an hour's walk in the Strand especially, and in the rest of the City, one has the spleen, one meditates suicide. The lofty lines of fronts are of sombre brick, the exudations being encrusted with fog and soot. Monotony and silence; yet the inscriptions on metal or marble speak and tell of the absent master, as in a large manufactory of bone-black closed on account of a death.

A frightful thing is the huge palace in the Strand, which is called Somerset House. Massive and heavy piece of architecture, of which the hollows are inked, the porticoes blackened with soot, where, in the cavity of the empty court, is a sham fountain without water, pools of water on the pavement, long rows of closed windows—what can they possibly do in these catacombs? It seems as if the livid and sooty fog had even befouled the verdure of the parks. But what most offends the eyes are the colonnades, peristyles, Grecian ornaments, mouldings, and wreaths of the houses, all bathed in soot; poor antique architecture— what is it doing in such a climate? The flutings and columns in front of the British Museum are begrimed as if liquid mud had been poured over them. St. Paul's, a kind of Pantheon, has two ranges of columns, the lower range is entirely black, the upper range, recently scraped, is still white, but the white is offensive, coal smoke has already plastered it with its leprosy.

These spots are melancholy, being the decay of the stone. And these nude statues in memory of Greece! Wellington as a fighting hero, naked under the dripping trees of the park! That hideous Nelson, stuck on his column with a coil of rope in the form of a pig-tail, like a rat impaled on the top of a pole! Every form, every classical idea is contrary to nature here. A swamp like this is a place of exile for the arts of antiquity. When the Romans disembarked here they must have thought themselves in Homer's hell, in the land of the Cimmerians. The vast space which, in the south, stretches between the earth and the sky, cannot be discovered by the eye; there is no air; there is nothing but liquid fog; in this pale smoke objects are but fading phantoms, Nature has the look of a bad drawing in charcoal which some one has rubbed with his sleeve. I have just spent half-an-hour on Waterloo Bridge; the Houses of Parliament, blurred and indistinct, appear in the distance but a wretched pile of scaffolding; nothing is discernible, and, more particularly, nothing is living, except a few steamboats skimming along the river, black, smoky, unwearied insects; a Greek watching their passengers embarking and disembarking would have thought of the Styx. He would have found that to exist here was not to live; in fact, life here is different from what it is in his country; the ideal has altered with the climate. The mind quits the without to retire within itself, and there create a world. Here one must have a comfortable and well-ordered home, clubs, societies, plenty of business, many religious and moral preoccupations; above all, instead of abandoning oneself to the influence of exterior impressions, it is necessary to extrude all the sad promptings of unfriendly Nature, and fill up the great void wherein melancholy and tedium would take up their abode. During the week one has work, constant, earnest work, wherewith to ward off and arm oneself against the inclemency of things. But what is to be done on the day of rest? There is the church or the pot-house, intoxication or a sermon, insensibility or refection, but no other way of spending a Sunday such as this; in that way, whether in thinking, whether in making a beast of oneself, one is absorbed, one attains forgetfulness. I observe many doors ajar in the spirit vaults, sad faces, worn or wild, pass out and in. Let us visit the churches.

I visited four, and I heard two sermons, the first in a church in the Strand. A naked, cold, and unornamented structure, with the exception of two allegorical figures at the end; large wooden pews in which one is ensconced up to the neck. The congregation which fills it is composed not of the commonalty, but of the respectable middle class, very well dressed, and with serious and sensible physiognomies. They come to provision themselves with moral counsels, to refresh their principles. The preacher chose for his text, " One mind, one spirit," and thereupon he advised his hearers to hold fast to their principles, yet to be conciliatory towards their fellows. The sermon was good—slightly commonplace, yet solid. When reading the numerous essays in English literature, and at the present day the moralisings of the *Saturday Review*, one perceives that commonplaces do not weary them; apparently they consider morality not as an object of curiosity, but as a practical tool, an instrument in daily use which must be sharpened every Sunday.

The books displayed on the ledges of the pews are the Psalms and the Book of Common Prayer—the mass book of England. It is marked by much elevation, and a certain Hebraic sublimity in the style of Milton; yet by no tenderness and outpourings as in the "Imitation," no flowers of rhetoric or sentimental namby-pambyness, as in our minor devotional works; but by an imposing, impassioned, and sometimes a lyrical tone. The Liturgy was compiled at the period of the Revival, and retains its accent. A noteworthy point is that here the date and origin of each piece are noted, this one being of the sixteenth century; this passage being taken from the Apocrypha, but retained on account of its elevation. The believer is instructed by these remarks, is informed about criticism and history; see the sermons of Tillotson and of Barrow at the era of Bossuet, with their Greek texts and discussions about the grammatical interpretation. Time being given, this necessarily leads to German exegesis.

The superb nave, the admirable Gothic architecture of Westminster Abbey, are alone adapted to the climate; this labyrinth of forms, these sweeping and huge mouldings, this profusion of delicate sculptures, are required to fill the dim air and people the void of such sombre interiors. I wandered about looking at the mortuary monuments, the numerous graceful sculptures of the eighteenth century, others of our own age so cold and pedantic, when suddenly the music pealed forth, not the monotonous psalmody of our Vespers, the rude and monkish chants, the verses and responses which seem to be the voices of ailing nuns, but beautiful pieces in parts, grave and noble recitative, melodious outbursts of harmony, the productions of the best epoch. Then after the reading of a passage about Sisera, the organ and the choristers, children's voices and bass voices, sounded forth a full and rich anthem. Such music as that is the worthy accompaniment to the psalms and to the prayers which I have just perused. Thus understood, worship is the opera of elevated, serious, and believing souls. Nothing is more important; it is essential that the church and the services should be on a level with the sentiments of a people, not merely of the crowd and of the uneducated, but of the select few.

I visited two other churches in the afternoon. There, too, the music was beautiful, and the edifice was filled with the well-to-do middle class. The large enclosed pews, all the galleries were filled with well-dressed persons; there are as many men as women, and many gentlemen; the public was not our public of women, old curmudgeons, servant girls, common people. Of the three clergymen I have seen, one worthy and polite, who spoke to me, had the air of a semi-professor and semi-magistrate. Another resembled a Parisian notary, mature and well preserved, who assumes soft tones and a sentimental look, in order to procure the signing of a marriage contract. I saw others last year in London and the country. With their short gown, the tone they use in the pulpit, one would take them for judges or chief justices; by their education, their marriage, their manners, their calling, they are laymen slightly graver than the others; their garb out of church is that of laymen, with the exception of the everlasting white tie; the moral difference is not much greater than the material difference. This is the essential point; to place the layman on a par with the priest, or at most separated by one degree only, is in truth the work of the Reformation.

On returning to my hotel I read the following proclamation in Friday's *Gazette*:—" Victoria R.: We, most seriously and religiously considering that it is our indispensable duty to be careful above all other things to preserve and advance the honour and service of Almighty God, and to discourage and suppress all vice, profaneness, debauchery, and immorality. . . . . we do hereby strictly enjoin and prohibit all our loving subjects, of what degree or quality soever, from playing on the Lord's-day, at dice, cards, or any other game whatsoever, either in public or private houses, or other place or places whatsoever; and we do hereby require and command them, and every of them decently and reverently to attend the worship of God on every

Lord's-day;" and the magistrates are enjoined "to take effectual care to prevent all persons keeping taverns, or other public houses whatsoever, from selling wine, beer, or other liquors, or receiving or permitting guests to be or remain in such their houses in the time of Divine service on the Lord's-day."

This order is not strictly observed; the tavern doors are closed during service, but they can be opened and drinking goes on in the back room. In any case this is a relic of the old Puritanism altogether distasteful in France. Prohibit people to drink and amuse themselves on Sunday? But to a French workman, and to a peasant, Sunday appears to have been made for nothing else. Stendhal said that here, in Scotland, in true Biblical countries, religion spoils one day out of seven, destroys the seventh part of possible happiness. He judges the Englishman, the man of the North, after the model of the man of the South, whom wine exhilarates and does not brutalise, who can without inconvenience give way to his instinct, and whose pleasure is poetical. Here the temperament is different, more violent and more combative; pleasure is a brutish and bestial thing: I could cite twenty examples of this. An Englishman said to me, "When a Frenchman is drunk he chatters; when a German is drunk he sleeps; when an Englishman is drunk he fights."

Other traces of Puritanical severity, among the rest, are the recommendations on the stairs which lead down to the Thames, and elsewhere; one is requested to be decent. At the railway-station there are large Bibles fastened to chains for the use of the passengers while waiting for the train. A tall, sallow, and bony fellow handed to me two printed pages on the brazen serpent of Moses, with applications to the present life: "You, too, oh reader, have been bitten by the fiery serpents. To heal yourself lift up your eyes to Him who has been elevated as the sign of salvation." Other tokens denote an aristocratic country. At the gate of St. James's Park is the following notice: "The park-keepers have orders to prevent all beggars from entering the gardens, and all persons in ragged or dirty clothes, or who are not outwardly decent and well-behaved." At every step one feels oneself further removed from France.

The population numbers three millions and a quarter; that makes twelve cities like Marseilles, ten cities like Lyons, two cities like Paris put together; but words upon paper are no substitutes for the sensation of the eyes. It is necessary to take a cab several days in succession, and proceed straight on towards the south, the north, the east, and the west, during a whole morning, as far as the uncertain limits where houses grow scanty and the country begins.

Enormous, enormous—this is the word which always recurs. Moreover, all is rich and well ordered; consequently, they must think us neglected and poor. Paris is mediocre compared with these squares, these crescents, these circles and rows of monumental buildings of massive stone, with porticoes, with sculptured fronts, these spacious streets; there are sixty of them as vast as the Rue de la Paix; assuredly Napoleon III. demolished and rebuilt Paris only because he had lived in London. In the Strand, in Piccadilly, in Regent Street, in the neighbourhood of London Bridge, in twenty places, there is a bustling crowd, a surging traffic, an amount of obstruction which our busiest and most frequented boulevard cannot parallel. Everything is on a large scale here; the clubs are palaces, the hotels are monuments; the river is an arm of the sea;

the cabs go twice as fast; the boatmen and the omnibus-conductors condense a sentence into a word; words and gestures are economised; actions and time are turned to the utmost possible account; the human being produces and expends twice as much as among us.

From London Bridge to Hampton Court are eight miles, that is, nearly three leagues of buildings. After the streets and quarters erected together, as one piece, by wholesale, like a hive after a model, come the countless pleasure retreats, cottages surrounded with verdure and trees in all styles—Gothic, Grecian, Byzantine, Italian, of the Middle Age, or the Revival, with every mixture and every shade of style, generally in lines or clusters of five, ten, twenty of the same sort, apparently the handiwork of the same builder, like so many specimens of the same vase or the same bronze. They deal in houses as we deal in Parisian articles. What a multitude of well-to-do, comfortable, and rich existences! One divines accumulated gains, a wealthy and spending middle-class quite different from ours, so pinched, so straitened. The most humble, in brown brick, are pretty by dint of tidiness; the window panes sparkle like mirrors; there is nearly always a green and flowery patch; the front is covered with ivy, honeysuckle, and nasturtiums.

The entire circumference of Hyde Park is covered with houses of this sort, but finer, and these in the midst of London retain a country look; each stands detached in its square of turf and shrubs, has two stories in the most perfect order and condition, a portico, a bell for the tradespeople, a bell for the visitors, a basement for the kitchen and the servants, with a flight of steps for the service; very few mouldings and ornaments; no outside sun-shutters; large, clear windows, which let in plenty of light; flowers on the sills and at the portico; stables in a mews apart, in order that their odours and sight may be kept at a distance; all the external surface covered with white, shining, and varnished stucco; not a speck of mud or dust; the trees, the turf, the flowers, the servants prepared as if for an exhibition of prize products. How well one can picture the inhabitant after seeing his shell! In the first place, it is the Teuton who loves Nature, and who needs a reminder of the country; next, it is the Englishman who wishes to be by himself in his staircase as in his room, who could not endure the promiscuous existence of our huge Parisian cages, and who, even in London, plans his house as a small castle, independent and enclosed. Besides, he is simple, and does not desire external display; on the other hand, he is exacting in the matter of condition and comfort, and separates his life from that of his inferiors. The number of such houses at the West-end is astonishing! The rent is nearly £500; from five to seven servants are kept; the master expends from twelve to twenty-four hundred pounds a year. There are ten of these fortunes and these lives in England to every one in France.

The impression is the same when visiting the parks; the taste, the area are quite different from what is the case among us. St. James's Park is a genuine piece of country, and of English country; huge old trees, real meadows, a large pond peopled with ducks and waterfowl; cows and sheep, in an enclosed space, feed on the grass, which is always fresh. There are even sheep in the narrow green border that surrounds Westminster Abbey; these people love the country in their hearts. It is sufficient to read their literature from Chaucer to Shakespeare, from Thomson to Wordsworth and Shelley, to find proofs of this. What a contrast to the Tuileries, the Champs Elysée, the Luxembourg! As a rule, the French garden, that of Louis XIV., is a room or gallery in the open air, wherein to walk and converse in company; in the English garden, such as they have invented and propagated, one is better alone; the eyes and the mind converse with natural things. We have arranged a park on this model in the Bois de Boulogne; but we have committed the blunder of placing therein a group of rocks and waterfalls; the artifice is discovered at a glance, and offends; English eyes would have felt it.

Regent's Park is larger than the Jardin des Plantes and the Luxembourg put together. I have often remarked that our life seems to them cooped up, confined; they need air and space more than we do; Englishmen whom I knew in Paris left their windows open all night; thus arises their longing for motion, their horse and foot races in the country. Stendhal justly said that a young English girl walks a greater distance in a week than a young Roman girl in a year; the Northern man, of athletic temperament, has a need of free respiration and of exercise. This park is in a retired neighbourhood; one hears no longer the rolling of carriages, and one forgets London; it is a solitude. The sun shines, but the air is always charged with damp clouds, floating watering-pots which dissolve in rain every quarter of an hour. The vast watery meadows have a charming softness, and the green branches drip with monotonous sound upon the still water of the ponds. I enter a hot-house where there are splendid orchids, some having the rich velvet of the iris, others a fresh colour of that inexpressible, delicious, mingled tint transfused with light like palpitating living flesh, a woman's breast; the hand desires yet dreads to press it; alongside, palm-trees raise their stems in a tepid atmosphere. A strange thing to us is that there are no keepers; admission is free, and no damage is done; I can understand that they must ridicule our establishments and public festivals, with their accompaniments of municipal guards. It is the same at the railway stations: every one is free to move about, to stand on the side of the line, to come and meet his friends at the carriage door; they are surprised and annoyed to see us caged in our waiting-rooms, enclosed, led like sheep, and always under the eye or the hand of an official.

I returned on foot to Piccadilly; again the London weather begins—the small and constant rain, the dissolving mud. F., who has spent the winter here, says that there is little snow, not more than in the centre of France; but, on the other hand, there is perpetual fog, rain nearly every day, and the most execrable muddy streets for pedestrians. As evidences, look at the foot-coverings and the feet of the ladies. Their boots are as large as those of gentlemen, their feet are those of watermen, and their gait is in keeping. My question continually recurs, How do the English spend their leisure hours, among others, their Sunday? They have the Club and often wine. F., in his club, had a neighbour who, in the reading-room, drank a large glass of wine, then went to sleep, drank a second half an hour afterwards and went to sleep again, and so on in succession without ever saying a word. Another of great wealth, a leading merchant, and who has sixteen gardeners at his country seat, is occupied all day with his business, returns home in the evening, speaks but seldom, lives like an automaton among his children; his daughter amuses herself by travelling about the entire year with a governess; in the family circle he merely finds the money—this is a common trait of the English character, deficiency in expansion and in amiability.

From Regent's Park to Piccadilly the spacious and interminable streets have a funereal aspect; the roadway is of black macadam; the rows of buildings, of the same cast, consist of blackened brick, where the window-panes shine with dark reflections; each house is separated from the street by railings and an area. There are few shops, not a single pretty one, no large plate-glass windows and engravings; that would be too dismal for us; nothing to attract and gladden the eyes; lounging is impossible; it is necessary to do one's work at home, or to take one's umbrella and go to business or to one's society.

Hyde Park is the largest of them all, with its small rivulet, its wide green-sward, its sheep, its shady walks, resembling a pleasure park suddenly transported to the centre of a capital. About two o'clock the principal alley is a riding-ground; there are ten times more gentlemen and twenty times more ladies on horseback than in the Bois de Boulogne on its most frequented days; little girls and boys of eight ride on ponies by the side of their father; I have seen ample and worthy matrons trotting along. This is one of their luxuries. Add to it that of having servants. For instance, a family of three persons which I visited keeps seven servants and three horses. The mother and daughter gallop in the park daily; they often pay visits on horseback; they economise in other things—in theatre-going, for example; they go but seldom to the theatre, and when they do it is to a box which has been presented to them. This vigorous exercise appears indispensable for health; young girls and ladies come here even when it rains. To keep three horses and a carriage costs nearly £200 a year. Looking at this crowd of persons on horseback one comes to the same conclusion as after seeing the houses and the staff of servants. The wealthy class is much more numerous in England than in France. Another index is the outlay in linen, clothes, gloves, and dresses always new. The climate dirties everything rapidly; they must be continually renovated. In every newspaper I find the addresses of dealers who come to the house and buy slightly soiled clothes; the obligation of a gentleman is to be always irreproachably well dressed; his coat when shabby is handed over to a man of the lower class, ends in rags on the back of a beggar, and thus marks the social rank of its possessor. Nowhere else is the disparity of conditions so clearly written in the externals of men. Imagine the evening dress of a man of fashion or the rose-coloured bonnet of a lady; you will find the former again on a miserable wretch squatting on one of the stairs of the Thames, and the latter at Shadwell on the head of an old woman groping amidst rubbish.

From five to seven o'clock is the review of ladies' dresses. Beauty and ornamentation abound, but taste is wanting. The colours are outrageously crude and the forms ungraceful; crinolines too distended and badly distended, in geometrical cones or bunched, green flounces, embroideries, flowered dresses, quantities of floating gauze, packets of falling or frizzed hair; crowning this display tiny embroidered and imperceptible bonnets. The bonnets are too much adorned, the hair, too shiny, presses closely on the temples; the small mantle or casaque falls formless to the lower part of the back, the petticoat expands prodigiously, and all the scaffolding badly joined, badly arranged, variegated and laboured, cries and protests with all its gaudy and overdone colours. In the sunshine, especially, at Hampton Court the day before yesterday, amongst the shopkeepers' wives, the absurdity was at its height; there were many violet dresses, one being of a wild violet clasped round the waist with a golden band, which would have made a painter cry out. I said to a lady, "The toilette is more showy among you than in France." "But my dresses come from Paris!" I carefully refrained from replying, "But you selected them."

Excepting only the highest class, they apparel themselves as fancy dictates. One imagines healthy bodies, well built, beautiful at times; but they must be imagined. The physiognomy is often pure, but also often sheepish. Many are simple babies, new waxen dolls, with glass eyes, which appear entirely empty of ideas. Other faces have become ruddy, and turned to raw beefsteak. There is a fund of folly or of brutality in this inert flesh—too white, or too red. Some are ugly or grotesque in the extreme; with heron's feet, stork's necks, always having the large front of white teeth, the projecting jaws of carnivora. As compensation, others are beautiful in the extreme. They have angelic faces; their eyes, of pale periwinkle, are softly deep; their complexion is that of a flower, or an infant; their smile is divine. One of these days, about ten o'clock in the morning, near Hyde Park Corner, I was rooted to the spot motionless with admiration at the sight of two young ladies; the one was sixteen, the other eighteen years old. They were in rustling dresses of white tulle amid a cloud of muslin; tall, slender, agile, their shape as perfect as their face, of incomparable freshness, resembling those marvellous flowers seen in select exhibitions, the whiteness of the lily or orchis; in addition to all that, gaiety, innocence, a superabundance of unalloyed sap and infantine expression, of laughter, and the mien of birds; the earth did not support them. Many of the horsewomen are charming, so simple, and so serious, without a trace of coquetry; they come here not to be seen, but to take the air; their manner is frank without pretension; their shake of the hand quite loyal, almost masculine; no frippery in their attire; the small black vest, tightened at the waist, moulds a fine shape and healthy form; to my mind, the first duty of a young lady is to be in good health. They manage their horses with complete ease and assurance. Sometimes the father or brother stops and talks business or politics with a friend; the ladies listen and thus habituate themselves to serious topics. These fathers and brothers, too, are a pleasant sight; expressive and resolute faces, which bear, or have borne, the burden of life; less exhausted than among us, less ready to smile and to execute the tricks of politeness, but calmer and more staid, and who often excite in the onlooker a vague impression of respect, of esteem at least, and often of trust. Perhaps this is because I am instructed as to their condition; yet it seems to me that mistake is difficult: whether nobles, members of Parliament, landed proprietors, their manners and their physiognomies are those of men accustomed to authority, and who have wielded it.

III.

ST. JAMES'S PARK, RICHMOND, THE DOCKS, AND EAST-END.

I HAVE paid many visits, and taken several walks. The things which please me most are the trees. Every day, after leaving the Athenæum, I go and sit for an hour in St. James's Park; the lake shines softly beneath its misty covering, while the dense foliage bends over the still waters. The rounded trees, the great green domes make a kind of architecture far more delicate than the other. The eye reposes itself upon these softened forms, upon these subdued tones. These are beauties, but tender and touching, those of foggy countries, of Holland. Yesterday, at eight o'clock in the evening, although the weather was fine, everything seen from the Suspension Bridge appeared vapoury; the last rays disappeared in whitish smoke; on the right, the remains of redness; over the Thames, and in the rest of the sky a pale slate tint. There are tones like these in the landscapes of Rembrandt, in the twilights of Van der Neer; the bathed light, the air charged with vapour, the insensible and continuous changes of the vast exhalation which softens, imparts a bluish tint to, and dims the contours, the whole producing the impression of a great life, vague, diffused, and melancholy—the life of a humid country.

At Richmond, I felt this still better. From the terrace can be discerned several leagues of country; the Thames, which is not larger than the Seine, winds through meadows, between clumps of large trees. All is green, of a soft green, almost effaced by the distance; one feels the freshness and the peace of the infinite vegetation; the grey sky extends over it a low and heavy dome; at the horizon are whitish mists in floating layers, here and there a darkened cloud, or the violet patch of a shower. From all the ground rises a sluggish mist; one watches it as if it were a piece of muslin drawn between the interstices of the trees, and gradually the floating gauze of the earth re-unites with the uniform veil of the sky. How still is the park! Troops of deer feed in the moist brake; the hinds approach the fence, and gaze on the passer by without fear. Can a tract of country be better arranged for relaxing the nerves of the man who struggles and toils? The oaks, the lime trees, the spreading and huge chestnut trees, are noble creatures which seem to speak in low tones with majesty and security; at their feet is thick and tall grass; the blades of grass, whereon the rain has left its tears, smile with a tender and sad grace. A sort of fond quietude emanates from the air, the sky, and all things; Nature welcomes the soul, weary and worn with striving. How one feels that their landscape suits them, and why they love it! Without doubt their climate befits trees, and, besides, they have had no invasion or popular rising to mutilate or cut them down; the national taste has favoured their preservation; olden things have been more respected and better preserved than in France, and among them must be numbered the trees.

Those of Windsor and of Hampton Court are as beautiful. From Kew Gardens to Hampton Court extends an alley of gigantic chestnut trees, of which the large pink and white bunches resemble girandoles. The foliage is so thick that underneath it is cool in the height of the sun. Upon the velvet of the grass, constellated with flowers and bordered by nasturtiums, stand forth clusters of rhododendrons, as tall as two men, entirely covered with rose-coloured flowers, amid which bees are humming. There are so many of them, they are so magnificent, of so tender a tissue and of so fine a tone, they are grouped with such profusion in a single clump wholly impregnated with light, that one remains dazzled; it is delicious, intoxicating; almost beyond Nature. A little way farther, in an enormous hot-house, palms, as large as oak, spread their curious vegetation, and bananas unfold leaves which would cover a child twelve years old. This is one of their talents; they admirably understand the architecture of trees, of grass, and of flowers; I have not seen even a classical palace or even a poor cottage where it was uncomprehended. Sometimes, indeed, the effect is too strong; in the sun, it is overpowering; the incomparable verdure then assumes tones so rich and intense that they cannot be transferred to canvas; they would offend, they would be too raw; it is necessary to enjoy them with the mind, not with the eyes; they are a feast, and, as it were, an outburst of delight; in order to prepare and maintain them, swell and expand the tissues, moisture was required, excessive moisture, the caress and the guardianship of soft vapour; beneath a warmer sky, such flowers would be stiffened and dried;

they are not accustomed to bear the full sun; hence it is that they break forth to-day under his blaze. They have the tint of a beautiful lady; they, too, are patricians developed, preserved, embellished by all the refinements of art and of luxury; I have had the same impression at a full-dress morning party, before a staircase filled from top to bottom with young laughing ladies in swelling and sweeping dresses of tulle, of silk, the head covered with diamonds,. the shoulders bare. This was a unique sensation, that of splendour and brilliancy carried to the highest pitch—all the flowers of civilisation and of nature in a single bouquet and in a single perfume.

Hampton Court is a large garden in the French style, laid out in the time of William III. Our style was then the reigning one in Europe. Yet English taste is discoverable here also: the borders have been planted with standard rosebushes, and these, closely trained along the slight espaliers, form columns of flowers. Ducks, swans swim in all the pieces of water; water-lilies unfold their velvet stars. The old trees are propped up by iron rods. When they die, in order that they may not be wholly lost, the remainder of their trunks are converted into a kind of huge urn. Clearly, they are cared for and they are loved. There are no fences. I noticed young boarding-school girls walking and playing on the grass, but they never pluck a flower. The following notice suffices to protect the garden:—"It is hoped that the public will abstain from destroying that which is cultivated for the public gratification." I have seen families of common people taking their dinners on the green sward of Hyde Park; they neither tore up nor spoilt anything. This is perfect; the aim of every society is

PRIVATE INCOMES.

that each one should be always his own constable, and end by not having any other.

My English friends confirm what I had guessed about the large number and the vastness of the private fortunes. "Take a cab from Sydenham; for five miles you will pass houses which indicate an annual outlay of £1,500 and upwards." According to the official statistics of 1841, there are one million of servants to sixteen millions of inhabitants. The liberal professions are much better remunerated than on the Continent. I know a musician at Leipzig of first-class talent; he receives 3s. a lesson at the Academy of Leipzig, 6s. in the city, and one guinea in London. The visit of a doctor who is not celebrated costs 4s. or 9s. in Paris, and a guinea here. With us a professor at the College of France receives £300, at the Sorbonne £480, at the School of Medicine £400. A professor at Oxford, a head of a house, has often from £1,000 to £3,000. Tennyson, who writes little, is said to make £5,000 a year. The Head Master of Eton has a salary of £6,080, of Harrow £6,280, of Rugby £2,960; many of the masters in these establishments have salaries from £1,200 to £1,240—one of them at Harrow has £2,220. The Bishop of London has £10,000 a year, the Archbishop of York has £15,000. An article is paid for at the rate of £8 the sheet in the *Revue des Deux Mondes*, and £20 in the English Quarterlies. The *Times* has paid £100 for a certain article. Thackeray, the novelist, has made £160 in twenty-four hours through the medium of two lectures, the one being delivered in Brighton, the other in London; from the magazine to which he contributed his novels he received £2,000 a year, and £10 a page in addition; this magazine had 100,000 subscribers;

he estimated his own yearly earnings at £4,800. It must be understood that I put on one side the enormous fortunes made in manufactures, those of the nobility, the profit or revenues of £200,000 yearly; their outlay is proportionate. A young engineer, a younger son, and who was obliged to make his fortune, said to me one day, " With £8,000 yearly one is not wealthy in England, one is merely very comfortably off." Another, who spends his summers in the country, added, "look at the family circles of our farmers; their daughters learn French and to play on the piano; they dress splendidly." The rule is to make much and to spend much: an Englishman does not put anything aside, does not think of the future, at the most he insures his life; in this he is the reverse of a Frenchman, who is saving and abstemious.

Whence comes all this money, and how is it distributed? I shall endeavour to procure the statistics; meantime, let us examine one of the great reservoirs whence gold flows through the people of all conditions, and over the whole country—the Docks of London.

I always find that London resembles ancient Rome as Paris resembles ancient Athens. This modern Rome, how heavily must it weigh, like the other, upon the labouring class! For every monstrous erection, Babylon, Egypt, imperial Rome, indicates an accumulation of efforts, an excess of fatigue. I have never seen a great city, whether a capital or place of manufactures, without thinking of the nations which have vanished from around the Mediterranean under the pressure of the Roman machine. It is true that to-day there are no more slaves before the law; yet frequently man is a slave in fact, and by the constraint of his condition.

THE DOCKS.

These docks are prodigious, overpowering; there are six of them each of which is a vast port, and accommodates a multitude of three-masted vessels. There are ships everywhere, and ships upon ships in rows, show their heads and their swelling bosoms, like beautiful fish, under their cuirass of copper. One of them has arrived from Australia, and is of 2,500 tons burden, others are 3,000 tons and upwards; some of them hail from all parts of the world, this is the trysting-place of the globe. For the most part they are magnificent. Seen from the keel they are leviathans, and they are slender and as elegant as swans. A merchant who is here superintending the arrival of spices from Java, and the transhipment of ice from Norway, tells me that about 40,000 vessels enter every year, and that on an average, there are from 5,000 to 6,000 in the docks or the river at one time.

In the wine quarter the cellars contain 30,000 barrels of port. A crane discharges them. They seem to move of their own accord. When brought on a little wheeled truck, they slide down an incline to their places, almost without labour. The machines work so well that they appear to be living auxiliaries, voluntary slaves. Note that bridge; it weighs a hundred tons; yet one man moves it by means of a screw-jack. There is a quarter for groceries, a quarter for skins and leather, a quarter for tallow. The cellars and the warehouses are colossal. Under their arch, equal to that of a large bridge, one beholds the peopled and profound obscurity recede far away. Rembrandt would have found ready-made pictures in their mysterious distances, in the flickering blackness of their choked-up air-holes, in these infinite receptacles where a hive of men is moving about. They roll the casks without confusion and with calmness One hears the voices of clerks calling out the numbers. In the middle of the cellar a foreman, seated at a small table, makes entries or looks on. The masters, who are grave, and in black hats, walk about superintending in silence. Yet around the capstans are creaking, and sailors in boats are scraping or scrubbing their ship. Thus occupied in their working coats, with their serious air, their phlegmatic or wearied faces, they form a pleasing sight; one feels that they are in their right places, every living being, animal or man, is beautiful in his proper place.

I was smoking, seated on a bale, when a man passing along said, without stopping, "Five shillings fine." "Is it forbidden then?" "Yes." Nothing more. There is no better way of working or making others work than to be sparing in gestures or words. At Hyde Park Corner there are two policemen whom I have frequently watched for a considerable time; they never speak; if there be a block of vehicles, they raise their arm to stop a coachman, and lower it as a sign that he may drive on: the coachman instantly and silently obeys. Our steward on board the steamboat, many servants, and merchants whom I have seen, do likewise; when, in giving orders and executing them, chattering, exclamations, tokens of impatience, fumbling, and disorder are thus suppressed, the command and the performance gear into each other as quickly and as surely as two wheels.

At the end of an hour the mind feels itself overstocked; it is requisite to permit the images to group and to arrange themselves. I was at the corner of Shadwell Basin and I gazed upon the slate-coloured river before me shining and exhaling mist; the northern bank winds and bounds the horizon with its blackish fringe mottled with red ; a few vessels descend with the supple and slow movement of a sea-bird; their sombre hulls and brown sails balance themselves upon the water which shimmers. To north and south a mass of ships raise their crowded masts. The silence is almost complete ; one hears but the strokes of distant hammers, the vague tinkle of a bell, and the fluttering of birds in the trees. A Dutch painter, Van der Heyden, Backhuysen, would have taken pleasure in beholding this plain of water, the distant tones of brick and tar, this uncertain horizon where stretch the sleeping clouds. I have seen nothing more picturesque in London. The rest is too scrubbed and varnished, or too bustling and too foul.

Shadwell, one of the poor neighbourhoods, is close at hand ; by the vastness of its distress, and by its extent, it is in keeping with the hugeness and the wealth of London. I have seen the bad quarters of Marseilles, of Antwerp, of Paris, they do not come near to it. Low houses, poor streets of brick under red-tiled roofs cross each other in every direction, and lead down with a dismal look to the river. Beggars, thieves, harlots, the latter especially, crowd Shadwell Street. One hears a grating music in the spirit cellars; sometimes it is a negro who handles the violin ; through the open windows one perceives unmade beds, women dancing. Thrice in ten minutes I saw crowds collected at the doors; fights were going on, chiefly fights between women ; one of them, her face bleeding, tears in her eyes, drunk, shouted with a sharp and harsh voice, and wished to fling herself upon a man. The bystanders laughed ; the noise caused the adjacent lanes to be emptied of their occupants ; ragged, poor children, harlots—it was like a human sewer suddenly discharging its contents. Some of them have a relic of neatness, a new garment, but the greater number are in filthy and unseemly tatters. Figure to yourself what a lady's bonnet may become after passing during three or four years from head to head, having been crushed against walls, having had blows from fists; for they receive them. I noticed blackened eyes, bandaged noses, bloody cheek-bones. The women gesticulate with extraordinary vehemence; but most horrible of all is their shrill, acute, cracked voice, resembling that of an ailing screech-owl.

From the time of leaving the Tunnel, street boys abound—bare-footed, dirty, and turning wheels in order to get alms. On the stairs leading to the Thames they swarm, more pale-faced, more deformed, more repulsive than the scum of Paris; without question, the climate is worse, and the gin more deadly. Near them, leaning against the greasy walls, or inert on the steps, are men in astounding rags; it is impossible to imagine before seeing them how many layers of dirt an overcoat or a pair of trousers could hold; they dream or doze open-mouthed, their faces are begrimed, dull, and sometimes streaked with red lines. It is in these localities that families have been discovered with no other bed than a heap of soot; they had slept there during several months. For a creature so wasted and jaded there is but one refuge—drunkenness. "Not drink!" said a desperate character at an inquest. "It were better then to die at once."

A trader said to me, "Look after your pockets, sir," and a policeman warned me not to enter certain lanes.

I walked through some of the broader ones; all the houses, except one or two, are evidently inhabited by harlots. Other small streets, dusty courts, reeking with a smell of rotten rags, are draped with tattered clothes and linen hung up to dry. Children swarm. In a moment, in a narrow court, I saw fourteen or fifteen around me—dirty, barefooted, the little sister carrying a sucking child in her arms, the year-old nursling whose whitish head had no hair. Nothing is more lugubrious than these white bodies, that pale flaxen hair, these flabby cheeks encrusted with old dirt. They press together, they point out the gentleman with curious and eager gestures. The motionless mothers, with an exhausted air, look out at the door. One observes the narrow lodging, sometimes the single room, wherein they are all huddled in the foul air. The houses are most frequently one-storied, low, narrow—a den in which to sleep and die. What a place of residence in winter, when, during weeks of continuous rain and fog, the windows are shut! And in order that this brood may not die of hunger, it is necessary that the father should not drink, should never be idle, should never be sick.

Here and there is a dust-heap. Women are labouring to pick out what is valuable from it. One, old and withered, had a short pipe in her mouth. They stand up amidst the muck to look at me; brutalised, disquieting faces of female Yahoos; perhaps this pipe and a glass of gin is the last idea which floats in their idiotic brain. Should we find there anything else than the instincts and the appetites of a savage and of a beast of burden? A miserable black cat, lean, lame, startled, watches them timidly out of the corner of its eye, and furtively searches in a heap of rubbish. It was possibly right in feeling uneasy. The old woman, muttering, followed it with a look as wild as its own.

She seemed to think that two pounds weight of meat were there.

I recall the alleys which run into Oxford Street, stifling lanes, encrusted with human exhalations; troops of pale children nestling on the muddy stairs; the seats on London Bridge, where families, huddled together with drooping heads, shiver through the night; particularly the Haymarket and the Strand in the evening. Every hundred steps one jostles twenty harlots; some of them ask for a glass of gin; others say, "Sir, it is to pay my lodging." This is not debauchery which flaunts itself, but destitution—and such destitution! The deplorable procession in the shade of the monumental streets is sickening; it seems to me a march of the dead. That is a plague-spot—the real plague-spot of English society.

IV.

VISIT TO EPSOM AND TO CREMORNE GARDENS.

RACES at Epsom : it is the Derby day, a day of jollification ; Parliament does not sit; for three days all the talk has been about horses and their trainers.

We start from Waterloo Station. The sky is cloudless, free from mist ; my English neighbours remark that they had never seen such a day in London. All around may be witnessed green husbandry, meadows encompassed with hedges, and the hedge-row is often interspersed with trees. The splendour of this green, the mass and the vigour of lustrous, golden, bursting flowers, are extraordinary. Velvets constellated with diamonds, watered silks, the most magnificent embroideries do not match this deep hue ; the colour is excessive, beyond the reach of painting : but never have the blooming and blossoming of plants, the luxury and the joy of the adorned earth, dazzled me with such bright pomp.

Epsom course is a large green plain, slightly undulating ; on one side are reared three public stands and several other smaller ones. In front, tents, hundreds of shops, temporary stables under canvas, and an incredible confusion of carriages, of horses, of horsemen, of private omnibuses; there are perhaps 200,000 human heads here. Nothing beautiful nor even elegant; the carriages are ordinary vehicles, and toilettes are rare; one does not come here to exhibit them, but to witness a spectacle; the spectacle is only interesting on account of its size. From the top of the Stand the enormous ant-heap swarms and its din ascends. But beyond, on the right, a row of large trees, behind them the faint bluish undulations of the verdant country, make a magnificent frame to a mediocre picture. Some clouds as white as swans float in the sky, and their shadow sweeps over the grass; a light mist, charged with sunshine, flits in the distance, and the illuminated air, like a glory, envelops the plain, the heights, the vast area, and all the disorder of the human carnival.

It is a carnival, in fact; they have come to amuse themselves in a noisy fashion. Everywhere are gipsies, comic singers and dancers disguised as nègroes, shooting galleries where bows and arrows or guns are used, charlatans who by dint of eloquence palm off watch-chains, games of skittles and sticks, musicians of all sorts, and the most astonishing row of cabs, barouches, droskies, four-in-hands, with pies, cold meats, melons, fruits, wines, especially champagne. They unpack; they proceed to drink and eat; that restores the creature and excites him; coarse joy and open laughter are the result of a full stomach. In presence of this ready-made feast the aspect of the poor is pitiable to behold; they endeavour to sell to you penny dolls, remembrances of the Derby; to induce you to play at Aunt Sally, to black your boots. Nearly all of them resemble wretched, hungry, beaten, mangy dogs, waiting for a bone, without hope of finding much on it. They arrived on foot during the night, and count upon dining off the crumbs from the great feast. Many are lying on the ground among the feet of the passers-by, and sleep open-mouthed, face upwards. Their countenances have an expression of stupidity and of painful hardness. The majority of them have bare feet, all are terribly dirty, and most absurd-looking; the reason is that they wear gentlemen's old clothes, worn-out fashionable dresses, small bonnets, formerly worn by young ladies. The sight of these cast-off things, which have covered several bodies, becoming more shabby in passing from one to the other, always makes me uncomfortable. To wear these old clothes is degrading; in doing so the human being shows or avows that he is the offscouring of society. Among us a peasant, a workman, a labourer, is a different man, not an inferior person; his blouse belongs to him, as my coat belongs to me—it has suited no one but him. This employment of ragged clothes is more than a peculiarity; the poor resign themselves here to be the footstool of others.

One of these women, with an old shawl which appeared to have been dragged in the gutter, with battered head-gear, which had been a bonnet, made limp by the rain, with a poor, dirty, pale baby in her arms, came and prowled round our omnibus, picked up a castaway bottle, and drained the dregs. Her second girl, who could walk, also picked up and munched a rind of melon. We gave them a shilling and cakes. The humble smile of thankfulness they returned, it is impossible to describe. They had the look of saying, like Sterne's poor donkey, "Do not beat me, I beseech you,—yet you may beat me if you wish." Their countenances were burned, tanned by the sun; the mother had a scar on her right cheek, as if she had been struck by a boot; both of them, the child in particular, were grown wild and stunted. The great social mill crushes and grinds here, beneath its steel gearing, the lowest human stratum.

However, a bell rings and the race is about to begin. The three or four hundred policemen clear the course; the stands are filled and the meadow in front of them is but a large black patch. We ascend to our places; nothing seems grandiose. At this distance the crowd is an ant-heap; the horsemen and the carriages which move forward and cross each other resemble beetles, May-bugs, large sombre drones on a green cloth. The jockeys in red, in blue, in yellow, in mauve, form a small group apart, like a swarm of butterflies which has alighted. Probably I am wanting in enthusiasm, but I seem to be looking at a game of insects. Thirty-four run; after three false starts they are off; fifteen or twenty keep together, the others are in small groups, and one sees them moving the length of the ring. To the eye the speed is not very great; it is that of a railway train seen at the distance of half a league; in that case the carriages have the appearance of toy-coaches which a child draws tied to a string; certainly, the impression is not stronger here, and it is a mistake to speak either of a hurricane or of a whirlwind. During several minutes, the brown patch, strewn with red and bright spots, moves steadily over the distant green. It turns; one perceives the first group approach. "Hats off!" and all heads are uncovered, and every one rises; a repressed hurrah pervades the stands. The frigid faces are on fire; brief, nervous gestures suddenly stir the phlegmatic bodies; below, in the betting-ring the agitation is extraordinary—like a general St. Vitus's dance; picture a mass of puppets receiving an electric shock, and gesticulating with all their members like mad semaphores. But the most curious spectacle is the human tide which instantaneously and in a body, pours forth and rolls over the course behind the runners, like a wave of ink; the black and motionless crowd has suddenly melted and become molten; in a moment it spreads itself abroad in vast proportions till the eye cannot follow it, and appears in front of the stands. The policemen make a barrier in two or three ranks, using force when necessary to guard the square to which the jockeys and horses are led. Measures are taken to weigh and see that all is right.

There is one imposing moment, when the horses are not more than two hundred paces of; in a second the speed becomes suddenly perceptible, and the cluster of riders and horses rushes onward, this time like a tempest.

A horse, of which little is known, has won, and very narrowly; the betting against him was 40 to 1; on the contrary, it was 3 to 1 or 9 to 2 against the two favourites; hence there were miscalculations and explosions. The prize, with its accessories, amounts to £6,775; bets included, the owner will have won nearly £40,000. We are told of enormous losses—£20,000, £50,000; last year a colonel committed suicide after the great race because he saw that he was bankrupt; if he had awaited the result of the others he would have won enough to pay all. The proprietor of one of the private stands shouted at the moment of departure, "Everything that I have just made on Buckstone." Several cabmen have lost their horses and their vehicles, which they risked in bets.

To my thinking, these bets are to the mind what

spirits are to the palate—an indispensable stimulant for heavy and rough frames; they require violent impressions, the sensation of a prodigious risk; add to that the combative and daring instinct; every wager is a duel, and every large bet a danger. As for the reasons which render the passion for horses and races so widespread and so national, it appears to me we must seek for them in the gymnastic and rural life; people in easy circumstances, or who are rich, spend a great part of the year in the country; in a miry country locomotion is not pleasant save on horseback; their temperament necessitates much physical exercise; all these habits lead to the Derby day, which is their chosen festival.

We descend; there is hustling and crushing in the staircases, at the refreshment counters; but most of the carriages are provisioned for the day, and the people feast in the open air in small knots. Good humour and unreserved merriment; classes mingle; P——, one of our party, has met his usual coachman at table with a gentleman, two ladies, and a child. The gentleman had employed and then invited the coachman; the coachman introduces P——, who is amicably compelled to drink port, sherry, stout, and ale. In fact, to-day it is hail fellow well met; but this lasts for a day only, after the manner of the ancient saturnalia. On the morrow distinctions of rank will be as strong as ever, and the coachman will be respectful, distant, as is his wont. Another of our friends perceives a gentleman of his acquaintance, who has come in an omnibus, bringing with him his daughter and his lady acquaintances—eight ladies in all; stopped in passing, we are all obliged to drink and eat; our reception is frank, jovial, and cordial; this gentleman, who had never seen me before, invites me to visit him in the country. Still, over the whole downs, jaws are at work, bottles are emptied, and towards evening the carnival is in full swing. Twenty-four gentlemen triumphantly range on their omnibus seventy-five bottles which they have emptied. Groups pelt each other with chicken-bones, lobster-shells, pieces of turf. Two parties of gentlemen have descended from their omnibuses and engaged in a fight, ten against ten; one of them gets two teeth broken. There are humorous incidents: three men and a lady are standing erect in their carriage; the horses move on, they all tumble, the lady with her legs in the air; peals of laughter follow. Gradually the fumes of wine ascend to the heads; these people so proper, so delicate, indulge in strange conduct; gentlemen approach a carriage containing ladies and young girls, and stand shamefully against the wheels; the mother tries to drive them away with her parasol. One of our party who remained till midnight saw many horrors which I cannot describe; the animal nature had full vent. There is nothing exaggerated in Rubens's "Kermess" in the Louvre. The instincts are the same, and are equally unbridled; only, in place of portly, overflowing, and ruddy forms, picture to yourself faces which remain grave, and well-cut modern garments. The contrast between the natural and the artificial human being—between the gentleman who, by habit, and mechanically, continues grave, and the beast which explodes, is grotesque.

On our return, the road is hidden by dust; portions of fields have been reddened by feet; everybody returns frightfully dirty, and powdered with white; there are drunken people along the whole road; up to eight o'clock in the evening they might be seen staggering and sick at Hyde Park Corner; their comrades support them, laughing, and the spectators' faces do not betoken disgust. To-day everything is allowable; it is an outlet for a year of repression.

About eleven o'clock in the evening we proceed to Cremorne Gardens, a sort of Bal Mabille, and where the folly of the day is continued throughout the night. At the entrance is crowding and jostling; a band of English force their way through, crying, "Make room for the Japanese Ambassadors." Within, especially at the turnings, the crowd is terrible, but one can find breathing space in sombre recesses. All the men are well or properly dressed; the women are harlots, but of a higher class than those of the Strand; they wear bright shawls, white stuffs of gauze or tulle, red cloaks, new bonnets; there is a dress which has cost £12; but the faces are rather faded, and sometimes, in the crowd, they raise terrible cries—the cries of a screech-owl. What is most comical, and proves their state of excitement, is their notion of pinching people, particularly foreigners. One of our party, who is forty years old, being sharply pinched and otherwise scandalised, leaves the place. Another woman beats a gentleman on the back with her fists for having trodden on her foot; he laughs, and all the on-lookers are pleased. They are decidedly good-natured folks; I saw no one lose temper in the scuffle; and they were provoked; one of my French friends imprudently jeered loudly; this must be witnessed in order to comprehend the joyous rustic festivals of the sixteenth century, Shakespeare's "Merry England," the abounding primitive sap of the tree which Puritanism has clipped, pruned, and rendered rigid as well as straight.

We sat down near three young women at a side-table, and we offered them sherry and beer; they did not drink too much. Our book-English and their emphasised speech became mixed in a ludicrous jumble. One of them is the gayest and most playful of creatures; I have never seen animal spirits equally redundant; another, modest, rather pretty, slightly sad, is a milliner, and lives by her needle; she has a friend who spends the Sundays with her; I looked carefully at her, and saw that she had the making of an amiable and honest woman in her like any other. In what lies the chance? It is impossible to state their number in London; it has been put at 50,000. Certain houses are filled with them from top to bottom. We escorted them to the gate, and paid for their cabs. Our conveyance returned through streets, crescents, squares, which I did not recognise. A sepulchral glare illumines the empty Babel, and covers the colossal architectures with the whiteness of a winding-sheet. The dense, unwholesome air seems to be still impregnated with human exhalations; at intervals, we perceive a hungry woman loitering, a poor wretch in rags, the feet covered with cloth. While walking through the nightly procession of the Haymarket, I thought about the Argyll Rooms, a sort of pleasure casino which I had visited the night before; the spectacle of debauchery here leaves no other impression than one of misery and degradation. There is no brilliancy, dash, and liveliness about it, as in France; when a gentleman wishes to dance, a master of the ceremonies, with a badge and a white tie, goes to find a partner for him; the two often dance together without exchanging a word. These poor girls are often beautiful, many have a sweet and honest look; all dance very properly, smile a little, and do not gesticulate; they are in low dresses, but when dancing they keep their cloaks on. As to the men, their external appearance is that of leading merchants, wharfingers, middle-class manufacturers, or their sons, their foremen, who have foresaken their accounts, their commerce, and their coal. They like a gaudy show, an illumination in coloured glass, women in full dress, showy and variegated dresses, white shawls embroidered with red flowers and exotic birds. They have plenty of money; a bottle of champagne costs twelve shillings; the price of the evening's amusement may be £6. A tragical thing is that men and women both drink, and begin by intoxication —it is the brutality and destitution which first meet together in traversing unreason, imbecility, and stupor. One returns deeply grieved, with a bitter and profound feeling of human grossness and helplessness; society is a fine edifice, but in the lowest story, what a sink of impurity! Civilisation polishes man; but how tenacious is the bestial instinct! I dare not yet pronounce judgment; however, it seems to me that the evil and the good are greater here than in France.

V.

TYPICAL ENGLISH MEN AND WOMEN.

AT bottom the essential thing in a country is **man**. Since my arrival I have made a collection of types, and I class them with those which I had collected last year. As the result of experience, the best method in my eyes is always that of artists and of naturalists; to note each face or very salient expression, follow its shades, its debasements, and its combinations; to verify its repetition in several individuals; to separate in this way the leading characteristic traits, comparing, interpreting, and classifying them. Painters and romance writers act thus by instinct, when by means of some personages they furnish us with an epitome of their era and of their society. Botanists and zoologists act thus on system when, choosing some plants or some animals whose characters are well marked, they exhibit to us in five or six representative types, all the species of a class.

Seated on a bench in a public walk, or stationed in the morning at the outlet from a railway-station, French eyes, accustomed to French physiognomies very quickly perceive differences; the memory keeps them in view, although the intelligence cannot, as yet, clearly comprehend them. One continues **to do this** daily at table, in a railway-carriage, in an omnibus, at an evening party, during a visit, in the city, in the country. At the end of some days certain new types, rare in France, common here, arise and stand forth; week after week, they become distinct, acquire completeness, call forth questions and answers, fit into one another, and end by forming a whole. Now, consider that in order to describe them it is often necessary to exhibit them in all their prominence—that is to say, in their excess, and that the excess is never the rule. The pure type, such as it can be rendered by pen or pencil, is an exception; in Nature it is almost always more or less changed. But in Nature its degrees and varieties are grouped around, and in accordance with it, while making the requisite deductions, the reader and spectator can picture it to themselves without very great incorrectness. Arranged in groups, the following are those which have struck me the most:—

I. The robust individual, largely and solidly built, the fine colossus, at times six feet high and broad in proportion. This is very common among soldiers, notably among the Life Guards, a select body of men. Their countenance is fresh, blooming, their flesh magnificent; it might be supposed they had been chosen for an exhibition of human products, like picked prize beets and cauliflowers. They have a fund of good humour, sometimes of good nature, generally of awkwardness. Their foppery is of a special kind. In light scarlet jacket, with a little cane in hand, they strut along displaying their shape and the lower part of their back; the distinct parting in their pomaded hair is seen under their small undress cap. One of them, stationary at a street corner, well set up, the shoulders down, majestically displays himself to the street boys. In point of mass they are monuments; but there may be too much of a good thing, and movement is so essential to matter! Other monuments, rather less tall, but even fresher and more varnished, are the servants of a great house. They wear white cravats with large faultless bows, scarlet or canary-coloured knee-breeches, are magnificent in shape and amplitude; their calves especially are enormous. In the fashionable neighbourhoods, beneath the vestibule, about five o'clock in the evening, the butler seated, newspaper in hand, sips a glass of port; around him, ushers, corded lackeys, footmen with their sticks, gaze with an indolent and a lordly air upon the middle-class passers-by. The coachmen are prodigiously broad-shouldered and developed; how many yards of cloth must be required to clothe such figures? These are the favourites of creation, the best fed, the most easy-going, all chosen and picked in order to act as specimens of the nation's physique. In the great houses their clothing is found them; the two lackeys must be of equal height, like two horses. Each of them states his height in the newspaper advertisements; 5 feet 9 inches and a half, 5 feet 11 inches. So much goes for the size of the calves, so much for the shapeliness of the ancles, so much for the commanding presence; the ornamental look is worth to them as much as an extra £20 a year. They are taken care of, and they take care of themselves in consequence. Their table is nearly as well served as that of their masters; they have several kinds of wine and beer, and hours of relaxation. It is necessary that their exterior should proclaim the wealth and style of the house; they know this, and they are proud of it. However, their stuck up airs have become proverbial. Thackeray has drawn upon them for several characters in his novels, and has made them the subject of one romance. *Punch* has caricatures on the same subject; a valet gives his master warning because he has seen his lordship on the top of an omnibus, another because the colour of the livery does not suit his complexion. The lackey behind a carriage is so fine that he resembles a big doll; street boys stick pins into his calves to see if they are real or stuffed.

There is the same athletic and full-fleshed type among the gentlemen; I know four or five specimens among my acquaintances. Sometimes the excess of feeding adds a variety; this was true of a certain gentleman in my railway-carriage on the Derby day; large ruddy features, with flabby and pendent cheeks, large red whiskers, blue eyes without expression, an enormous trunk in a short light jacket, noisy respiration; his blood gave a tinge of pink to his hands, his neck, his temple, and even underneath his hair; when he compressed his eyelids, his physiognomy was as disquieting and heavy as that seen in the portraits of Henry VIII.; when in repose, in presence of this mass of flesh, one thought of a beast for the butcher, and quietly computed twenty stones of meat. Towards fifty, owing to the effect of the same diet seasoned with port wine, the figure and the face are spoiled, the teeth protrude, the physiognomy is distorted, and turn to horrible and tragical caricature, as, for example, a fat and fiery general at the Volunteer Review in Hyde Park, who had the air of a bulldog and had a brick-dust face, spotted with violet excrescences. The last variety is seen among the common people, where spirits take the place of port, among other places in the low streets which border the Thames; several apoplectical and swollen faces, whereof the scarlet hue turns almost to black, worn-out, blood-shot eyes like raw lobsters; the brute brutalised. Lessen the quantity of blood and fat, while retaining the same bone and structure, and increasing the countrified look; large and wild beard and moustache, tangled hair, rolling eyes, truculent muzzle, big knotted hands; this is the primitive Teuton issuing from his woods; after the portly animal, after the overfed animal, comes the fierce animal, the English bull.

All that is rare enough; these are the extremes of the type. Much more common is the labouring animal, the great bony body, full of protuberances and projections, not well set up, ungainly, clumsy, slightly automatic, but of strong build, and as capable of resistance as of effort. It is not less common among gentlemen, clergymen, the liberal professions, than among the people. I have three specimens of it before my eyes. (1.) A tall clergyman, stiff, frigid, and who will never thaw; gestures of a semaphore, narrow and dogmatic opinions, yet charitable, and who demonstrates his devotedness; this stout framework was required to endure for thirty years the apostolic profession; constant sermons, visits in noisome lanes, night-watches, long walks on foot in the mud of the suburbs. (2.) A member of Parliament, with the shoulders, feet, and hands of a carman, large white teeth too close together, strong jaws which scarcely open to speak, irregular and very marked traits, his whole person largely and rudely shaped as if by strokes of a pruning-knife, and insufficiently cut down; the modern dress, the gloves, the blue cravat, the dazzlingly white linen, are out of place on these muscles, which might draw a dray, and engage in a boxing match. His eye is dim, his gestures are few, he is sparing of speech, he has no wit, nor, it seems, any ideas; he is not a leader, he is but a member of a party, he votes and works. But for the long night sittings, for the scrutiny of blue-books, and the verification of accounts, for meetings, committees, clubs, for wearying and indefinite labour he is well-built and admirable. (3.) The third is an Englishman of the middle-class, whom I met yesterday in an omnibus with his family. He was thirty-two, dressed in new clothes, with an income, I should suppose, of from £480 to £600 a year; had an air of solidity and of resolution, being a good machine, well mounted, well constructed, well kept, untiring and regular, the true budding paterfamilias; cold in appearance, correct, motionless, slightly heavy, and dull. At his side, a young wife in black velvet, too showy bonnet and finery, innocent and pleasing, always occupied with her baby, which is very white, over-abounding in flesh, health, and fat, with stuck-out and embroidered petticoats which make a bunch and a display. In front is the nurse, thirty-five years old, who strives to please and to smile respectfully. That is a good specimen of an English family; the husband energetically, conscientiously, and without yawning drags his conjugal chariot; his happiness must consist in taking tea, with slippers on, at his home in the evening; he will have many children who, not knowing how to gain a livelihood, will emigrate, and who will require to have a constitution like his own to undergo their hardships. Place in this powerful frame of bones and muscles the lucid, calm, active intelligence developed by special education, or by complete education, and you will have the fine variety of the same type, the serious, capable man, worthy of commanding, in whom, during the hour of need, one might and one ought to place confidence, who will accomplish difficult tasks. In spick-span new clothes, in too light a dress, the disparity between the habit and its wearer is not far from being grotesque. But fancy him on the bridge of a vessel, in battle, or simply in a counting-house at the head of twenty clerks, on the bench and pronouncing decisions, governing fortunes or lives, he will be beautiful, morally beautiful. This body can contain the soul without succumbing.

Many of the women have the same power of growth and structure, more frequently indeed than in France, out of every ten young girls one is admirable, and upon five or six a naturalist painter would look with pleasure. On horseback especially, and in full gallop, they are amazons, not only by their skill and the firmness of their seat, but on account of their figure and their health. In their presence one thinks of the natural form of life, Grecian and gymnastic. Yesterday one of them in a drawing-room, tall, with well-developed bust and shoulders, blooming cheeks, active, and without too much expression, seemed to me to be made to live in the avenues of a park, or in the great hall of a castle, like her sister, the antique statue, in the free air of the mountains, or under the portico of a temple upon the sea-shore; neither the one nor the other could breathe in our small Parisian dwellings. The mauve silk of the dress follows the form from the neck to the hips, descends and spreads forth like a lustrous wave; in order to depict her as a goddess it would require the palette of Rubens, his rosy red spread over a tint of milk, his large masses of flesh fixed by one dash of the brush; only here the contour is more severe, and the head is nobler. Lady Mary Wortley Montague, who came to see the Court of the Regent in France, severely rallied our slim, painted, affected beauties, and proudly held up as a contrast "the natural charms and the lively colours of the unsullied complexions" of English women. By way of compensation one may sometimes recall this mocking sketch by Hamilton:—"Madam Wetenhall was properly speaking a beauty wholly English: permeated with lily and roses, with snow and milk, as regards colours: formed of wax with regard to her arms and her hands, her throat and her feet, but altogether without soul or air. Her visage was the tiniest, but it was always the same visage; one might say that she took it out of the case in the morning and put it back in the evening, without having used it during the day. What else would you expect? Nature had made her a doll from infancy, and the white Wetenhall remained a doll till her death." Yet, even when the physiognomy and the form are commonplace, the whole satisfies the mind; a solid bony structure, and upon it healthy flesh, constitute what is essential in a living creature; the impression is the same as that produced by a house built of well-hewn stone, whereof the plaster and polish are new; one does not require that it should be architecturally perfect nor even elegant; it will withstand bad weather, it is comfortable, suits its occupant; that suffices.

There are two probable causes. The one, which is of a special character, the hereditary conformation of the race; the other, which is the custom of open-air living and bodily exercise. A *Review* spoke recently about the rude, unfeeling health which slightly startles delicate foreign ladies, and attributes it to riding on horseback and the long walks which English ladies take in the country. To these advantages are joined several inconveniences: the fair complexion is easily and quickly spoilt; in the case of many young ladies, the nose reddens early; they have too many children, and this deteriorates them. You marry a blonde, slender, and clear-complexioned woman; ten years afterwards you will perhaps have at your side a housekeeper, a nurse, a sitting hen. I have in my mind two or three of these matrons, broad, stiff, and destitute of ideas; red face, eyes the colour of blue china, huge white teeth—forming the tricolour flag. In other cases the type becomes exaggerated: one sees extraordinary asparagus-sticks planted in spreading dresses. Moreover, two out of every three have their feet shod with stout masculine boots; and as to the long projecting teeth, it is impossible to train oneself to endure them. Is this a cause, or an effect, of the carnivorous régime? The too ornate and badly-adjusted dress completes these disparities. It consists of violet or dark crimson silks, of grass-green flowered gowns, blue sashes, jewellery— the whole employed sometimes to caparison gigantic jades who recall discharged heavy cavalry horses, sometimes vast well-hooped butts, which burst in spite of their hoops. Of this cast was a lady, in Hyde Park, one of these days, on horseback, followed by her groom. She was fifty-five, had several chins, the rest in proportion, an imperious and haughty mien; the whole shook at the slightest trot, and it was hard not to laugh.

Another specimen is the children. I have seen Eton and Harrow-on-the-Hill. The small ones in the nursery are living flowers—full-blown roses; in the country especially, the large cherub cheeks, the firmness and quantity of the flesh proclaim the abounding sap which will afterwards produce a sturdy fellow. About seven and upwards, it is not intelligence which predominates, but physical and moral energy. The manner is often rude, very unamiable; one thinks of young bull-dogs. For example, the young ones of H—— and M——, sons of great families, seem to be and are simple cubs averse to culture, good only for hunting and school-fights. An observer said to me—"A young Englishman is ferocious, unconquerable; the blood of the Scandinavian rover is in his veins; hence the usage of the birch; in our schools we could not dispense with it." He is not very precocious and vivacious, but has plenty of daring and tenacity. George Eliot has given a very good specimen of this in the character of Tom in "The Mill on the Floss." Very often he is a blockhead; the caricatures have represented this trait. A little fellow of eight says to his sister of eighteen, "Charlotte, lend me your paint-box." "No, sir, you know how you spoiled it the last time." "Very well, then I shall put my guinea-pig on your neck." And he raises the guinea-pig to perform his threat. The animal instincts are too powerful in him, he is too full of health, he hates books, he neither will nor can learn. He prefers eating, boxing, playing at cricket, riding on horseback. Owing to another effect of the same instincts, he is brave, patient, hardy, inured to blows and risks of all kinds. The author of "Tom Brown's School-days" says, "It is strange to see how fond nearly all young English boys are of danger; you will find ten ready to join in a hunt, climb a tree, swim across a stream, if there be a chance of their breaking their necks or drowning themselves; and out of them you will not find more than one to play at marbles, remain on dry land, or bathe within his depth." Young Tom, when going to school, passes a very cold night on the top of the coach, and, frozen though he be, he persists in doing so, because he has the "silent pleasure, so dear to every Englishman, of enduring, resisting, and struggling with something, and not giving way." I can call to mind fifty similar minor facts. On the whole, I am certain that the animal physique, the primitive man, such as Nature bequeathed to civilisation, is of a stronger and rougher species here. The following are some of these minor facts. During these days I have seen farm and draught horses in breweries and in two farms: they resemble elephants; one of the farmers has twelve of them which cost from £50 to £60. They are the athletes of the species; lustrous hair; reins full of muscle, colossal cruppers. The smallest one among them is French, and the farmer says it is the weakest, the least capable of standing changes of temperature. Now, I have everywhere found this kind of consanguinity between the horse and the human being; for example, follow it up successively in the Department of the Var, at Orleans, in Normandy, and in England. On the other hand, a skilful physician who prescribes for a Frenchman here does not give him more than half a dose; the English dose would be too strong for him, and would hurt him; if you ask a chemist for a purge, he hands calomel to you; an Englishman often keeps it by him, and takes a pill of it when his head feels rather heavy; the medicines here might be compounded for French horses. In like manner their common wines, port, sherry, very hot, very spirituous, are loaded with brandy in addition; this mixture deprives them of delicacy, yet if they were pure the English would consider them insipid; our Bordeaux wines and even our Burgundies are too light for them. Amongst the middle class, ale, stout, or porter are preferred, especially brandy and water, a kind of grog in which the half is spirit; to please them it is necessary that the beverage should be rough or fiery, their palate must be either scratched or scraped. The same impression is made on trying their cookery, which, excepting that of their very fine clubs, and of the "Continental" English, who keep a French or Italian cook, has no savour. I have purposely dined in twenty taverns, from the lowest to the highest, in London and elsewhere. I got large portions of fat meat and vegetables, without sauce; one is amply and wholesomely fed, but one has no pleasure in eating. In the best Liverpool eating-house they do not know how to dress a fowl. If you would tickle your palate, there is a cruet filled with pickles, peppers, sauces, and Chili vinegar. I once inadvertently put two drops of it into my mouth. I might as well have swallowed a hot cinder. At Greenwich, having already partaken of plain whitebait, I helped myself to some out of a second dish; it was devilled, and fitted for skinning the tongue. Lastly, on the coaches and on the bridge of the steamboats many gentlemen, and even ladies, remain out of choice in the wind and rain, exposed to be blown about and drenched; the inclemencies of the weather please them. In my opinion, all these traits denote senses less delicate and a temperament more robust.

Such a robust frame has vast wants. They consider us sober; yet we ought to consider them voracious. Economists say that on an average a Frenchman eats a sheep and a half yearly, and an Englishman four sheep. At the tables of the eating-houses you are served with a small piece of bread along with a very large helping of meat. *Punch* contains caricatures of juvenile gluttons:—"What a horrible life," said a young girl on seeing two enormous pigs which were being fattened, "to do nothing but eat and sleep." Her brother of ten replies, "There is nothing in the world which I should like better." The exaggeration is clear, but it denotes a trait of manners. Vanbrugh in his "Journey to London" had previously depicted the little gluttonous squire, a being unknown in France. From all time they have gloried in being meat-eaters and substantially fed; in their eyes this was a privilege of their race and an aliment of their courage. Mr. Froude calls them "a sturdy, high-hearted race, sound in body and fierce in spirit, and furnished with thews and sinews which, under the stimulus of those 'great shins of beef,' their common diet, were the wonder of the age. . . . . Again and again, a few thousands of them carried dismay into the heart of France. Four hundred adventurers, vagabond apprentices from London, who formed a volunteer corps in the Calais garrison, were for years the terror of Normandy. In the very frolic of conscious power they fought and plundered without pay, without reward, except what they could win for themselves; and when they fell at last they fell only when surrounded by six times their number, and were cut to pieces in careless desperation. Invariably, by friend and foe alike, the English are described as the fiercest people in all Europe (the English wild beasts, Benvenuto Cellini calls them), and this great physical power they owed to the profuse abundance in which they lived, and the soldiers' training in which every man of them was bred from childhood."

An Englishman with whom I conversed at the Derby was influenced by the same principle in wholly disapproving of temperance societies: according to him the race required stimulants; even in India, where he had lived five years, the English would make a mistake in entirely abandoning spirituous liquors. "Our sailors cannot do without their glass of spirits. We are eminently an energetic people; we require strong meat and drink to sustain our frames; without them we should have no animal spirits; it is on account of this régime that our mariners are so hardy and so brave. When they board, after discharging their pistols, they fling them at random on the enemy's deck, saying that they are certain to find them again after the victory." It is possible that he was right. Certain organisations are prodigal; there are chimneys which draw badly unless the fire be great; besides, the climate, the fog, the large expenditure of physical and mental labour necessitate copious repasts; an English workman, who does as much work with his own hands as a Frenchman and a half, and lives amidst the fog of Manchester, is a locomotive of which the boiler produces steam only by using spirits and meat. Pitt did not find two bottles of port wine too large a quantity to take with his dinner; but I return to my types.

II. The Phlegmatic: On him impressions are made without inducing expression, or, for a stronger reason, shock, agitation, explosion. This is exactly the opposite of southern petulance and passion. He has a frigid and starched air, the gestures of an automaton, motionless physiognomy, he speaks little, or not at all. B——, being introduced to a family, pays a visit, is beginning to chat with the mistress of the house, the husband arrives, notices him on entering the door, walks silently across the room, his eyes turned in another direction, sits down, and after the lapse of a minute, says, "Glad to see you, sir." Nothing more. At the end of five minutes he takes up a newspaper and reads it. This was not churlishness; he is hospitable and kind. An officer relates that an English admiral, after a long fight, forced the enemy's vessel to surrender, and received the captain, whom he had made prisoner, on the poop, with the single phrase, "Fortune of war." This was politeness, but abbreviated, in laconic fashion. Here is a portion of a letter from one of my friends, after some weeks' stay :—" Shall I tell you what has struck me the most in this country? It is the inertness of the nervous system. The other day I witnessed a game of cricket on Kew Green; seven or eight English boys were there pitching the ball. Certainly they could not help blundering and missing now and then. Yet, during upwards of an hour and a half there was not a single cry, not a single remark made in a loud voice and in a tone of reproach. They pitched the ball about, changed places, doing it all with the utmost calmness, and generally in silence. You must have remarked that the English speak exceedingly low. An Italian society into which I strayed by chance, actually deafened me; I had become accustomed to the moderate tone of English voices My coachman, the other day, thought fit to rattle down a mews at full speed; he frightened two carriage horses which were being harnessed to the carriage. The groom advanced, took hold of the bits, and calmed the horses. Not a single word passed between these two men. Picture to yourself the same scene in France—the taunts of the lackey, proud of his master; the blackguardism of the jealous menial, &c. That is, my dear friend, what I have seen of most significance in England, and by means of which I figure to myself English liberty. These people have water mixed with their blood, exactly as their cattle are deficient in juice. Compare the gigots of St. Léonard with those of London. That is why they are allowed to combine together, to brawl, to print what they please. They are primitive animals, cold-blooded, and with a sluggish circulation."

Among the persons with whom I have associated there are two or three very well instructed, highly educated men, who have written and who talk well. But talking is distasteful to them. They do the honours of their house and take part in the most interesting conversations almost without saying anything —not because they are inattentive, wearied, absent; they listen, that suffices them. If they are addressed directly they summarise their experience in a sentence. That debt discharged, they become silent again, and this excites no surprise; it is merely said in explanation of their manner, "He is a man of few words." Now, join to this disposition the robust and slightly rough temperament which I have just described, and you will have a particular variety—that is, the sluggish, slow, heavy, dull, material one, unfit for all fine culture, satisfied with its mechanical occupation, the true Flemish boor of Van Ostade. The following is a biography which exhibits this character, combined with a practical aptitude and a special talent:—

John S. is the son of a workman in the environs of Bristol; he has laboured from infancy in his father's small smithy; possessing a turn for mechanics, he invented a species of bolt for affixing the rails to the sleepers; on that account a wealthy and well-brought-up gentleman, who knew him, offered him money for the purpose of establishing a factory. John consulted his father, who had remained a mere workman, narrow-minded, and who refused to enter into partnership. John persevered, studied hard, learned what he required in mechanics, spent much time in practising, received the funds, and established the factory; last year it returned £20,000 net profit to the partners. At present he is twenty-eight; he is rich already, and spends the day in the following manner. In the morning he goes to the factory, inspects, supervises, takes a file in hand to show the clumsy workman how to use it properly, returns home frightfully dirty, washes himself, and breakfasts. He does likewise in the afternoon. He dines. In the evening he seats himself in a small neighbouring tavern, drinks sixpennyworth of beer, smokes his pipe, and returns home to go to bed at ten o'clock. For three or four years he has had an intended, and does not marry her; yet she is twenty-four, he loves her, he intends to marry—he will marry her; but he is sluggish; considers himself comfortable as he is; this is inertia, moral inertia. As for her, she waits patiently, she is gentle, submissive. He goes to see her on Saturday night, makes short excursions with her, visits friends; both sleep away from home, returning together on Monday. All this is quite proper; custom permits these freedoms, and no one takes notice of them. Nevertheless he has neither an idea, nor any curiosity; he can barely spell; he never reads, his own condition alone interests him; a shabby coat for work, and a good coat for Sunday; nothing beyond that; his circle is traced out; he rests like a snail in its shell. Yet, on the advice of the gentleman, who is his partner, he has just built himself a fine house, but he is not at his ease in it. George Eliot, in her novels, has admirably painted these heavy, narrow-viewed natives so common in England, who remain fixed, and, as it were tethered, in animal, manual, or local life, preserve a tradition, and do not swerve from it except at intervals, as an exception, and only on one point. Witness also the landlord, John Willet, in "Barnaby Rudge," by Dickens, an excellent caricature. The personage is half ox, half bull; in this solid mass of flesh the few and brief ideas are, as it were, congealed, and no new idea gains entrance. On the contrary, when the person is an intelligent and a cultured gentleman, the phlegmatic temperament imparts to him a perfectly noble air. I have several of them in my memory, with pale complexion, light blue eyes, regular features, constituting one of the finest types of the human species. There is no excess of cavalierism, of glitter, and gallantry, after the style of the French gentleman; one is conscious of a mind wholly self-contained; and which cannot lose its balance. They elevate this quality of their temperament into a virtue; according to them the chief merit of a man is always to have a clear and cool head. They are right; nothing is more desirable in misfortune and in danger, and this is truly one of their national traits, the gift by which they succeed. A French officer who fought in the Crimea related to me how an English battalion of infantry destroyed two Russian regiments; the Russians fired incessantly, and did not lose a foot of ground, but they were excited and aimed badly; on the contrary, the English infantry avoided undue haste, took steady aim, and missed scarcely a single shot. The human being is ten times stronger when his pulse continues calm, and when his judgment remains free. The consequences and the shades of a type are innumerable. If one starts from the principle that in the case of the phlegmatic, movement and expression are wanting, rare, or unwonted, one will understand the following figures; I copy sketches taken on the spot:

The swell, or dandy of the second class.—Absolutely a cut from a plate of fashions; everything is bran new, and most exact in his linen and attire; the whiskers, moustache, and hair come from the hairdresser's hands, and he himself has the air of a hairdresser's puppet; his clear complexion and his glassy eyes would suit a waxen face; rigid in attitude, measured in movement, he will not disarrange a fold of his cravat; his clothes are put on him as if to show them off. The diversified, unexpected movements, the pleasing, gay, and amusing physiognomy which could alone render this specimen endurable, are wholly wanting, and he remains but a stuffed fool. The stiff personage who walks as if he had swallowed a poker. Very common among clergymen. The large machine, badly put together, whereof the wheels are rusty—witness many tall young folks, and also men of fifty, who have worked hard—all the parts composing them grate at being together. The gestures and the physiognomy have not the necessary agility, move maladroitly, at the wrong time, and with a discordant explosion. This is chiefly visible in the convulsive movement of the mouth.

The timid. Finding expression difficult, he exaggerates its difficulty. If he possess a little cleverness, his habitual silence sinks him still deeper in his inborn silliness; if he possess much, he becomes moody, he lives lonely in a world of inner sentiments to which he forbids ingress to any one, and in proportion as he feels himself more a stranger, he concentrates himself the more. These two descriptions of character are so frequent here that they cannot be noted. Not only young girls, but women of forty, are startled at a new face; I was told of a lady of the highest class, accustomed to important ceremonies, and who becomes dumb, blushes when a stranger is introduced to her. There are men well-educated, even learned, having travelled, knowing several languages, who are embarrassed in company; one might live six months with them without detecting their merits; they have neither the art nor the desire to display themselves; to unseal their lips, a great shock, an urgent interest, are requisite. I know one of them who stammers in a drawing-room, and who on the following day has addressed eight meetings with great eloquence. This kind of awkwardness and bashfulness, wholly physical, is a peculiarity of Teutonic nations. On the other hand, an Italian, a Frenchman, speak naturally, with ease and confidence; the Frenchman still more than the Italian, because he instantly becomes the comrade of his interlocutor. An old historian has remarked this trait, that the Frenchman is he, of all others, who speaks with least hesitation to kings and to princes. Owing to another effect of this temperament, the human being is backward, by no means precocious; it dares not develop itself, it continues longest in the animal and infantine stage of existence; it is often artless innocent, original. The physiognomy remains youthful here much later than amongst us, especially than at Paris, where it withers so quickly; sometimes it remains open even in old age; I recall at this moment two old ladies with white hair whose cheeks were smooth and softly rosy; after an hour's conversation I discovered that their minds were as fresh as their complexions. Like every trait somewhat general, this one produces grotesques and masterpieces. The dignified stick; body and mind puffed out; plenty of principles. The bewildered, who opens the mouth idiotically and has the look of not understanding. The large fat heifer, lymphatic, with white eyelashes. The female goose, with large silly goggle eyes, long waist badly set up above expansions of crinoline. The young chittish girl, rosy, playful, with sparse locks over the neck, a real bird who incessantly laughs and chirps, and without more ideas than a bird. Dickens has pourtrayed this type in Dora, the child-wife of David Copperfield. The blonde maiden with downcast eyes, purer than one of Raffaelle's Madonnas, a sort of Eve, incapable of falling, whose voice is music, adorable in candour, gentleness, and goodness, and before whom one is tempted to lower the eyes out of respect. Since Virginia, Imogen, and the other women of Shakespeare or of his great contemporaries, to Esther and to the Agnes of Dickens, English literature has placed them in the foreground; they are the most perfect flower of the land. The purely virtuous woman, calm, serious, and whom temptation has never approached, and whose life is planned in such a way as to banish all curiosity, every evil thought, every chance of stumbling. In this class many young Quakeresses are conspicuous; with poke bonnets, or covered with a white veil, the subdued complexion of a nun. The expression is that of a person who has lived in a moral enclosure without having ever had a notion of leaving it.

As dress is a sort of expression, an exterior superimposed upon other exteriors, it denotes what the **physi-**

ognomy and gestures have already manifested—to wit, awkwardness, want of skill, of flexibility, of tact. As a general rule, costume ought to image the body, and here it nearly always does so badly. Two exceptions are the riding dress, the black habit which fits the shape, which is simple, devoid of ornament, and exhibits hardihood, strength, physical health; the travelling dress, the little straw hat with a single ribbon, the plain gown, the small boots of solid leather, everything showing the good walker, without trace of coquetry, capable of ascending with her husband the top of a diligence, of being a man's real companion, and not a delicate troublesome doll. With the exception of these two costumes, their showy and overdone style of dress is that of a lorette or an upstart; one is surprised to see such gear on the back of a young virtuous woman. In Hyde Park, on Sunday, the exaggeration of the dresses of the ladies or young girls belonging to the wealthy middle class is offensive; bonnets resembling piled-up bunches of rhododendrons, or as white as snow, of extraordinary smallness, with packets of red flowers or of enormous ribbons; gowns of shiny violet silk with dazzling reflections, or of starched tulle upon an expanse of petticoats stiff with embroidery; immense shawls of black lace, reaching down to the heels; gloves of immaculate whiteness or bright violet; gold chains; golden zones with golden clasps; hair falling over the neck in shining masses. The glare is terrible. They seemed to have stepped out of a wardrobe, and to march past to advertise a magazine of novelties. Not that even; for they do not know how to show off their dresses. They have the head firmly set on the neck, like the beadle in a procession; their hair is too much plastered or too loose; their garments are displayed upon them as upon a wooden puppet. The crinoline is like a tub at the bottom, the cloaks are tucked up behind in clumsy and pretentious puffs; there are not three pretty shapes. The white row of teeth is a crude patch on the red of the lips; black feet, strongly shod, show themselves below the balloon petticoats. Thus bulged out, they walk along rustling; their dress follows and precedes them like the ticking of a clock. Compared with the supple, easy, silent serpentine undulation of the Spanish dress and bearing, the movement here is energetic, discordant, jerking, like a piece of mechanism.

III.—The last type is the active, energetic human being, capable of enterprise, of efforts, of endurance, of perseverance, and who loves effort as effort. The elements of such a character are numerous, and I have not reduced them to order. Turn, then, to particular instances—to examples.

One day, when returning from a visit in the country, two young men asked me if I would take them in my fly to the station, offering to pay the half of the fly. Naturally I agreed to the first part of the proposal, and I declined the conclusion. We chatted. They were two brothers, the one nineteen, the other seventeen years of age; they have ten brothers and sisters, and start for New Zealand; they count upon being twelve years there, and returning with a fortune, becoming sheep farmers. It is impossible to reproduce the zeal, the ardour, the decision of their gestures and of their accent; one was conscious of a superabundance of energy and of activity, overflowing animal spirits. They had the look of strong-limbed greyhounds, sniffing the air in full hunt. According to the elder, there

are already cities of ten thousand inhabitants in New
Zealand. With a capital of £2,000 one may bring
back £20,000 at the end of twelve years. "You will
be thirty years old then. You will return at the proper time to marry." "Yes, sir." This was uttered
with the most powerful tone, with an admirable juvenile outburst. The first year he would learn his business; then he would launch out, shift for himself.
There one must be his own labourer. "Build, fell
trees, plough, reap, pasture cattle, shear sheep, all with
these hands!" He laughed with the ruest and
most joyous spirits. He has had some training; he
has lived on a farm, he has a slight acquaintance with
applied mathematics, with German, but not with
French, and he has travelled in France, in Germany,
in Switzerland; his sentences are disjointed, sounding,
and, as it were, shot forth: "Obliged to go to the
colonies; large family, you know; obliged to look
out for oneself." These two lively, hardy, enterprising
young men pleased me; that is a fine style of beginning life; one risks much here; the world is open,
and one takes the cream of it. England remains the
place to which the return will be made, the treasure to
which all gravitates and flows back. The fortune
once made, the zeal continues; the children of a rich
father are bound to work on account of their number,
and because the law of inheritance awards the largest
share to the eldest. Besides, whether rich or enriched,
they find occupation in politics, associations local or
general, public life. Labour always appears as the end
or aim of labour. Amongst us, a fortune is made in
order to retire, to rest, to remain unemployed, and to
procure the means for children being so.

Subtract youth · with calmer externals, the same

longing for working and doing subsists in mature age. On this head witness the story of a life known to me. M. W—— is the son of a small shopkeeper who had six children. The father caused him to be educated as a practical engineer, and, as soon as the son was eighteen ordered him, not with harshness, but on principle, to provide for himself. Many parents here think that they are only bound to educate their children. .W—— went to Scotland, procuring a situation at £40 a year. Some years afterwards he was sent to India to erect a lighthouse; salary £300 a year. The lighthouse was well done; he returned, and erected a second; salary £400 a year, and a present of £100. On his return, he worked at the construction of a tubular bridge, made reports concerning it; became secretary to a company in London— fixed salary, £500; he married a governess who had not a penny. At present he is secretary to a large establishment, and gets £600 a year. He goes there every day, and works at his desk for nine or ten hours at full steam. He writes from thirty to seventy letters, receives nearly twenty-five visits, and inspects an infinity of objects and persons. Returned home, he helps to compile a dictionary of Grecian antiquities. In order to do that, he first perused the classics in translations; then, aided and counselled by his learned friends, the undertakers of the dictionary, he succeeded in reading them fluently in the originals. He spends a portion of his nights thus; observe that he has selected the short, troublesome articles, because no one would take them, and to do them somebody was required. The end being the first consideration, he supplied a willing man himself. Besides that, he has found time for acquiring and well understanding German, French, music, for educating himself in every way, for being abreast of everything. He avows that work is a necessity to him, that once having been two days in entire idleness, he almost expired from weariness; that he likes to travel, because every day one gets stuffed with facts, with new ideas; he maintains that need of work to be the English resource; the machine would grind itself away if it turned in a vacuum. The grandfather of his pleasing young wife, well trained and instructed, was the carpenter of a college. Her father, the carpenter's son, entered the college by favour, distinguished himself as a student, took honours, left it a tutor; having taken noblemen to board with him, he obtained through their influence a cure worth £500; moreover, he was a good preacher, his sermons sold largely. Aided by his reputation, he came to London, founded a chapel with the help of some rich people, and ended by making £1,200 a year. Twice married —the first time to a woman possessing nothing, the second to one well off—he has had fourteen children by the former and six by the latter; his sons are professors, lawyers, clergymen—nearly all in good circumstances; among the daughters, several have remained at home, others have gone out as governesses, among others Mrs. W———, in order "to be independent." This last phrase is thoroughly characteristic, and, in my opinion, admirable. W———, his wife, and three children, live comfortably. They rent a cottage in the environs of London for £200 a year. Every year they take a trip together. It is evident to me that they expend everything; if they provide for the future, it is at most by means of a life assurance. A very good specimen of English life; to be thrown early upon one's resources, marry a woman without fortune, have plenty of children, expend one's income, save up nothing, work prodigiously, put one's children to the necessity of working also, lay in continuously stores of facts and positive information, find distraction from one labour in another labour, recruit oneself by travel, always producing and always acquiring; they desire nothing better, either for themselves or for their children.

Such a disposition of heart and mind is explicable by many concurrent causes; the following are those which I partially discern :—The law of primogeniture, and the large number of children; as a consequence, each one is bound to help himself, and acquires, when quite young, the idea that he must be the architect of his fortune. But in order to furnish an explanation of the large number of children, it must be admitted, among other causes, that the parents possess more courage, and, above all, more insensibility than among us; more courage, because they fear less the embarrassment of a numerous family, and the obligation of working in their old age; more insensibility, because they accept beforehand the idea that their children must struggle and toil, that their daughters will quit them for ever, going to settle in India, in Australia. On the contrary, the first desire of a French father is to spare his son the privations which he has undergone himself; he stints himself to dower his daughters, and cannot bear the thought of having half-a-dozen who will be governesses, or of whom he will rid himself by exportation.

Second cause, the climate; I always recur to this, because there is no greater power. Consider that this humidity and this fog existed, and even worse, under the Saxon kings, and that this race has lived amid, as far as can be traced, even in its earliest country on the coasts of the Elbe and of Jutland. At Manchester, last winter, one of my friends informed me that in the principal hotel of that city it was necessary to keep the gas burning for five days; at midday it was not clear enough to see to write; the sixth day the fog still lasted, but the supply of gas was exhausted. During six months, and during several days in the other months, this country seems to have been made for wild ducks. After having seen London, the country houses, all the luxury and all the comfort, I said to an Englishman—" The drawing-room and the dining-room are perfect; I have yet to see the kitchen—the manufactories, Manchester, Birmingham, and Liverpool How do your working men live down there? They labour; what else can one do in these streets and in that fog?" The dismalness and severity of Nature cut off clean and by the root every voluptuous conception of life. The ideal, under this sky, is a dry, clean, well-closed, well-warmed habitation; a chat with a faithful wife, a good housekeeper, dressed with care; rosy-cheeked children well washed and in clean clothes; abundance of furniture, commodities, useful and pleasing knick-knacks nicely ranged and polished, the presence of them recalling to man that he is sheltered against inclemencies of weather and weariness, that provision has been made for all the possible wants of his body and of his mind. On the contrary, in Provence, in Italy, in southern countries, the ideal is lounging in the shade, on a terrace, in the open air, with a mistress, before a noble landscape, amid the perfume of roses, amid statues and the music of instruments. In order to relish delicately the beauty of the light, the balmy air, the delicious fruits, and the configuration of the landscape, the senses have but to expand themselves;

here the climate closes them, and, by dint of repressing, blunts them. Take an example in little: a poor person at Marseilles, or at Milan, buys a pound of grapes for a halfpenny, worthy of being placed on the table of gods, and thus he acquires the idea of exquisite sensation. How can you suppose that a like idea can be engendered in the brain of one whose palate knows nothing beyond a morsel of meat and a glass of gin or of ale? Shut out from this path, the man never dreams of fine and sensual enjoyment; he would not understand how to essay it, he is hardened, stiffened, habituated to the exigencies and hardship of his lot. However, his thoughts are turned elsewhere, and this is an obvious necessity, for he would not have time to dawdle, to taste, and to enjoy if he desired it. Cold, rain, mud, bad weather, a barren soil are the foes he is bound to combat without ceasing; in addition, his frame consumes more, and needs more powerful restoratives; it could not subsist without spirits and heavy food. A poor person is not wretched in the South; he obtains the most beautiful and the best things gratis, the necessaries of life for next to nothing, so many things which are necessaries in the North, he does not need: abundance of nourishment, artificial light, fire, a well-protected dwelling, warm clothing, frequent changes of linen, and much more. Here he is a painful sight. Nothing can be more horrible than the coat, the lodging, the shirt, the form of an English beggar; in Hyde Park, on Sunday, when a poor family sits on the grass it makes a stain. Possess £20,000 in the Funds here, or else cut your throat: such is the idea which constantly haunts me, and the omnibus advertisements suggest it still more in informing me that "Mappin's celebrated razors cost only one shilling" They are of the same mind, and say, to excuse themselves, that, very commonly, among them, poverty debases. It is partly to avoid this downfall that the English are so eager in quest of wealth. They prize it because, in their eyes, it is the accompaniment, the aliment, the condition of morality, of education, of all the qualities which make a gentleman. Under the lash of this perpetual whip each one advances, pulling his car. Now, custom turns into necessity; even after reaching the end, he continues to pull, and, if his own be lacking, he harnesses himself to that of his neighbour, of his parish, of his association, or of the State.

Another incentive: he has a longing for rough exercise; he has fighting instincts, consequently the desire to conquer, and to earn the proud testimony that he has performed a difficult task. There are a thousand signs of this. I have previously noted the necessity for physical movement, the long walks of young girls, the general habit of riding; the moist and cold climate impels the play of the muscles; add the innumerable pleasure yachts, the dangerous steeplechases, hunting. An ambassador named to me spent the whole summer in Scotland when he was young. During six days of the week he hunted with a companion in the Highlands, slept in the open air, returned home on Saturday evening, started off again at four on Monday morning. A number of young and grown-up men go every year to fish for salmon in Norway, shoot deer in Canada, or elephants at the Cape. As for journeys full of dangers and hardships, even women brave them, and alone. On this head I have fifty instances; and besides, their reputation is well known. Applying this longing for action and for struggle to trades and to professions, it will produce the requisite energy for supporting their fatigue and yoke, more especially if we take into account two circumstances which greatly lessen the principal weight of modern toil, I mean weariness. The one is the phlegmatic temperament which represses the springs of ideas, the improvisation, the petty intervening emotions, and enables the man to work with the regularity of a machine. The other is the want of nervous delicacy, the acquired insensibility, the being accustomed to dull sensations, which suppress in man the desire for keen and varied pleasure, and hinder him from rebelling against the monotony of his business. I have distinctly seen this in France when following, in a calico-printing establishment, the proceedings of two English workmen among thirty Frenchmen; long, cold faces, silent, expressionless, without distraction, without haste, giving themselves just the necessary movement, never becoming animated or unbending, and working as well during the tenth hour as during the first. To sum up, there is no other outlet for the faculties save useful action; the tyranny of numerous wants which labour alone can satisfy, the natural taste for physical effort and moral struggle, no aversion for the monotony of uninteresting toil: in all that there is stuff for forming, in every manual or liberal career, powerful and patient workers.

Owing to a very natural consequence, this character has become here the ideal pattern; for every people hallows and places on a pedestal the type which best exhibits its own faculties, and best supplies its wants. This is why opinion and morality repeat to an Englishman, " Labour and compete in some useful undertaking; if you refuse, you are not a man, and have no title to esteem." That is a fresh impetus, which is the reverse of those which precede, but which is none the less distinct from them, and which is of chief importance here. For it is an idea, a mental conviction; now, among the men of this country pure ideas, convictions, the deliberate opinions of a reasoning brain, are much more dominating and efficacious than elsewhere. Nothing is more rare than this supremacy among the lively and southern races. In my opinion, a Frenchman argues for the sake of arguing; it is so agreeable to him to string one idea after another; if the conclusion be new and its import great, his delight is extreme; but he stops there: he has furnished himself with a fine spectacle of a lofty kind; that suffices him On the contrary, for a Teutonic head, especially for an English head, the slowly elaborated conclusion is but a starting-point; it becomes a principle, a spring of action, one of the powers, often the greatest of the powers, governing his conduct. He does not act, like the other, by impulse, on the spur of the moment, under the influence of lively passions which reflection has left intact, and which boil over spontaneously in hot resolves. In his case these impulses retire into the background; it is his idea which occupies the foremost place and determines it. Having admitted that a man ought to strive and render himself useful, he requires no other motive for striving and rendering himself of use. I quoted above the remark of Mr. W———, relating to the short, wearisome articles which he had undertaken in the Dictionary: "It is necessary that they should be done." In like manner Arthur Young, who, during two years visited in succession all the provinces of France on horseback, in the interests of agriculture, could scarcely get the French to whom he told this to understand him; in their eyes the thing looked well in words; but to leave his family and his business, undertake such a long task, of such remote return, of so problematical success, all by himself, without a mission, from personal choice, without other determining motive than a wholly abstract, cold idea, that appeared strange to them. The same causes, as those above-mentioned, explain this power of an idea, especially of a moral idea. In the first place, in a phlegmatic and hardened nature, the rival powers are fewer; there are fewer spirits, seductions, rashnesses, casting themselves across and breaking the uniform line of conduct. Besides, the attraction of sensible happiness is smaller, less penetrating, and less seductive. In fine, when one voluntarily gives oneself a watchword, when on reflection it is considered noble, when put to the test it is found hard, pride and the spirit of struggling cleave to it unto the end. Such is the sentiment of duty; the English say that in all degrees it is one of the essential traits of their national character. This being settled, let us review the types. When at eight o'clock in the morning, at the terminus of a railway, one sees people arriving from the country for their daily avocations, or when one walks in a business street, one is struck with the number of faces which exhibit this type of cold and determined will. They walk straight, with a geometrical movement, without looking on either hand; without distraction, wholly given up to their business, like automatons, each moved by a spring; the large, bony face, the pale complexion, often sallow or leaden-hued, the rigid look, all, even to their tall, perpendicular, black hat, even to the strong and large foot-covering, even to the umbrella rolled in its case and carried in a particular style, display the man unsensitive, dead to ideas of pleasure and elegance, solely preoccupied in getting through much business well and rapidly. Sometimes one detects the physiognomy of Pitt—the slight face, impassive and imperious, the pale and ardent eyes, the look which shines like the fixed gleam of a sword; the man is then of finer mould, yet his will is only the more incisive and the stouter; it is iron transformed into steel. The effect is at its height when this expression is perceived on the countenance of a young girl; I have seen it several times, and the accent, the words, and the thought were in unison; at the end of two minutes the cutting of the knife was felt. Probably these are the sort of women who, as if taking a walk, go alone from Alexandria to Khartoum, or, out of philanthropy, conduct bands of women from London to Australia.

I transcribe a note written at the close of a previous journey, and confirmed by what I have seen during the present one: "If we except the beaux and belles of the public walks, four times out of five the English type is the following: as regards women, a capacity for enduring much, and frequently the physiognomy of a person who has borne much, yet with resigned, worn, or determined air, which excites the remark, 'She has made up her mind;' as regards men, a capacity for doing much, for long-sustained effort, the imprint of sustained attention, contracted traits, not at all enervated or visionary, the jaw clenched, the face impassive, steadfast." The excess of this faculty and kind of life is exhibited on all hands, and notably among the poorer classes. A number of faces among the workmen, the day labourers of the country, are hollowed, blanched, spent with fatigue, and recall the screws in the cabs, which stand patiently and inert, the four feet apart, while the rain pours over their old lean flanks. Greyish and straight hair, in scanty locks; the mouth remains half open, as if due to an involuntary relaxation of the muscles; the eye has no longer any meaning. The man moves still, but this seems as if owing to the effect of an imparted movement; he has become a machine. When a trace of expression returns, he seems to awake out of a bad dream. The consumption, the wear and tear of life, the exhaustion of the being harnessed to a load too heavy, jaded, flurried, is still more visible in the women. Sometimes, during a visit made to them, upon a question being put, their lips endeavour to recall a smile; but one turns away with a heavy heart when one has seen this attempt to smile.

The strong, the phlegmatic, the worker; around these three types group several varieties, according to the differences of class, of education, of employment, of sex, of age, these again being complicated by the different degrees of purity and force, which each type may present. But all this is a sketch only; it must now be verified, corrected, investigated — always in contact with living things.

VI.

ENGLISH GIRLS AND AUTHORESSES.

NUMBERS of dinners or luncheons in town, walks in the country, with persons belonging to the upper middle class, and with some of the nobility. The drawing-rooms and the dinners are the same as everywhere else; there is a certain level of luxury and of elegance where all the wealthy classes of Europe meet. The only very striking thing at table, or in the evening, is the exceeding freshness of the ladies and also of their toilette; the hue of the skin is dazzling. Yesterday, I was placed beside a young lady whose neck and shoulders resembled snow, or rather mother-of-pearl; this extraordinary white is so powerful, that, to my eyes, it is not life-like. She wore a rose-coloured dress, wreath of red flowers, green trimmings, and a golden necklace around the throat, like a savage queen : they have rarely a feeling for colours.

Great reception at a minister's; the staircase is monumental, and the drawing-rooms are lofty, princely; but this is uncommon; in general the house is not well arranged for receiving guests. When one has a large company, the two drawing-rooms on the first-floor do not suffice; very rich people who are obliged to make a display, give their entertainment on two floors ; the ladies, for lack of room in order to get air, seat themselves on the steps of the stairs. To-day several distinguished persons were pointed out to me, but I have not the right to describe them. Some young ladies and young girls are extremely beautiful, and all the company are excessively dressed; many ladies have their hair decked with diamonds, and their shoulders, much exposed, have the incomparable whiteness of which I have just spoken, the petals of a lily, the gloss of satin do not come near to it. But there are many storks in gauze and tulle, many skinny jades, with prominent noses, jaws of macaws; ugliness is more ugly here than among us. As to the men, their physical type and their expression badly harmonize with their position; they are often too tall, too strong, too automatic, with eyes inert or wild, with angular and knotty features. I met again the two Frenchmen belonging to the Embassy; how agreeable as a contrast are their intelligent and lively, gay faces! It is sufficient to be introduced in order to be greeted with perfect politeness. The French wrongly think that they are privileged in this matter. In this respect, throughout Europe, all well brought up people resemble each other.

Another evening at Lady S———. One of her daughters sang a Norwegian song at the piano, and sang it well, with animation and expression which are not common. According to the opinions of my musical friends, the English are still worse endowed than we are with respect to music; however, on this subject, all illusions are possible; Miss B———, having pitilessly strummed a sonata, finished amidst general attention; her mother said to me, "She has quite a genius for it." Two other young girls are beautiful and pleasing; but too rosy, and upon this rosiness are too many adornments of staring green which vex the eye. But as compensation, how simple and affable are they! Twice out of three times when one converses here with a woman, one feels rested, affected, almost happy; their greeting is kindly, friendly; and such a smile of gentle and quiet goodness! No after-thought; the intention the expression, everything is open, natural, cordial. One is much more at ease than with a Frenchwoman; one has not the vague fear of being judged, rallied; one does not feel oneself in presence of a sharpened, piercing, cutting mind, that can quarter you in a trice; nor a vivid, exacting, wearied imagination which demands anecdotes, spice, show, amusement, flattery, all kinds of dainties, and shuts you up if you have no tit-bits to offer her. The conversation is neither a duel, nor a competition; one may express a thought as it is without embellishment; one has the right to be what one is, commonplace. One may even, without wearying her or having a pedantic air, speak to her about serious matters, obtain from her correct information, reason with her as with a man. I transcribe some conversation taken down on the spot.

Dined with Mrs. T——; her two nieces are at table. They have the small, plain dresses of boarding-school girls. The eldest never raises her eyes during the repast, or timidly glances around. This is not silliness; after dinner I talked freely for an hour with them. Their silence is mere bashfulness, infantine modesty, innocent wildness of the startled doe. When spoken to, their blood ascends to their cheeks; for myself, I love that youthfulness of the mind; it is not necessary that a young girl should too early have the assurance and the manners of society; the French girl is a flower too soon in bloom. They spend the winter and the summer in the country, twenty miles distant from the city. They talk for at least two hours daily; then they work in the family circle, where they listen to something read aloud. Their occupations are drawing, music, visits to the poor reading (they are subscribers to a circulating library). They read novels, travels, history, and some sermons. On Sunday there is church, and the school for the poor village children. They do not weary; they have no desire to see company. This winter they came to France, and found Frenchwomen very agreeable, amiable, engaging, and sprightly. But they are surprised and hurt at the constant supervision which we keep over our girls. In England they are much more independent. Even in London, each of them may go out alone, or at least with her sister. Yet there is excess; they censure the fast girls who follow the hounds, treat men as comrades, and sometimes smoke. All is commonplace in these two young girls, education, mind, character, face; they are very healthy, they are fresh, nothing more; they are average girls. But this modesty, this simplicity, this health, this good sense, suffice to make a good wife who will be contented with her household, will have children without being sickly, will be faithful to her husband, and will not ruin him in dress.

The chief point is the absence of coquetry; I proceed to cite trifling instances, extreme, unfavourable. This winter in a Paris drawing-room where I was, a stout, red-faced, bald man, related to a rather great English personage, entered leading his daughter of sixteen; pretty gentle face, but what ignorance of dress! She had dark brown gloves, hair in curls, not glossy, a sort of badly fitting white casaque, and her waist resembled a log in a sack All the evening she remained silent, like a Cinderella amidst the splendours and supreme elegances of the dresses and beauties surrounding her. Here, in St. James's Park, at the Exhibition, in the picture galleries, many young ladies, pretty, well dressed, wore spectacles. I put aside several other traits; but it is clear to me that they possess in a much lesser degree than Frenchwomen the sentiment which ordains that at every moment, and before every person, a woman stands with shouldered arms, and feels herself on parade. However, naturalness is less restrained, and breaks forth more freely. Recently, at thirty miles from London, we took a long walk with the daughters of the family, and we climbed a rather steep height. Still very young, they are true goats, always leaping, even when ascending, upon the sharp slopes and among the stones. Exuberance and freedom of the circulation, and of the animal forces; nothing feminine; in the carriage, before arriving, their noisy babble, excitedness, their sparkling eyes, above all their energy, the emphasis of their pronunciation, gave the idea of merry English boys during the holidays. The youngest had bright crimson cheeks like a rosy apple; both of them had full jaws and large feet. Miss Charlotte, aged fifteen, told me that she could easily walk twenty miles. They first learned German from a nurse; but they do not know French yet. "Yet you have a French governess?" "Yes, but when one is stupid!" Then an outburst of laughter. Certainly, self-love does not constrain them; they never dream of acting a part; tall and developed as we see them, daughters of a nobleman who is wealthy, they are children still; not one of their ideas, not one of their gestures, betrays the woman. Neither precocious nor worldly; these two traits coincide and engender a multitude of others. I can bear the testimony of my eyes to the great freedom which they enjoy; I see many of them in the morning in Hyde Park who have come to take a turn on horseback, without other companion than a groom. Two days after arriving in the country I was asked to give my arm to a young daughter of the family, in order to escort her to a place a mile off. S———, who has spent a year here, considers this loyal and free intercourse charming; a gentleman to whom he was introduced said, "Come to my house and I will make you acquainted with my daughters." They are more amiable and honest comrades. One rides with them on horseback, one accompanies them to archery meetings, one chats familiarly with them on all, or nearly all, subjects; one laughs without afterthought; it would be impossible even for a coxcomb to treat them otherwise than as if they were his sisters. At Manchester two of my French friends went to dine at a house. At eleven in the evening they were requested to escort home two young girls who were there. All the four entered a cab, and rode for half-an-hour. They chatted gaily, and without any trouble or embarrassment on either side. Thanks to these manners, the man most inured to the harshnesses and villanies of life, must keep a corner of his soul for poetry, for tender sentiments. In this we are deficient; an Englishman who has travelled among us is astonished and scandalised to see men in Paris staring women in the face, not yielding the pavement to them. It is necessary to have lived among foreigners to know how much our manners, our remarks on this subject are displeasing, and even offensive; they consider us bag-men, fops, and blackguards. The truth is that we feel with difficulty the sentiment of respect; sex, condition, education, do not create as great distinctions among us as among other nations. Moreover, in addition to individuals being more equal among us, they experience the necessity in a higher degree of being sensible of this equality.

Dined with F——. The ladies explained to me the training of young girls. In well-to-do or wealthy families they all learn French, German, Italian, in general from infancy, through nurses and foreign governesses. Commonly they begin with French; nearly all speak it fluently, and several without any accent; I have cited the sole exception I have encountered. They read Dante, Manzoni, Schiller, and Goethe, our classics, Chateaubriand, and some moderns. Many learn a little Latin; that will be serviceable for the education of their children, or of their young brothers. Several learn natural history, botany, mineralogy, geology; they have a taste for all natural things; and in the country, at the sea-side, in their frequent journeys, they can see minerals, herbs, shells, form collections. Besides, that suits the English habit, which consists in storing up facts; thus they are more instructed, and more solidly instructed, than among us. Another motive is that many of the young girls never marry, and that it is requisite to prepare an occupation for them beforehand. Lady M—— cited the case of a family in her neighbourhood, where there are five unmarried daughters, all beautiful; the older ones are thirty-five and thirty-six; this is because they have been brought up in luxury, and have scarcely any dowry. Frequently a father only gives his daughter a sum equivalent to the income of his eldest son and heir; and, moreover, he obliges the gentleman who offers himself, to make a settlement on his daughter of £200, £300, £400 sterling yearly, whereof she will have the entire control when married, and which will be her pin-money. This condition keeps away many suitors; besides, it is granted that one must marry for love, settled liking; now, it often happens that one does not feel this liking, or that one does not inspire it. Hence many girls miss the chance, and remain spinsters. There are some in almost every family, the position of aunt being very well filled. They help to rear the children, superintend a part of the household, preserve-making or the linen cupboard, make herbariums, paint in water-colours, read, write, become learned. Many compose moral romances, and sometimes very good novels; Miss Yonge, Miss Kavanagh, Miss Bronte, the author of "John Halifax," Miss Thackeray, and others, are known; talent is frequent among authoresses, there are some of the first class— Mrs. Gaskell, Miss Evans, Elizabeth Browning; the two last possess genius. Reckon again the translations: numerous German and French works have been translated — and well translated — by women. Others write in magazines, compose small popular treatises, join a society, teach classes of poor children. The constant concern is to find an employment for their faculties, or to acquire a talent which serves as a remedy for weariness. The highest rank is not absolved. Witness the occupations of the Royal Family : the Queen and her daughters send water-colours, engravings, drawings done by themselves, to charity sales; Prince Albert was one of the most cultivated and most active men in the kingdom; each one thus takes up one or two special subjects, labours at some improvement in agriculture, in science—some beneficent work or institution.

Thus life is serious, and all, even young girls, know that they must prepare themselves and provide themselves for it. N——, who comes to England every year, visited one of his old friends, wealthy, and the father of a family, who said to him—"I am put out; my daughter Jane is twenty-four, does not marry, frequently shuts herself up in the library, and reads solid works." "What dower will you give her?" "Two thousand pounds sterling." "And your sons?" "The eldest will have the estate; the second a mine which yields two thousand pounds." "Give five thousand pounds to Miss Jane." This phrase opened up vistas to the father; he gave her the five thousand pounds. Miss Jane has been married, she has a baby; she was made to be a mother; it would have been a pity to have converted her into a learned, spectacled spinster; if suitors do not offer themselves it is because the style of the house is too great. As for me, what I admire here is the coolness, the good sense, the courage of the young girl who, seeing herself in a blind alley, alters her course without a murmur, and silently sets herself to study. In none of the houses which I have entered in London or in the country have I seen a journal of the fashions. One of my English friends who has sojourned in France informs me that here no well brought up woman reads such platitudes. On the contrary, a special review, "The English Women's Review,' contains in the number of which I am turning over the pages, statements and letters on emigration to Australia, articles on public instruction in France, and other essays equally important; no novels, neither chit-chat about theatres, nor review of fashions,

&c. The whole is serious—substantial; witness as a contrast in a provincial mansion among us the journals of fashions with illuminated sketches, patterns of the last style of bonnets, explanations of a piece of embroidery, little sentimental stories, honeyed compliments to female readers, and, above all, the correspondence of the directress with her subscribers on the last page, a masterpiece of absurdity and inanity. It is shameful that a human intellect can digest such aliment. A dress badly made is more bearable than an empty head. I copy the titles of some articles, all written by women in the *Transactions of the National Association for the Promotion of Social Science.* "Education by Means of Workhouses," by Louisa Twining; "District Schools for the English Poor," by Barbara Collett; "Application of the Principles of Education to Lower-class Schools," by Mary Carpenter; "Actual State of the Colony of Mettray," by Florence Hill; "Hospital Statistics," by Florence Nightingale; "The Condition of Working Women in England and France," by Bessie Parkes; "Slavery in America, and its Influence upon Great Britain," by Sarah Redmond; "Improvement of Nurses in Agricultural Districts," by Mrs. Wiggins; "Report of the Society for Furnishing Employment to Women," by Jane Crowe. Most of these authoresses are not married, several are secretaries of active associations, of which the Review I have just cited is the central organ; one of these associations supplies women with work, another visits the workhouses, another the sick. All these articles are instructive and useful, the custom of keeping classes, of visiting the poor, of conversing with men, discussion, study, personal observation of facts, have yielded their fruits; they know how to observe and reason; they go to the bottom of things, and they comprehend the true principle of all improvement. Mary Carpenter says, "It is necessary above all, and as the first aim, to develop and direct the infant's will, enrol him as the principal soldier, as the most serviceable of all the co-operators in the education which is given to him." One cannot be corrected, improved but by oneself, instinctive personal effort, self-government are indispensable; the moral rule must not be applied from without, but spring up from within. Whoever has perused English novels knows with what precision and what justice these authoresses depict characters; frequently a person who has lived in the country, in a small set, busied with domestic cares, finds herself obliged to write a novel in order to gain her bread, and one discovers that she understands the human heart better than a professional psychologist. To be instructed, learned, useful, acquire convictions, impart them to others, employ powers and employ them well, that is something; one may laugh if one likes, say that these manners form schoolmistresses, female pedants, blue-stockings, and not women. As you please; but contrast this with our empty provincial idleness, the weariness of our ladies, the life of an old maid who rears canaries, hawks scandal, does crotchet-work, and attends every service. This is the more important because in England all are not female pedants. I know four or five ladies or young girls who write; they continue none the less pleasing and natural. Most of the authoresses whom I have cited are, on the authority of my friends, domestic ladies of very simple habits. I have named two among them who possess genius; a great French artist whose name I could mention, and who has spent several days with each of them, did not know that they had talent; not once did a hint of authorship, the need of speaking of oneself and of one's books, occur during twenty-four hours of talk. M——, being invited to the country, discovered that the mistress of the house knew much more Greek than himself, apologised, and retired from the field; then, out of pleasantry, she wrote down his English sentence in Greek. Note that this female Hellenist is a woman of the world, and even stylish. Moreover, she has nine daughters, two nurses, two governesses, servants in proportion, a large, well-appointed house, frequent and numerous visitors; throughout all this, perfect order; never noise or fuss; the machine appears to move of its own accord. These are gatherings of faculties and of contrasts which might make us reflect. In France we believe too readily that if a woman ceases to be a doll she ceases to be a woman.

VII.

ENGLISH MARRIAGES AND MARRIED WOMEN.

A CONVERSATION with several Englishmen about marriage; they have lived abroad, and I think them impartial; besides, their statements agree. A young English girl will not marry unless through inclination; she weaves a romance for herself, and this dream forms part of her pride, of her chastity; thus many, and of exalted character, think they have fallen short should they marry without experiencing the enthusiasm suited to an absolute preference. To marry is to abandon oneself wholly and for ever. Witness, with regard to this deep sentiment, the novels by ladies—above all, " John Halifax, Gentleman," and others by the same authoress. These are the theories of a pure, exclusive mind, which seems to have traversed the whole world without receiving, I will not say a stain, but the shadow of one.

In this romance of the heart, the young girl continues English, that is to say, positive and practical. She does not dream of outpourings, of sentimental walks, hand-in-hand in the moonlight, but of her share in an undertaking. She wishes to be the helper, the useful partner of her husband in his long journeys, in his difficult enterprises, in all his affairs whether wearying or dangerous. Such, for example, were Mrs. Livingstone and Lady Baker; the one traversed Africa from side to side; the other went to the sources of the Nile, and narrowly escaped dying in consequence. I have seen an English Bishop of a large island, a country of beasts and cannibals; his poor wife carried on her countenance the marks of that terrible climate. A young girl of the neighbourhood, rich and of good family, is at this moment making her preparations, packing up her piano, &c.; the gentleman she is about to marry will take her to Australia; she will return once only in five or six years to kiss her old parents. Another young lady of twenty-four, very weak and delicate; her husband is in the Punjaub (£6,000 of salary, £1,200 for the expenses of his establishment); she has been for two years in Europe with an affection of the throat, which will return as soon as she returns to India; four young children; they are sent to Europe before they are two years old; the Indian climate kills them; there are here entire boarding schools here recruited by these little Anglo-Indians. Very often a lady, daughter of a marquis or baronet, having a dowry of £3,000 or £3,250, marries a simple gentleman, and descends of her own free will from a state of fortune, of comfort, of society, into a lower or much inferior grade. She accustoms herself to this. The reverse of the medal is the fishery for husbands. Worldly and vulgar characters do not fail in this respect; certain young girls use and abuse their freedom in order to settle themselves well. A young man, rich and noble, is much run after. Being too well received, flattered, tempted, provoked, he becomes suspicious and remains on his guard. This is not the case in France; the young girls are too closely watched to make the first advance; there the game never becomes the sportsman. Commonly, the dowries are very small. I have been told of several families in which the eldest son has one or two hundred thousand pounds sterling; the daughters receive from three to five thousand. However, in order to marry, it is necessary that they should feel a passion. Many do not marry in consequence of a thwarted inclination, and continue to live with their eldest brother. Every Englishman has a bit of romance in his heart with regard to marriage; he pictures a home with the wife of his choice, domestic talk, children; there his little universe is enclosed, all his own; so long as he does not have it he is dissatisfied, being in this matter the reverse of a Frenchman, to whom marriage is generally an end, a makeshift. Frequently he is obliged to wait, especially if a younger son, because he has not sufficient as yet wherewith to maintain his wife. He goes to India, to Australia, labours with all his might, returns, and marries; here the passions are tenacious and deep. When an Englishman is in love, one of my entertainers said to me, he is capable of anything. Thackeray has very well marked the intensity and the persistence of this sentiment in his portrait of Major Dobbin, the lover of Amelia, in "Vanity Fair;" he waits fifteen years without hope, because for him there is but one woman in the world This causes silent rendings of the heart and long inner tragedies. Numbers of young men experience it; and the protracted chastity, the habits of taciturn concentration, a capacity for emotion greater and less scattered than among us, carries their passions to the extreme. Frequently it ends in nothing, because they are not beloved, or because the disparity of rank is too great, or because they have not money enough wherewith to maintain a family—a very costly thing here. Then they become half insane; travel to distract their minds, proceed to the ends of the earth. One who was mentioned to me, very distinguished, was supplanted by a titled rival; during two years apprehensions were felt for his reason. He went to China and to Australia; at present he occupies a high post, he has been made a baronet, he presides over important business, but he is unmarried; from time to time he steals off, makes a journey on foot, in order to be alone and not to have any one to converse with.

I have previously noted that young people see and associate together in perfect freedom, without being watched, they can thus study and understand each other as much as they please; for four months, for five months and more, they ride on horseback and chat together during several successive seasons in the country. When the young man has made up his mind it is to the young girl that he addresses himself first, asking the consent of the parents in the second place; this is the opposite of the French custom, where the man would consider it indelicate to utter a single clear or vague phrase to the young girl before having spoken to her parents. In this matter the English find fault with us, ridicule our marriages summarily settled before a lawyer. Yet C——, who is English, and knows France well, allows that their love-matches end more than once in discord, and our marriages of arrangement in concord. The wife's dowry is nearly always placed in the hands of trustees, who take charge of it on their own responsibility, handing over the interest only to the family; in general this income is the wife's pin-money: with it she must dress herself and dress her children. The fortune becomes thus a kind of dotal or paraphernalia fund, secured against the accidents which may happen to the husband. This precaution is taken, because, according to law, all the wife's property is engulfed in that of the husband; without this clause, she would enter the married state deprived of all share in the common fund; she can hold nothing in her own right; she is a simple infant in presence of her husband. Such is one of the reasons inducing Mr. J. Stuart Mill to protest so vigorously against the subjection of women. In fact they are kept in subjection here by the law, religion, manners, and much more closely so than among us. The husband is their lord, and very often he accepts the title seriously; as the wife brings but little money into the establishment, and as her small share remains apart, he thinks himself authorised to say nothing to her about his concerns. Sometimes she is unacquainted with what he does, how he makes the money which he acquires; he gives so much monthly for the household expenses, and renders no account of the rest. Whether he speculates, builds, sells, or buys, is none of her business: frequently ruin arrives without her being able to foresee it. She is merely a housekeeper; she must not busy herself about anything save her household and her children. Most frequently she contents herself with that part; owing to her conscience and education she is gentle and submissive. Nevertheless, on the avowal of my friends, this inequality has grave inconveniences; the husband is often a despot, and, should he die, the wife, kept all her life in ignorance and dependence, is not capable, as with us, of clearing up the affairs, of governing the children, of replacing the head of the family.

Marriage is encompassed with profound respect, and as regards this matter, opinion is unbending; it is quite sufficient to read books, newspapers, especially the writings in which anonymous authors indulge in the greatest license, for example, romances, comic journals; adultery is never excused; even in the latitude of intimate conversations between man and man, it is always held up as a crime. Breaches occur, of which I shall speak later, among the class of tradesmen; and in the lower order of the nobility which is fashionable, travels, and copies Continental manners. But, in the mass of the nation, among well brought up persons in the great world, the wives are almost always faithful. C—— tells me that I might remain here for eighteen months, and visit all the drawing-rooms, without meeting an exception, one only is cited among the highest class. More such cases occurred fifty years ago, in the time of Byron and Alfieri; since then, opinion has become severe, and the Queen has laboured with all her might in this direction, firstly, by her example, secondly by her influence; she excludes ladies of doubtful reputation from her Court; the extreme urgency and pressure of affairs were needed during the Crimean war for her to tolerate under the same roof with her, at Windsor, a statesman known as a profligate. Another guaranty is the dread of publicity and of the newspapers. On this head our free and rakish manners grievously offend them. C—— related to me that in a Parisian circle he heard a man of the world observe to another—"Is it true, then, that your wife has got a lover?" This remark he considers monstrous, and he is right. A book like Balzac's "Physiologie du Mariage" would give great offence; perhaps the author would be prosecuted by the Society for the Suppression of Vice, and probably it would not have been accepted by any publisher. As regards our ordinary novels, a liberal review, the *National*, could not find a strong enough expression wherewith to designate them—"nameless ignominy, the morality of stockjobbers and lorettes." They forget three things. In the first place, these irregularities are not habitual among us, excepting in the case of fashionable upstarts; they very rarely reach the rich or well-to-do middle-class which possesses family traditions. Besides, in the provinces, life goes on openly, and scandal-mongering, which is greatly feared, performs the part of the police. Finally, the Frenchman flaunts that which a foreigner conceals; he has a horror of hypocrisy, and he prefers to be a braggart of vice. According to my friends, the good conduct of English ladies is explainable by the following causes: 1. They are more habituated to take care of themselves, having been free from their infancy. 2. They are less accessible to illusion, to enthusiastic dreams, because they have mixed with young men, and had some experience of the world. 3. They have habits of reflection, and a fund of good sense, because they have received a more serious education, having learned several languages, gained a smattering of science, travelled nearly always in England, and often abroad, and heard their father discuss politics and grave subjects with his friends. Besides, Protestantism develops habits of reflection and reasoning. Lastly, the novels are always moral; and in contact with the poor, in charitable societies, they have gathered some knowledge of real life. 4. They live for eight or nine months of the year in the country, and are there sheltered against temptation. 5. They have many children, who occupy their time; a full nursery, with its train of nurses and governesses, requires continual supervision. 6. They give themselves all manner of occupations in addition. Sunday schools, country sewing classes, visits to the poor, botany, mineralogy, collections of plants and of butterflies, reading. Every family in easy circumstances, when in the country, receives in addition to the *Times,* in addition to other journals and very solid reviews, numbers of new books sent from the circulating library. Mudie's, which is the principal one, purchases one hundred and fifty thousand volumes yearly; it took three thousand copies of Livingstone's "Travels in Africa;" two thousand five hundred of Macaulay's "History of England." A quantity of serious books arrive in this way, and are renewed monthly on the library table in country seats. Among these books the most common are works of political economy, natural history, history, and, above all, travels. Each year scores of them are published. Next to the pleasure of travelling, the greatest pleasure for an Englishman is to read a volume of travel; in this way he augments his store of facts. The ladies have the same taste; all those with whom I am acquainted have visited France, Italy, Germany; a young wife with whom I dined yesterday will pass the winter in Rome, the spring in Jerusalem; those who have delicate chests go to Cairo as readily as we go to Nice. During the journey they take notes, keep a journal; on their return, some of these are printed, others are communicated to their friends in manuscript. They thus keep the globe perpetually at their finger ends; and I have seen those who, with a knowledge of the subject, interested themselves in the settlements of Australia, the oil springs of Pennsylvania, the revolt of the Taepings in China, and the annual massacres of

Dahomey. Add lastly, the great amount of physical movement and the talents which are cultivated; there are always one or two painters in water-colour in a family, and every one rides on horseback once a day. By these occupations the mind is engaged, the time is filled, and that closes the door against unhealthy ideas. These are the auxiliaries of the moral principle; but the principle itself must also be taken to account. In France it is based on the sentiment of honour; in England on the idea of duty. Now, the former is rather arbitrary; its reach varies in different persons. One piques himself upon being rigid on a certain point, and thinks himself free on all the rest; in the circle of bad actions, he cuts off a segment from which he excludes himself; but this part varies according to his preferences—for example, he will be truthful in speaking, but not in writing, or the reverse. My honour consists of that wherein I place my glory, and I can place it in this as well as in that. On the contrary, the idea of duty is strict, and does not admit of the slightest compromise. The Englishwoman knows that in marrying she has vowed fidelity, and the remembrance of this remains anchored in her conscience. According to my friends, this anchorage is so strong that frequently after a slip the wife breaks off altogether; all her past flows back upon her like a flood, till she is well-nigh choked with shame and sorrow. Besides, she has not the elasticity of mind, the manual dexterity, necessary for harmoniously conducting an intrigue and a household; ambiguity is repugnant to her decided character; division revolts her; the obligation to lie unceasingly is insupportable to her. She insists upon being carried off in order to bring about a divorce.

I continue to reproduce conversations. I find nothing

more agreeable than an evening spent in this way with one or two sincere, friendly, unprejudiced interlocutors, who have lived and travelled. National self-love does not interfere; one talks to learn, not to compete or shine. One ventures to give the minor characteristic fact, the precise and genuine detail; each supplies, as briefly as possible, the cream of his experience, his provisions made during a lengthened period, his choice dishes. The following are those of my friends. My mind has never been so fully or so well fed; I continued questioning and listening to them till one o'clock in the morning. Generally an English woman is more thoroughly beautiful and healthy than a Frenchwoman. The principal cause of this is the hygiene; the children ride on horseback, are much in the open air, do not dine with their parents, do not eat sweetmeats. Moreover, the nerves are less excited, and the temperament is calmer, more enduring, less exacting; what is the most wearing in these days, are incessant and unsatisfied desires. For example, in the Crimea the French wounded recovered less frequently than the English, because they resigned themselves less rapidly. This is still truer in the cultivated class, notably among the wives; in their case the uneasy or ardent brain deadens and dries up the springs of life; in our day, a wife must accept her condition, if she wishes to be well. On the other hand, the Englishwoman is less agreeable; she does not dress for her husband, she does not know how to make a pretty woman of herself; she has no talent for rendering herself fascinating and enticing at home; she is unacquainted with a number of fine and delicate graces; she considers it unworthy of her to employ minor means for re-awakening love or fondness; more frequently still she is not clever enough to invent them. She puts on handsome new dresses, is most careful about cleanliness, but nothing more; she is not attractive; one soon wearies beside her. Fancy a very beautiful pink peach, slightly juicy, and alongside of it a perfumed strawberry full of flavour. It is the same with respect to the other affections. B—— says that they have more charm in France when they are sincere and strong. In all things there is a turn, a manner, a degree; among the sentiments these consist of forethought, attentions, certain phrases, the tone in which they are uttered, the considerations, the caretakings which constantly renew and diversify the softer emotions.

According to C——, an Englishwoman is incapable of presiding in a drawing-room as cleverly as a French woman; I mean a drawing-room like those of Paris in which one is amused; he barely knows two or three married ladies of his country who could do it. The Englishwoman has not sufficient tact, promptitude, suppleness to accommodate herself to persons and things, to vary a greeting, comprehend a hint, insinuate praise, make each guest feel that she thinks his presence of much consequence. She is affable only, she merely possesses kindness and serenity. For myself, I desire nothing more, and I can imagine nothing better. But it is clear that a woman of the world— that is to say a person who wishes to make her house a place of meeting frequented and valued by the most distinguished persons of every species—requires to have a more varied and a more delicate talent. C—— greatly admires the facility with which a young married lady among us gets to know the world. A month after her marriage she knows how to do the honours to everybody in her house. In like manner a shopkeeper's wife takes her place at the desk the day after her wedding—understands the tricks of the trade, chats, smiles, retains the customers. I have seen the contrast in a restaurant at Dieppe. The French husband, always attentive and smiling, sped around the tables bowing and scraping, and seemed to take pleasure in waiting on the people; his English wife, stiff and solemn, said in an icy tone to the persons rising from the table, "'Ave yer paid, sir?" She never suspected that such a question put in this way could annoy. As a compensation, my friends said that French politeness was but veneer—an ornament; many foreigners misinterpret it. You have received them well, they think you their friend, and are greatly surprised to be forgotten by you three days afterwards. Our obliging demonstrations are not all the effect of true sympathy, but of natural goodness; we perform them, owing to education, custom, as a matter of honour, and even a little through egotism. They are a proof of our good breeding; we vaguely feel that the same will be done us in return; for a quarter of an hour we enter an agreeable atmosphere of respect and mutual civilities; we lay hold of this pleasant opportunity, and we give ourselves up to it, without its leading to any result in our eyes. A piece of politeness is repaid by a piece of politeness, as one anecdote by another anecdote; I have repaid you; the exchange made, we are quits; I go my way, you go yours; neither of us has anything more to claim from the other, save at the next meeting a smile and a bow. The Englishman is more thoroughly cordial and serviceable. He puts himself to inconvenience for the foreigner who is introduced to him; he goes about to serve him; he gives himself trouble on his behalf. As well as I can decide from my own experience, this judgment is correct. In the first place, I have never found the English selfish and discourteous, as they are represented to be. In London and in the country I I have inquired my way hundreds of times; every one pointed it out, and several gave themselves trouble, accompanying me far enough to put me in the right path. In an omnibus or in a railway carriage, when I have requested my neighbour to inform me, he has always done so with good grace; when I attempted to converse, he did not smile at my blunders of speech, and he talked with me in a kindly fashion. One evening lately, when on foot at some distance from my hotel, a gentleman whom I accosted wished to accompany me back, spoke in praise of France, asked me what I thought of London, and shook hands with me at parting. Another, on a like occasion, made me enter his carriage and drove me to a cab-stand. The newspapers announcing the arrival of three thousand French Orpheonists, remarked that they must be welcomed with heartiness, in order that they might return home with a good opinion of England. On no single occasion has a policeman, an official, a cabman, or conductor been rude or insolent to me. But what is altogether admirable, and perhaps unique in Europe, is their manner of practising hospitality; I cannot think without grateful feelings of that which I have received. The person to whom one presents a letter of introduction does not consider himself quits by an invitation to dinner; he gives you information, acts as your guide, traces out your plan, charges himself with occupying and amusing you, takes you to his Club, introduces you to his friends, takes you to his parents, introduces you to his set of acquaintances, invites you to visit him at his country house, and gives you other letters of introduction when you take your departure; you end by saying to him, "This is too much; I shall never be able to make a return in Paris for what you have done for me here." The like reception is met with among those to whom you have been introduced in the second place, and the same in succession; sometimes, after an hour's conversation, the gentleman whom you see for the first time books you to come and spend a week at his country seat. Should you go, you will be treated as a member of the family. Still more striking is the opening of the heart; frequently at the end of one or two days a gentleman does not hesitate to tell you about his private affairs. I requested information concerning domestic matters. Sometimes my host, in order to be precise, told me the amount of his income, of his expenses, the amount of his rent, the history of his fortune, of his family, of his marriage, a quantity of minor domestic and personal facts. Persons in society are more reticent in France.

We seek for the causes of this difference; the following is a summary of them:—The Englishman is hospitable; 1st. On account of weariness: most of the persons in society live in the country for eight months of the year; sometimes at a distance from a town, and very solitarily; they have need of conversation, new ideas. 2nd. As an effect of social customs, in London they scarcely speak; they live moving about; they remain too short a time, sometimes less than three months; there is too great a crowd, and too much to do; the country-house is the true drawing-room, the place for associating together

3rd. As an effect of domestic habits; many children, many servants; in a well-appointed great house order and a certain reserve are indispensable; the habitual stoicism of characters and manners operates in the same sense. Then, the presence of a stranger does not have the result, as among us, of interrupting acquaintance-ship, stopping the general impulse, the gaiety, the chit-chat, compelling people to be on their guard, to restrain their familiarity and their heedlessness. There is only another chair filled at table, in the drawing-room, nothing more; the tone has not changed. 4th. By the arrangement for comfort and the service: the organisation is perfect, and the machine in order; the domestics are punctual, the rooms ready, the hours fixed; there is nothing to undo or do over again; nor, above all, is there any makeshift required to entertain a visitor. 5th. By kindliness, humanity, and even by conscience; to be useful is a duty, and a foreigner is so thoroughly lost, so little at his ease in the new **country where** he has landed! He ought to be helped.

VIII.

ENGLISH HOUSEHOLDS.

THIS leads to a consideration of the interiors Rule and discipline are more strongly felt therein than among us. In this department, as in the others, the meshes of the social net-work are loosened in France and tightly drawn in England.

I have three households in view; in the one are seven domestics, cook and scullery maid, two housemaids, lady's maid, coachman, valet; in the second, fifteen; in the third, eighteen. A man servant has from £40 to £50 wages, and, if he be on board wages, which is common enough in London, twelve shillings a week are added for his board. Each has his post rigorously defined. The work is divided, no one either trespasses on, or trusts to another. For example, in the last of the houses which I have just cited, there is a special man for sweeping, carrying coal, lighting and keeping up the fires. There are two classes of servants, the lower and the upper, the latter are responsible and transmit the master's orders; at their head is the butler for the men, and the head lady's maid for the women; if a groom should appear with a dirty coat, his master says nothing to him, but reprimands the butler. These upper servants are a species of sergeants, who have an opinion and the authority of their position: defined distribution of employment, hierarchy of powers constitute the leading traits of a workable organisation. And the latter traits complete the former. These servants stand on their dignity; they will enter none but a respectable mansion. S——, requiring to add a housemaid to his staff, thought of a country girl, who, not having been married, had a child; but before taking her, he placed the matter before his servants. They consulted together, and, owing to the good character given of her, admitted the poor girl among them. Generally their manners are correct, though many are young, unmarried, and under the same roof; in S——'s whole life but one accident had happened in his house. On the other hand they do their work conscientiously, with perfect punctuality and regularity, at the appointed time, without fail; they have a watchword which they obey to the letter. However, it appears as if the machine works of its own accord; the masters have scarcely any need to interfere; on this head S—— maintains again that at bottom, in an Englishman, there is the sense of duty, that this sentiment reigns in the kitchen and the ante-chamber as well as in the ship or the workshop, that none other reconciles the subordinate with subordination. Two circumstances concur in alleviating it. The servants retain their share of independence, and they cleave to it. In London many of them have a club, an association whereof the members agree not to continue longer than two consecutive years in the same house, this is in order to leave less power to the masters. Moreover, as their hours are regulated, they are their own masters during the intervals of their service. They have their hall, a large room wherein they take their meals and sit. In the house of which I spoke, their dinner and their breakfast are served half an hour before those of their masters. They have a small library for their use, draughts, chess; after dinner they may go out; one only is kept to answer the bell. In order to obtain much, too much must not be demanded; he who commands must provide for the physical and moral welfare of his subordinates. If he desire the obedience of the heart, he must be their leader, a true chief, a general and responsible official, the accepted and authorised governor of their conduct. In this respect, on Sunday evening, he is their spiritual guide, their chaplain; they may be seen entering in a row, the women in front, the men behind, with seriousness, gravity, and taking their places in the drawing-room. The family and visitors are assembled. The master reads aloud a short sermon; next a prayer; then everyone kneels or bends forward, the face turned towards the wall; lastly, he repeats the Lord's Prayer, and, clause by clause, the worshippers respond. This done, the servants file off, returning in the same order, silently, meditatively. I have observed them several times—not a muscle of their countenance moved. By this community and direction of the moral sentiment, the master succeeds in filling his true place. In France he is very far from possessing in his house, amongst his servants, and even amongst his children, legitimate authority and entire authority. I note at once the inconvenience, the opposite side. In the habitual commerce of life the English are not easygoing; conditions among them are separated by a barrier, and in place of making a passage through it, they strew it with thorns. For example, Mr. N——, an

Englishman settled in France, chose a French tutor for his children. At the end of a month Mrs. N—— ceased to find him to her taste, spoke no more to him, communicated with him by letters only. One evening, in the drawing-room, Mr. N—— went to sleep, and Mrs. N—— began to read. The young man not daring to take up a book, and not being able to converse with any one, ended, after many struggles, by going to sleep also. Next day she said to him, in a dry and arbitrary tone, "Sir, your conduct last evening was very improper; I hope that it will not be repeated." Some days afterwards a young lady being invited with whom he was acquainted, he went and seated himself next to her at table. Mrs. N—— said aloud to him, "Sir, that is not your place; come and sit beside your pupil." He refused, left the table, quitted the house, and demanded, according to agreement, a year's salary. This was refused. A lawsuit followed. Mr. N—— was defeated. This recalls an anecdote of the last century. Lord A—— having engaged a French tutor, advised him not to speak anything but French to his children. "I am charmed, my lord, to find that you lay such store on that tongue." "Sir, we despise it, but we wish that in France our children should know how to speak as well as the natives." One can picture the smiling, effusive air of the Frenchman in quest of a compliment, and the immovable features, the haughty tone of the Englishman, who returns him a slap in the face.

The post of governesses in England is not a pleasant one; witness on this head the novels of Charlotte Bronte. The majority of those I have seen, had assumed a wooden face; nothing is more surprising when such a face is youthful. The tone, the demeanour, the whole is artificial and made to order; composed and maintained in such a way as never to give an opening; even after several days of familiarity, and out of the house in which they teach, they remain on the defensive; the habit of self-observation and of control is too strong; one might say they were soldiers on parade. As to the servants, their expression of humble and subdued respect greatly surpasses that of those whom we can have known; it is even unpleasant to observe this attitude of a man face to face with a man.

There is the same fund of stiffness in the intercourse of relations. A son when speaking familiarly of his father, says, my governor. In fact, by law and custom, he is the governor of his house, which is his castle, and of the garrison that lodges there. Except in the case of an entail, he can disinherit his children, and it has been seen that his wife is subject to him. Mr. W——, a rich landed proprietor, and a gentleman of the old school, has, among other children, a son in consumption. The poor young man, who returned from Nice and felt himself dying, stopped at Boulogne; he wished to end his days with his father, in the house wherein he was born; but he neither durst go thither without being invited, nor even ask permission. His mother, who is ill and wishes to embrace her son again, dare not take upon herself to rejoin him. At length, one of these days, he received a letter from his father, and set off on his journey. The inequality of positions is another cause of coldness. Between the eldest son, who will be a nobleman with an income of £8,000 a year, and the younger son, who will have £200 a year, who inhabits two furnished rooms, and spends the day in a machine shop in order to become an engineer, the distance is too great; real familiarity, fellowship, is impossible. Even when similarly educated they feel their separation. Two brothers were mentioned to me who were both at the University of Oxford, but the elder brother had one hundred pounds sterling a year more than the younger. Final cause of division is the independence of the children: a son, a daughter, can marry without their parents' consent, and very often exercise this right; hence occur squabbles which last a lifetime. Meantime, the father knows that his child can leave him, run directly counter to his will in the most mortifying manner. Frequently he says: " Since you have the right, you must take the consequences." Reasoning thus, many, above all those who have a legion of children, do not trouble themselves about marrying their daughters; they leave that to them; it is their business, as it is the business of the sons to gain a livelihood. That differs greatly from our homes, where the parents give themselves up wholly and without restriction to their children, where the elder sons, the younger sons, the brothers and the sisters are so equal among each other, and almost on a footing of equality with their parents, the familiarity and the intimacy being so complete, where each one considers it natural to enter, every day and at every hour, by their questions and their counsels, into the thoughts, the sentiments, the actions of their relatives, where nothing is enclosed nor reserved, where every mind is disclosed, opened by an hundred thousand apertures to the curiosity and to the sympathy of his kindred.

The English are surprised at this; S—— greatly admires our sociability in this particular, our kindly character. He has often seen in France two or three families together under the same roof and at the same table, during six months in the country, sometimes the entire year in the country, in town; at one time two married brothers, at another the parents with their son-in-law and their daughter, or with their son and their daughter-in-law. Nothing is rarer than this in England." Characters clash; "each family requires to possess its independence as well as its abode. We coalesce, we hold everything in common; as for them, even when living together, they maintain distinctions, they draw lines of demarcation. Self is more powerful; each of them preserves a portion of his individuality, his own special and personal nook, a kind of forbidden field, enclosed, respected by every one, even by the brother and the father, even by the sister, even by the mother; to enter it would be an intrusion; no one gains admission, save perhaps the beloved person, the husband, the wife, to whom all one's life is pledged. This reserved circle is larger or smaller according to the personages." It includes at one time business matters, questions of money and of ambition, at another certain profound sentiments, a hope, a love disappointment, an old and protracted mourning; at another intimate and lofty ideas, for instance religious beliefs; sometimes it embraces them all; then the personage is tongue-tied, and does not like to be spoken to." But in every case the line he has traced around him remains intact; he does not overstep it when unreserved. "If over-leapt by any one, it is owing to an indiscretion which cuts him to the quick; his relatives abstain from doing so as they would from housebreaking. Thus a father or mother is more imperfectly informed than among us as to the sentiments of their daughter, as to the business and the pleasures of their son."

To make this obvious, would require too lengthened detail. I shall cite but one trait. In France a son tells his mother everything, even about his mistresses; the usage is ancient. Madame de Sevigné received from her son secrets which she related to her daughter—very improper and very distinct secrets—and which she was only able to express, owing to her verve, her gaiety, her wonderful lightness of touch. Even at the present day, without going so far back, very many young men make similar avowals to their mothers, or at least hint—allow them to suspect, an affair of gallantry. The mothers are not scandalised at this, they are too happy to be made confidants, almost companions. They scold a little, smile faintly, and, lifting the finger, send away the naughty fellow, telling him to take care. B—— is of opinion that this is impossible in England; the son would not dare do it, the mother would be shocked or indignant. So in other matters; they have no acquaintance with these boundless conversations, these complete outpourings, where the differences in age compensate for the difference of sex, where the son entering the world finds in his mother separating herself from the world his most skilful guide and his most thorough friend.

These habits of reserve lead to a kind of stoicism. Even among their kindred they are not expansive, they are self-restrained. In a family which has lost a very near relative, a father, a son, there are never cries nor outbursts. From the morrow every one comes down, taking their places at table at the ordinary hour, and in the same manner; they merely talk rather less than their wont; it is all very well to feel sorrow, they have to do their work, whatever it be, as well and as conscientiously as before. When the Queen, after Prince Albert's death, shut herself up alone and appeared to have given up the receptions and other occupations of her post, the newspapers, after allowing several months to elapse, began to blame her, and declared to her that a private loss did not absolve any one from public obligations. A writer in the *National Review* praises Eugenie de Guérin, so pure and so melancholy; but, according to him, she is wrong in giving expression to her sadness and even in being sad. "An Englishwoman of right and healthy mind would consider cheerfulness a duty in itself, and would refrain from expressing distaste for life." I have badly translated the word "cheerfulness" (*gaieté*), being unable to render it; it means the opposite of dejection, a sort of smiling serenity. Nowhere is this sentiment nobler, more touching to notice than on the face of old ladies. One of them, bed-ridden for ten years, was still kindly and composed. The children were taken to her night and morning, she knew and laid down their daily programme, exacted an account of the whole family doings, did fancy work, read, and prayed, was never a moment idle; weariness had not stamped one wrinkle on her brow. Another, seventy-five, a great-grandmother, had the smooth complexion of a nun. Two among them are engraven in my memory like a fine Dutch picture. It was in the country, in a lofty drawing-room papered with white and pearl-grey; the clear colour was softened by the shades of evening. The large central window curved outwards above a flower bed, and, through its shining squares of glass, green fields were seen. On a chair, close to the light, a beautiful young girl, intelligent and cold, gravely read a small religious work. In the middle, two old ladies, before the tea-table, entertained their guest. Faces with large features, serene, determined, even commanding; in this single respect, they differed from the Flemish portraits. For costume they had dresses of black silk in ample folds, lace at the neck and wrists, rich caps of falling gauze, white embroideries at the stomacher as in the figures of Mierevelt; the degree of stiffness and opulence which displeases in the attire of young ladies was well adapted to their years and to their gravity. All around were the marks of perfect independence, of an undisputed position, of a balanced mind, of a healthy soul, of a worthy life. The one who was seventy and had the look of fifty is unmarried; through her family relations she has mixed with the first spirits of France and of England; during the season she goes to stay with friends, at home she reads. Dickens and the moderns appear to her low and strained, she enjoys more the writers who possess elevation and solidity—M. Guizot, M. Mignet, Hallam, Macaulay, the last rather less than the others, Arnold, Dean Stanley, others besides who write about morality and religion as respectful liberals, just as in France, among the upper middle-class, in the seventeenth century, the ladies read Du Guet and Nicole. The second has four sons settled abroad, the most of them Consuls or Chargé d'Affaires, one in Africa, another in Turkey, another in Sweden; every two years each of them comes and spends a fortnight with her. She is not melancholy on account of being alone and so far from them; she is contented, like a Roman mother, to know that they are all "in a position so honourable and so useful to their country."

Amid all this, I think, two things are visible; the one is the native and acquired energy, the force of character by which a man masters himself, always keeps himself in check, is self-sufficing, risks and resists misfortune, sorrow, and disappointment; the other is the institution of a hierarchy which, even in private life, upholds inequality, subordination, authority, and order. But there is the reverse of every medal. As far as I can judge this character and this system of rule produce many tyrants, louts, mutes, down-trodden and eccentric persons. A certain number of homes resemble that of the Harlowe family in Richardson; but on that head an observer's mouth is closed. I send the reader to the pictures of George Eliot, of Dickens, and of Thackeray; see, in particular, in Thackeray, the portraits of Lord Steyne, of Barnes Newcome, of Lady Kew, of old Osborne, and of the step-mother of Clive Newcome.

IX.

ENGLISH SCHOOL BOYS AND SCHOOL LIFE.

EXCURSION to Harrow-on-the-Hill; I have also seen Eton. Harrow, Eton, Rugby, are the principal places of secondary instruction, and nearly correspond to our large lyceums; at Eton there are about eight hundred boys, and five hundred in each of the others, from thirteen to eighteen. But, between these schools and our lyceums, the difference is enormous, and no other comparison gives greater prominence to the contrast between the two nations. I am told that I may take Harrow as a specimen.

This is an independent, private establishment, without State aid, originally founded by a legacy, and, consequently, provided with landed estate and an hereditary revenue. Sometimes the revenue yielded by such a property is very large; at Harrow it is small (£1,100). Large or small, it is administered by a body of trustees who are renewed by election. Here there are six, great lords and proprietors of the neighbourhood, who are empowered to make considerable changes, and to appoint the head-master. But the principal part of the machine is the staff of under-masters; each of them undertakes a course of study (Greek, Latin, French, Mathematics, &c.), and, in addition, lodges and feeds in his house from ten to thirty boarders. When there is but a dozen of them they take their meals at his table with his family; sometimes, when they are more numerous, they take their meals at two tables presided over by the ladies of the house. Commonly, two occupy the same bedroom; the oldest have rooms to themselves. Thus, the child transplanted into the school, finds there a likeness to the paternal mansion, the more so because families are so large in England. He has his room, he dines at three paces from a lady, he is a person among persons, he lives in a natural and complete position, and is not, as among us, subjected to the communism of a barrack.

Another difference; among us a lyceum is a large box of stone which one enters through a single hole, furnished with a grating and a porter; in the interior are some courts resembling yards, sometimes a wretched row of trees, by way of compensation plenty of walls. As the box is always in a great city, the young man who passes without the grating does not find beyond any more than within it, anything but stone and brick. Here the school is in a little town, with a hundred free openings upon the country. At Eton, around the old central quadrangle, I saw roses, ivy, honeysuckle climbing everywhere along the buildings; in the distance are rich meadows, wherein huge elms spread their venerable branches; close to them is a green and shining river; upon the water are swans; in the islands cattle ruminate; the current winds and disappears towards the horizon amidst foliage. At Harrow, the landscape is less pleasing, but verdure and the open air are not wanting; a meadow of ten or twelve acres belongs to the school, and supplies a ground for cricket. I met the little boys in black jackets, the big ones in black coats, all wearing on their head a small straw hat, not only in the town, but without the town, along the hedgerows, on the banks of the pond; their muddy boots show that they are always on the roads or in damp meadows. Thus, while among us the season of youth is spent under a bell-glass through which penetrates the moral and physical atmosphere of a capital, among them it is spent in the open air, without imprisonment of any sort, in the constant companionship of fields, of waters, and of woods. Now it is a great point for the body, the imagination, the mind, and the character to be developed in a position healthy, calm, and conformed to the mute exigencies of their instincts.

On the whole, human nature is more respected here and more unaffected. Under this education, the children resemble the trees of an English garden; under ours, to the clipped and ordered yews of Versailles. For instance, here the children are almost as free as students; they are bound to attend classes, lessons, dinner, to enter at an appointed hour in the evening, nothing more; the remainder of the day is their own; it can be spent in their own fashion. The sole duty weighing upon these hours of freedom is the obligation to perform the prescribed task; but they may do it where they please and when they please; they work in their own rooms or elsewhere. I have seen some studying with the librarian, others reading seated on a balustrade. They follow their taste, wander where they like. They are to be seen in the streets, in the pastrycooks, in the cookshop; they scour the country, fish, skate, bathe, go birds'-nesting. They are masters of their time and of their money also, give themselves treats, purchase ornaments for their rooms. It appears that they get into debt, their little private furniture is sold to the highest bidder. They have initiative and responsibility; it is curious to see youths of twelve elevated to the dignity of men.

Eight hours' work daily is the maximum; most frequently six or seven; among us eleven, which is irrational. The young have need of physical movement; it is running counter to nature to oblige them to be pure brain, sedentary, cripples. Here, athletic games—tennis, football, races, boating, and, above all, cricket, occupy a portion of every day; in addition, twice or thrice weekly, the classes are suspended in the afternoon in order to give place to them. Self-love is mixed up with this; each school endeavours to surpass its rivals, and sends, to the trial of strength, oarsmen and players carefully trained and chosen. Harrow beat Eton last year, and hopes to win this year also. To-day, eleven of the oldest and best players uphold the reputation of the school against eleven players from London; two flag-bearers, flag in hand, mark the bounds, hundreds of youths line the sides, at a distance, and applaud happy strokes. The affair is serious; their opponents belong to a celebrated cricketing club, all being admirably skilled, strong, and cool; the youths have a right to be passionately fond of an exercise which grown-up men make the principal object of their life. Indeed, there are gentlemen in this country whose ambition and course of living are those of a Grecian athlete; they subject themselves to a particular diet, abstaining from all excess at table and in drinking; they develop their muscle, and submit themselves to a wise system of training. When prepared, they proceed and compete for the prizes for boating or cricket at all the great competitions in England, even farther off, in America. I was informed of a cricketing eleven who went to Australia with this design, just as in other days the athletes of Pontus and Marseilles went to Olympus. It is not at all surprising if the youth become enthusiastic for games so much in repute; the head of the eleven cricketers, the captain of the eight oarsmen, is a more important personage in the school than the best scholar.

These already constitute germs of association, an apprenticeship in commanding and obeying, since each lot which plays at cricket submits to discipline and selects a head. But the principle is still more widely applicable; youths and young men form together an organised body, a kind of minor State apart, having its chiefs and its laws. These chiefs are the boys of the sixth form, more particularly the fifteen monitors, and in each boarding-house the first pupil. They keep order, enforce the rules, and, in general, hold the place of our ushers. They hinder the strong from bullying the weak, are arbitrators in disputes, intervene when a boy has got into a scrape with a villager or a shopkeeper, punishing the delinquents. In short, here the pupils are governed by pupils, and each one after having submitted to authority exercises it in turn. During the last year he is enlisted on the side of the regulations, he makes them prevail, he feels their utility, he adopts them with all his heart instead of kicking against them, as a French schoolboy does not hesitate to do. Hence, when he leaves school and enters life he is less disposed to consider rule absurd and authority ridiculous; he understands freedom and subordination; he has more nearly comprehended the conditions of a society, the rights and the duties of a citizen. Besides this general preparation, there is a special one. The bigger boys form debating societies amongst themselves, where they discuss moral and political topics; the head-master is only the honorary president. After the young speakers have addressed the meeting, the vote is taken, the arguments and the debate are summarised in a report; it is a parliament in miniature. In addition, three of the oldest boys edit a review—*The Triumvirate.* Their aim "is to arouse in their comrades extended ideas of patriotism and to interest them in the affairs of the country." They belong to the Conservative opposition, argue about the French alliance, about the elections, about the right of election. There are some commonplaces and there is a little inflation, but good sense is not absent; for example, with regard to the right of representation which they wish to extend, but up to a certain limit only, they appeal to their young reader's experience; during the holidays in the country he has seen that the villagers, the shopkeepers of the proposed class, are sufficiently intelligent and educated to vote rightly; thus the argument is practical, drawn from facts, and not from a pompous theory. I have just read a number of this review; certainly our students of rhetoric have by no means anything approaching to the same degree of culture and political information. Add another trait still; all, or nearly all, are religiously disposed; they would be shocked at an irreverent word; they sing earnestly in chapel. Since Arnold's time, the aim of education has been to produce Christian gentlemen; most of them are professedly religious, take the Sacrament, and pray nightly of their own accord. Thus when they enter the world, they are the upholders, and not the adversaries, of the great ecclesiastical establishment, of the national religion.

On all hands I arrive at the same conclusion: in

England there is not a profound separation between the life of the child and that of the adult; the school and society are on an equal footing, with no intermediate moat or wall; the one leads to and prepares for the other. The adult does not, as among us, leave a hothouse in compartments, "an exceptional rule, a special atmosphere." He is not troubled, taken out of his element by the change of air. Not only has he cultivated his mind, but he has also undergone an apprenticeship to life. Not only does he possess ideas, but these ideas are suited to the world which receives him. In politics, in religion, he finds a place quite ready for him at twenty, for which his tastes and his faculties have been adapted beforehand. In this manner he most easily escapes scepticism; he more rapidly settles down; he experiments less to find an employment for his powers. All those whom I have seen in the class, in the fields, and in the streets, have a healthy and active, decided, and energetic air. Evidently, to my eyes at least, they are greater children and more manly; greater children, that is to say, more addicted to play and less inclined to pass the limits of their years; more manly, that is to say, more independent, more capable of governing themselves and of acting. On the contrary, the French schoolboy, above all the inmates of our colleges, is wearied, embittered, rendered acute, precocious, and too precocious; he is caged up, and his imagination ferments. In all these respects, and in what relates to the formation of character, English education is superior; it better prepares for the world and forms healthier minds.

The author of "Tom Brown's School-days" says, "When I formed the project of writing this book I endeavoured to represent to myself the most common type of a little English boy of the upper middle class, such as I had witnessed in my experience; and I faithfully maintain this type from the beginning to the end of my story, while merely striving to give a good specimen of the species." The book thus conceived had an enormous success. Youths and adults all recognised themselves in the picture, and we can make use of it, in admitting with the author that the portrait, if not flattered, is at least kindly. Neither Tom nor his father cared much for education properly so called. His father asks himself, "Shall I tell him to mind his work, and say he's sent to school to make himself a good scholar? Well, but he isn't sent to school for that —at any rate not for that mainly. I don't care a straw for Greek particles, or the digamma, no more does his mother. What is he sent to school for? Well, partly because he wanted so to go. If he'll only turn out a brave, helpful, truth-telling Englishman, and a gentleman, and a Christian, that's all I want." And when Tom, several years afterwards, asks himself what he came to school for, he replies:—"I want to be A 1 at cricket and football and all the other games, and to make my hands keep my head against any fellow, lout or gentleman." . . . "I want to carry away just as much Latin and Greek as will take me through Oxford respectably." . . . "I want to leave behind me the name of a fellow who never bullied a little boy or turned his back on a big one."

'Remarkable words, and well summarising the ordinary sentiments of an English father and child; science and mental culture occupy the last place; character, heart, courage, strength, and bodily skill are in the first row. Such an education produces mo*t*, and physical wrestlers, with all the advantages, but also with all the drawbacks, attached to this direction of the mind and the body.

Along with other unpleasant effects the rude instincts are developed. An Eton master states that "play takes the first place, books the second." The child makes it his glory, like Tom Brown, to be a good athlete; he spends three, four, five hours daily in rough and violent exercises. At hares and hounds one flounders for hours in ploughed fields and in muddy meadows, one stumbles in the mud, one loses one's shoes, one picks oneself up as well as possible At football the sides precipitate themselves upon each other; the child underneath bears the weight of the entire mass, arms and legs are dislocated, collar-bones broken. At cricket the great heavy ball is thrown with such force that the unskilful wicket-keeper is knocked down, if struck by it. Nearly all the games habitually yield bruises; pride is taken in not minding them; and by a natural consequence, there is no more hesitation in inflicting than in submitting to them. The child becomes a fighter, a boxer; the author of "Tom Brown" says, "To fight with fists is the natural and English way for English boys to settle their quarrels." All the men I have met did so when at school, and this is still common. This kind of duel has its rules, its appointed place, its audience, its witnesses. Each combatant has two seconds who sponge his face, and put forward their knee for a seat during the rounds; these encounters are renewed, and sometimes prolonged during half-an-hour. The maxim is to go on fighting as long as one can see clearly and stand upright; after the fight there are black eyes, swollen and livid cheeks.

sometimes a thumb put out of joint, or a lip cut open.

Unfortunately the school arrangements operate in the same direction; in addition to impositions, the being kept from play and confinement, the birch is used; in certain schools, it is enough for a boy to appear three times on the black list, for him to have to prepare for a flogging. This morning four were flogged at Harrow (fourteen strokes, not drawing blood). In all the schools it is the head-master to whom this amiable office appertains; there is hardly a head-master in France who would accept, at such a price, a salary of £6,000. In principle all are liable to the birch, ever the bigger boys; yet scarcely any but the younger and smaller ones are subjected to it. A strange thing is that it is not unpopular. Fifty years ago at the Charterhouse the boys, hearing that it was proposed to substitute a fine for it, rebelled, crying, "Down with fines! hurrah for the birch!" and on the morrow they renewed acquaintance with the beloved birch. The teachers with whom I have conversed consider that this chastisement is not humiliating, and that it develops special courage in the child; according to them the strokes are a natural form of repression; it is enough that opinion does not regard them as shameful, and that the sufferer does not feel himself insulted. Under the head-master, the big boys entrusted with maintaining discipline have the right to inflict the same punishment. For this purpose they carry a cane in certain schools, and use it.

Here a shocking institution must be referred to— this is "fagging," or the obligation of the little boys to be the servants of the bigger. It has been modified, softened, at Harrow, at Rugby, and in some other establishments; but in itself it always continues **bad**; for it is a school of brutality, and pushes the English child towards the side to which he inclines, towards all the excesses which the energetic, violent, tyrannical, and hard temperament admits of. A lady whom we know, and who is in truth of foreign extraction, could not bring herself to subject her son to fagging, and has put him in a Parisian lyceum. According to official inquirers the small boys are valets and slaves. Each big boy has several, who are bound to run errands for him, to sweep his room, to clean his candlesticks, to toast his bread and his cheese, to call him at the appointed time, to help him at his games, frequently during two or three hours daily, to run after his balls, and return them to him, to be at his orders during all the time he is awake, to endure his caprices. "At Westminster School the life of a foundation scholar for the first year is such an uninterrupted servitude that it is impossible for him to find the necessary time for his studies." "I state as a fact," said one witness, "that from the 1st of January to the 31st of December, the young foundation scholar has not a single moment which is not exposed to interruption. At half-past three in the morning, two of the younger, chosen in succession, rise to light the fire, boil the water, call up those of the big boys who have ordered this to be done. Frequently, the senior, awakened at four o'clock, does not get up till half-past seven; he must then be called every half hour. This task falls to each of the small boys two or three times weekly." Add all those of the day, all those of the evening. "The seniors are very fond of tea, they must have it three times in the course of the evening, without saying anything of coffee. Every two minutes the kettles must be filled for them."

One of the witnesses relates that on Saturday night, a holiday at Westminster, when his son arrived home from school he was so thoroughly broken down for want of sleep, that he had no other desire than to go to bed. In order to maintain such an exact and minute obedience the big boys use terror. "Boxes on the ears, kicks are mere common pranks of theirs, these not counting among the numerous punishments. . . . . In the first degree the real punishments are systematic boxes on the ears; the offender must keep his hands at his sides and hold his head forward to receive a dozen slaps applied right and left." On other occasions he places the palm of his hand on the table, the back of the hand is then beaten with the blade of a paper-knife till sometimes a gash is made. Caning comes next, then two kinds of tanning. The boy is beaten on the fleshy part of the leg with a racket-bat, which breaks the skin and makes the blood flow. He places his foot on a sink the height of a table, the executioner then takes a run of two or three paces and kicks the part exposed. The reporter states, "I have heard of two or three cases in which the boys were so cruelly bruised, that they were unable for a long time to join in the games and other exercises." Tom Brown was tossed in a blanket, and thrown upwards with such force that he struck the ceiling. One day having refused to sell his lottery-tickets to the big boys, he was seized hold of, held up before the blazing fire, and roasted (literally) and till he was ready to faint. This actually occurred, the romance being but a reproduction of an authentic fact. Besides, in the lives of Cowper, Lord Byron, Sir Robert Peel, other cases, equally revolting, are to be found. Doubtless the instances just cited are the darkest, and, as the English are persevering in matters of reform, the picture is becoming brighter Yet, even supposing the reform completed, the impression continues unpleasant; for, on the whole, a school conducted in this style is a sort of primitive society, where force reigns almost uncontrolled, all the more so because it is considered a point of honour among the oppressed not to denounce their oppressors. The master interferes as little as possible; he is not, as among us, the perpetual representative of humanity and justice; very seldom and in very few schools is an appeal made to him or to the governing body. The weak are left to themselves, they have but to suffer and be patient. Now what a temptation is it for a vigorous youth to possess the power and the right to flog! It is not a good thing to give the rein to the instincts of domination and of brutality. The use always leads to the abuse; an incentive to what is unreasonable is given by the irrationality which is practised, to blows by the blows which are given; a man ought never be allowed the opportunity for becoming a despot and an executioner. On the whole, education thus understood is not destitute of resemblance to that of the Lacedemonians; they hardened the body and tempered the character, but, as well as I can conjecture, they often ended by producing hunters and louts.

Naturally, the cultivation of the mind must suffer from such a training. Mr. Farrar writes: "When seeing young men ready to sacrifice everything to cricket, when seeing them devote to it a number of hours and an enthusiasm out of all proportion to that which they give to their work, when seeing that their mind is so emphatically taken up with it that they speak, think, and dream of nothing but cricket, it is not surprising to find many persons attributing to this affectation of muscularity the miserable poverty of the intellectual results which we obtain." A vice unknown among us, which is due to this preponderance of the physical over the moral faculties, is gluttony, and, above all, the fondness for wine; hence one of the faults punishable by flogging is drunkenness; many stuff themselves with eatables, and among them are to be found precocious drunkards.

The teaching is not what is requisite for counterbalancing these gross tastes; there is nothing attractive about it; it can hardly be considered by the young people as other than a task; it is very slightly literary and altogether technical. The chief aim is to know Greek and Latin well, to write correctly in verse and prose in these two languages; in fact, by dint of memory and exercises, the most clever succeed in doing so. On one point, the knowledge and the manipulation of Greek, they are far superior to the pupils of our lyceums; I have in my hands prize exercises, in which scenes from Shakespeare are very well translated into Greek iambics in the style of Sophocles. But on other points I consider them inferior. Their Latin, prose and verse, is less elegant and less pure than that of our good compositions of the class of rhetoric. They do not appear to be really acquainted with history; they recount the legends of Curtius and of Regulus as authenticated facts. They descant on chivalry and the Middle Age in vague generalities, as was done in our old University. They do not appear to apprehend the difference of manners, of sentiments, of ideas, of characters which is the result of centuries. They do not seem to have read, like our good scholars, the works of a genuine historian, of a Thierry, of a Michelet, of a Guizot. In general, they have few ideas; if the questions relating to existing and practical contemporary politics are excepted, a student of rhetoric in a Parisian lyceum possesses more. They have read many classical texts; but the explanation which is given to them is wholly grammatical and positive. Nothing is done to set forth the beauty of the passage, the delicacies of the style, the pathos of the situation; nor is the process of the writer indicated, the character of his talents, the turn of his mind; all that would seem vague. The master does not speak to the pupils as a critic to persons of taste; he does not endeavour to refine their literary touch; he does not comment upon the great writers of their country. It is the same in mathematics; he teaches formulas rather than the spirit; the manual of geometry is always the text of Euclid learned and said by heart; reason and reasoning hold but a secondary place. " Too frequently this teaching tends to form Greek scholars and calculators." On the contrary, the young Frenchman of nineteen possesses, if he be intelligent, and if he has been studious, general instruction, a quantity of ideas blocked out, some half ideas of his own, a decided preference for certain authors and a certain form of style, the embryos of theories, vague views about the beautiful, about history, about philosophy, at least the sentiment that there are vast questions of first importance on which he requires to form an opinion, a requirement all the more pressing because around him scepticism floats in the air, because, most frequently, he has lost his religious beliefs, because no prevailing doctrine, imposed or accepted, is at hand to arrest his fluctuating mind, and because, if he desires to cast anchor in a port, he is obliged to seek for the port and forge the anchor. Here many distinguished Englishmen whom I have known consider their school and even their university education as a simple preparation, a gymnastic, a training of the attention and of the memory, nothing more. They said to me, "When finished with that, we have been obliged to undo, or rather to form, our education; to acquire by personal reading all that we have succeeded in learning about philosophy, about history, about political economy, about the natural sciences, about art, about literature." A remedy is being found for this defect, the circle is now being enlarged; but it is still narrow, always having Euclid and Sapphic verse as its centre. In consequence, the mind, becoming adult at a later period, arrives later at forming comprehensive views.

Final detail, and a crowning one, marks the difference between the two countries: the average outlay for keeping a boy at Harrow is £200 yearly. How many fathers among us would be able to expend £200 yearly on their son's education? In France a functionary, a man attached to one of the professions called liberal, makes most frequently £120 at thirty, and £200 at fifty; and, commonly, he has for addition the interest on a very small capital. Then, as compensation, to keep his son at college costs him £40 only, £20 at a minor seminary, and the bursaries given by the State are numerous. It may be calculated, I think, that a classical education is five times cheaper in France than in England. They admit themselves that one of their national vices is the habit of lavish expenditure. As regards primary instruction, the parliamentary grant merely aids 8,500 schools; the same grant would maintain 25,000 in France. It would entirely educate 1,500,000 French children in place of 950,000 English. Mr. Arnold estimates that the expense of maintaining and administering the French schools, in proportion, is the fourth of that of the English schools. At Oxford, whither I shall go to-morrow, and in the Universities in general, B—— tells me that on an average an undergraduate spends £300 a year; however, £200 yearly are sufficient; some, by dint of economy, live upon £100. The author of "Tom Brown at Oxford" mentions that a very poor student managed with £75, but only because he was lodged gratis, and on condition of being despised. Among us, a student of medicine or of law who should have £75 and his lodgings found him, would consider himself well off; many of them have no more than £60, and it never enters into the head of the richest to despise his poor comrade.

X.

LIFE AT THE UNIVERSITY.

HERE am I at Oxford, in the company of a Fellow who replies to all my questions with extreme courtesy. We are in a garden full of flowers; at the side, separated by a wall, is a fine kitchen garden, the one and the other are the dependencies of the residence of a professor; a more pleasant and poetical abode for a studious man cannot be imagined. But I shall return to that; I now proceed to transcribe our conversation.

Oxford is a collection of twenty-four colleges or distinct, independent foundations, having each an average revenue of £15,000; Magdalen College has £40,000 and upwards. In addition, the city contains a University of professors, serving as a centre for the colleges.

A college is composed (1) of a head, having from £1,000 to £3,000 yearly; (2) of fellows having from £200 to £300; (3) of tutors, paid in part out of the college chest, in part by the undergraduates, having from £400 to £500; (4) of scholars, students who have obtained scholarships through merit, having £30 and upwards; (5) of undergraduates who pay, to the number of from forty to eighty. The rest of he revenues of the establishment pays servants — the cooks, the porters, &c.; and, in addition, the stewards who administer the properties.

The University is a body of professors analogous to our College of France; an undergraduate is not obliged to attend their lectures. Most of the professors have salaries of from £500 to £600; two or three chairs yield less than £800; as compensation, another yields £1,000, and certain professors of theology have as much as £1,600; sometimes a canonry, cathedral deanery, is attached to the chair, and yields from £1,000 to £3,000, besides the use of a large house and a garden. But they are obliged to live handsomely, to display hospitality, to contribute to all sorts of subscriptions, &c., so that, like the Bishops and the high public officials, they often expend their whole salary.

There are about thirteen hundred undergraduates at Oxford, eleven hundred at Cambridge; there are also some at London. But, as a general rule, this high finishing place of education is for the aristocracy, for the rich, for the minority; in the first place because it is expensive (from £200 to £300 yearly, and the temptation to expend more is very great), next because it is a luxury of intelligence (pure mathematics, Greek, Latin), and retards the entry into lucrative careers.

The undergraduates have each two or three rooms in a college, and thus form hives. They are obliged to attend chapel at eight, dine in hall at five, to be indoors by nine, and in general to attend a tutor's class in the morning and a lecture in the afternoon. Breaches of rules are noted and punished, especially if repeated. To return after nine constitutes a fault; after midnight a grave fault; to sleep out of college a very grave fault. The punishments are, in certain colleges, a fine of from 5s. to £1 ; in others an imposition longer or shorter, more frequently a reprimand from the Head, withdrawal of the right of going out, temporary expulsion, and lastly permanent expulsion. This detail is important; for it is seen that here the schoolboy is freer and the undergraduate less free than among us. The youth, on becoming a young man, does not pass from cloistered discipline to complete independence; the passage is regulated. At school, as regards many of his actions, he has been previously left to himself; at the University he is not wholly left to himself. Such a precaution is excellent; against the abuse of liberty, the habit of liberty is a moral guaranty, and supervision a physical guaranty. Another check: Oxford and Cambridge are small places. The young man is not, as among us, thrown amidst the temptations of a capital, reduced to sedentary and cerebral life, without the necessary counterpoise of physical exercises, led to seek variety at the theatre, in the café on the Boulevards, in the excitement of the world, of conversation, and of pleasure. There is no debauchery at Oxford; the University officers walk the streets after nine, and can enter every tavern or publichouse. The libertines go to London or to the neighbouring villages; my friend estimates that the half of the undergraduates is pure. The principal failing is the taste for wine; fifty years ago drunkenness prevailed here as among the entire upper class; at present, here, as among the entire upper class, it has become rare. A last favourable circumstance: the undergraduate, like the schoolboy, remains a good Protestant; he is religious, or at least he has a respect for religion. Out of an hundred young men whom one of my friends had occasion to examine, two only declared themselves free-thinkers; seventy belonged to the Broad Church, the others to the two varieties called High Church and Low Church, the one liking fine ceremonies, pompous ritual and approaching Puseyism, the other being altogether Calvinistical and slightly iconoclastic.

The studies last about three years; during the first year scarcely anything is done but to resume and repeat the lessons learned at school. The first two examinations are chiefly grammatical and linguistic; they comprise two or three Greek and Latin authors, Greek and Latin compositions in prose and verse, some questions about the Old and New Testament. The third comprises the same subjects, but more carefully studied, considered from a new point of view, from the critical, historical, and philosophic point of view. Next, the undergraduate has the choice between three final examinations, the one in mathematics, the other in physical and natural sciences, the other in languages, history, law, and political economy. An undergraduate who has failed enters another college and begins again; on the second failure he generally quits the University. There are two sorts of undergraduates. The one aspires to honours, which are most useful, and lead to high position in the University, in the Church, and elsewhere. The other which, as in France, forms the majority, has no other ambition than to obtain a degree; its members scarcely do anything but attend the tutor's class, never the lectures of the Professors, and restrict themselves to the minimum of study. The distinguished men produced by this education are principally mathematicians (notably at Cambridge) or classical scholars. But for the last ten years the routine is modified; contemporary sciences and modern ideas have infiltrated, gained a place. New chairs have been founded, other chairs have widened their teaching. See the writings of Stanley, of Jowett, the celebrated book styled "Essays and Reviews;" Max Müller, the Sanscrit scholar, lectures here on the history and philosophy of language.

All that is but the bark; the thing it is important to know about is always morality, the turn of mind, the dominant inclination of man. How do these young men live, and what do they love? In order to reply, it would be necessary to reside six months here; in default of personal experience the following pictures of manners are said by my friends to be correct: "Pendennis," by Thackeray; "Tom Brown at Oxford," and a rather lively little romance, illustrated by the author, "Adventures of Mr. Verdant Green." The first point is that Oxford and Cambridge being the gathering-place for sons of good family, the tone of the place is suited to the character and the position of the residents; an English University is in many respects a club of young noblemen, or at least of rich men. Many who have acquired wealth send their sons there, solely for the purpose of their making good acquaintances; certain poor or low-born undergraduates become the toadies of their noble comrades, who later on will be able to present them with a living. The very usages of the University tend to favour this distinction of ranks. In certain colleges the noble undergraduates have a separate table, a particular dress, divers minor privileges. Imagine, if you can, a like system introduced into a great French school!

At St. Ambrose, the author of "Tom Brown" instances a class of poor students, a kind of semi-bursars, named servitors (who are now abolished), whom their rich or noble comrades look down upon Among us, at the Polytechnic School, the pupils are unaware of the bursars' names; their names are known only to a committee pledged by honour to silence; such is the delicacy of the spirit of equality. The author of "Tom Brown" says that "tuft-hunting and the worship of money are the most shameful and wide-spread of our vices," at Oxford, as well as throughout the rest of England. Elsewhere, speaking of his hero, he adds, " his instinct, again, sad to say, was already teaching him that poverty is a disgrace to a Briton, and that, until you know a man thoroughly, you must always seem to assume that he is the owner of unlimited ready money." One of the personages says, " If the Black Prince were here we would change his motto, ' Ich dien ' (I serve), into ' Je paye ' (I pay)." Many of these young men have £500 a year and upwards, which they regard as pocket-money; moreover, the shopkeepers give them credit. They hold it honourable to spend money, to cut a dash; they keep horses, dogs, a boat; they furnish their rooms with elegance and richness. "London wine merchants furnished them with liqueurs at a guinea a bottle, and wine at five guineas a dozen." "Their cigars cost two guineas a pound; pine-apples, forced fruit, and the most rare preserves figured at their wine parties." "They dined like gourmets; drove tandems, scattering silver in all the taverns of Oxford and the neighbouring roads." "They hunted, rode steeple-chases by day, played billiards until the gates closed, and are then ready for vingt-et-un, unlimited loo, and hot drink in their own rooms, as long as anyone could be got to sit up and play."

The appointed task scarcely hampers them; during the first year especially it is more than trifling. "Twelve lectures of two hours each weekly upon the New Testament, the first book of Herodotus, the second of Euclid; in addition two hours of work daily; everything is over by mid-day, or at one o'clock at the latest; there is no supplementary exercise in the shape of themes, verses, or other exercises. A moderate scholar does not require to prepare anything; he has previously studied all that; he knows beforehand by heart the subject of the lecture." Thus the leisure hours are still more numerous than among us during the first years of law studies. Under such circumstances it is necessary, in order to study, to be naturally very studious or very ambitious, which it is given only to a very small number to be. The others follow their instinct, and it is here that the difference between the English and French temperaments is openly exemplified.

In France the temperament is precocious; the imagination of a collegian, shut up and sealed, during long hours of weariness, grows heated; the dangerous atmosphere of a great city penetrates to him; the conversation of seniors, our too free literature has done the rest; frequently he has the folly to think that it is honourable to be a man before the time. Set free at a stroke, and let loose uncontrolled in a capital, he is there exposed to the contagion of example, to the conveniences of being unknown, and, in all public places, to the temptations which are flaunted before him. Besides, in this respect, opinion is more indulgent; it speaks to him only in the name of prudence and good taste; it only decidedly condemns drunkenness, gross debauchery, lasting low alliances which may degenerate into marriages; it tolerates escapades. A mother said to me, "When my sons go to Asnières I know it, but I appear not to be aware of it." Have tact, moderation, foresight; in that, as in everything, the morality of the world prescribes nothing more. The young man does not know that there is no worse diminution of power, that intercourse of this sort abases the heart, that after ten years of such a life he will have lost the one-half of his will, that his thoughts will have an habitual after-taste of bitterness and of sadness, that his inner spring will be weakened or broken. He excuses himself in his own eyes by saying that a man must handle everything in order to know everything. In fact, he learns life; but very often also he loses energy, the warmth of soul, the capacity for acting, and at thirty he is merely fit for becoming an official, a provincial, a dilettante, or a fundholder. Here, as far as I can judge, the human being continues more intact; in the first place, because he is subject to discipline, is better watched, and less tempted; next, because written and spoken opinion is more severe. It will permit drunkenness, it will not sanction profligacy. A book like the "Vie de Bohème," by Henry Murger, would be placed beside the old free and easy novels, and regarded as the delineation of merry-andrews, perfect scoundrels, and half-sharpers. In the three novels I have cited, the decency is extreme. A phrase in "Tom Brown at Oxford" indicates a group of wealthy loose fish, who have each a mistress hidden in a village; but they are censured, even by many of their comrades. As regards the three heroes, their hearts are smitten, they experience calf-love for a milliner; but they stop short, or are stopped in time; and the loose fish themselves admit in principle that the seduction of an innocent girl is the act of a scoundrel.

Two derivatives are the auxiliaries of these maxims. The first is the precocity of love and of marriage; they are smitten young, sometimes at twenty, and frequently they marry a few years afterwards. The second is the keen, popular, almost universal taste for bodily exercises. In this respect the university is a continuation of the school. To play at cricket, row, steer sailing-boats, keep dogs, set them upon a band of rats, fish, hunt, ride on horseback, drive four-in-hand, swim, spar, fence, and, since a recent period, drill as volunteers, are for them the most interesting occupations. These do not fit in too well with studies; Plato, a long time ago, in his Dialogues, put in opposition the life of the athlete and that of the thinker. According to a learned foreigner who has much frequented Oxford, if refined philology and the lofty philosophical speculations are acclimatised here with difficulty, it is because the undergraduates eat too much and make too much use of their muscles.

But sport is an excellent vent for the strong and superabundant sap of youth, and here again, as at school, rivalry serves as a spur. Each college has its boat, its eight oarsmen and coxswain, all selected and exercised with care. Five or six weeks before the races, the training begins. To traverse from ten to twenty miles of the river every day, dine early on stale bread, milk, meat, and very little wine; to have tobacco rationed; two pints of beer at the most daily; no pastry, no ices; not to sup late, and to go to bed early; such was the discipline imposed on Tom Brown. During the first days, one is disjointed; during the last, one is dying of thirst; during the race, the exertion is so enormous, that one runs the risk of breaking a blood-vessel, and on arrival many are giddy and cannot speak All Oxford is there—the University and the townsmen. When the boats start, an excited crowd follows them, running and crying, out of breath, leaping ditches, their feet in the water panting along the bank. The description must be perused in order to conceive the seriousness and the enthusiasm of the crews. The last minute, that which precedes the report of the cannon fired to announce the departure, is solemn. "Short minute, indeed! you wouldn't say so if you were in the boat, with your heart in your mouth, and trembling all over like a man with the palsy. Those sixty seconds before the starting-gun in your first race—why, they are a little lifetime. . . . . During the first ten strokes, Tom was in too great fear of making a mistake to feel, or hear, or see. His whole soul was glued to the back of the man before him; his one thought to keep time, and get his strength into the stroke. . . . Isn't he grand, the captain, as he comes forward like lightning, stroke after stroke, his back flat, his teeth set, his whole frame working from the hips with the regularity of a machine." Trumpets sound, acclamations continue swelling forth like thunder, embroidered handkerchiefs are waved. In the evening the victors feast in the great hall of the college; there are speeches, cheers, toasts, choruses sung in unison, a gorgeous and glorious hubbub; it is clear that such a triumph must be almost as greatly desired as the palm of the ancient Olympian Games. The interest is greater still when, in the month of March, the race takes place on the Thames between the crews of the two Universities; nothing else is talked about in London during two days.

Doubtless muscular culture thus understood leads to a certain rudeness of manner. Town and gown fight on occasion in the streets. But, as compensation, the gymnastic and athletic life has this twofold advantage, that it blunts the senses and stills the imagination.

Moreover, when the moral and mental life is afterwards developed, the mind has for its support a healthier and more robust body. The young men who walk about here in the odd traditional costume (a short black gown and a kind of flat cap) are full of sap and strength, have a fine and frank deportment, are muscular and strong-limbed, and, in my opinion, have a phsiognomy less perturbed, less worn than those of our students. During twenty years, a gradual reform has been in operation, and many traits in this picture are softened. At present, in each college, several Fellows may marry; Dissenters and Roman Catholics are admitted to the course of study. The passion for boating is rather less; the undergraduates of different classes are less unequal; in certain colleges their table expenses are supervised and limited. Oxford is gradually ceasing to be an aristocratic club, an athletic gymnasium, an ecclesiastical and Anglican preserve; it is on the way to become a modern school, a lay and liberal academy.

At two o'clock there is a ceremony in the great hall of the University. The costumes are grotesque, like those at the distribution of prizes at our great competition; a Latin speech which recalls the antiquated forms of the Sorbonne; a piece of English verse, composed and read by the student laureate; its subject is Sir John Franklin; the verses are rhetorical phrases. Five or six foreigners of distinction receive the honorary title of Doctor of Law, *in jure civili;* this is pronounced *in ioure çaivaïlai.* An Englishman quoting Cæsar's phrase, *Veni, vidi, vici,* and pronouncing it in the same fashion, *Vénai, vaidai, vaiçai,* my neighbour replied to him, "Cæsar could never have pronounced a similar phrase."

In the evening there is a meeting, with experiments

and lectures on physical and natural sciences, in a museum—a vast building of a somewhat Gothic character, erected by subscription, and still unfinished. Bands of ladies walk about there in staring, showy attire, many, who are young and in low dresses, wear spectacles. But it is certain details only which are disagreeable; the whole—town, buildings, landscape—is admirable. I had previously traversed the town; I wander about there again at the close of the day. What a number of colleges, each with its chapel and its high surrounding crenellated walls; these diverse and multiplied architectures of every age, in the Gothic style, in the Tudor style, in the style of the seventeenth century; these large courts, with their statues and central fountain of spouting water; these balusters which cut the tender azure of the sky at the summit of the edifices; these windows latticed with delicate mouldings, or cut into sculptured crosses, after the manner of the Revival; these pulpits in wrought stone; at each turning of the street some lofty conical spire; —what a number of noble forms in a small space! It is a natural museum, in which are accumulated the works and the inventions of six centuries. The stone, worn, exfoliated, is all the more venerable. One is so well-pleased with any olden things! The more so, that here they are only old; not neglected or half ruined, as in Italy, but piously preserved, restored, since their foundation, have been always in the hands of rich, considerate, and intelligent guardians. Ivy covers the walls with its ample drapery; honeysuckle climbs around the pillars; wild flowers plume the tops of all the walls; rich turf, carefully kept, extends its carpet up to the arcades of the galleries; behind the apse of a chapel one sees a garden in flower, thousands of blooming roses. One goes onward. At the extremity of the town, venerable trees form a walk; beneath their branches two living streams flow along; beyond, the eyes rest delightedly on meadows running over with plants in bud and flower. It is impossible to imagine a vegetation more magnificent, a verdure more opulent and yet better tempered by the blended tones which the buttercups, the daisies, the wild sorrel, the greyish grasses throw over its dazzling tint. The country is in all the luxury of its freshness. As the sun slightly blinks forth, it smiles with a charming joy; one might liken it to a beautiful timid virgin, happy under the veil which is being withdrawn. However, the day closes, and indistinct whitenesses ascend above the meadows; under their soft gauze, the river shines with black reflections; all is still, excepting the bells which chime melodiously in the chaste tower of Christ Church. One would never believe one's self to be at an hundred paces from a town. How contemplative and poetical is study here!

A walk in Magdalen College. I never weary of admiring these old edifices festooned with ivy and blackened by age, these crenellated clock-towers, these mullioned windows; above all, these vast square courts, of which the arcades form a promenade like that of the Italian convents. In the afternoon, with the exception of one or two passing undergraduates, they are solitary; nothing is sweeter than this architectural solitude, poetic, intact, where there is never a trace of neglect, of ruin, and of death. Flocks of deer browse peacefully beneath the gigantic elms; a long road, bordered with the finest trees, winds between two rivers. Oxford is in an ancient hollow; hence this softness, this freshness, this incomparable opulence of the verdure. At Worcester College an ample sheet of water, on which swans float, moistens with its slow undulations the green sward constellated with flowers. On every hand cedars, huge yews, oaks, poplars raise aloft their trunks, and expand their foliage; from branch to branch honeysuckle, Virginia creepers hang and extend. The large gardens of St. John's, the little garden of Wadham, are masterpieces of a unique sort, beyond art itself, for nature and time have been the artificers. Can human art produce anything so beautiful as a group of perfect trees three hundred years old?

On returning, I recast this judgment in regarding the architecture anew; it also is three centuries old, and seems rooted in the soil by the same right as the trees; the tint of the stone is accommodated to the climate; age has imparted to it something of the majsty of natural things. One does not feel there the mechanical regularity, the official imprint; each college has been developed by itself, each age has built in its fashion: here the imposing quadrangle of Christ Church, with its turf, its fountains, and its staircases; there, close to the Bodleian library, a mass of edifices, sculptured portals, lofty bell-towers, all flowered and embroidered, cupolas circled with small columns. Sometimes the chapel is a small cathedral. In several colleges the dining-hall, sixty feet in height, vaulted, appears the nave of a church. The council-hall, wholly lined with antique wood, is worthy of our venerable old halls. Imagine the life of a Master of Arts, of a Fellow, amid these monuments, beneath that Gothic wainscoting, before the windows of the Revival or of the Middle Age, in the midst of severe luxury and in the best taste, engravings, copper-plates, admirable books. In the evening, when descending the stair, when the light flickers upon the large black forms, one thinks that one is walking in a true piece of scenery.

Nothing is wanting here, neither the beauties of art, nor the freshness of nature, nor the great and grandiose impressions of history. A moment since, when going through the colleges, I was told the names of their ancient occupants, students for ever famous— Wycliffe, the Black Prince, Sir Walter Raleigh, Pym, Hampden, Archbishop Laud, Ireton, Addison. At each building the guide pointed out the dates and the authors of the foundation, the embellishments, the restorations. All these old men seem living still; for their work has survived them and endures. The wisdom of ancient times remains written in Latin sentences upon the walls; on a sun-dial, above the hours, this solemn phrase may be read—*pereunt et imputantur*. And this is not a dead city, nor is it asleep; the modern work completes and increases the ancient work; the contemporaries, as in former times, contribute their buildings and their gifts. When at the Bodleian library one has seen the manuscripts, the precious volumes, the portraits of Vandyck, Lely, and Kneller, one finds further on a recent collection of sketches and original drawings by Raffaelle and Michel Angelo, where the vitality, the sentiment of nudity, the superb Paganism of the Revival, are displayed with incomparable freedom. The collection cost seven thousand pounds sterling; Lord Eldon alone contributed four thousand. I have visited two or three professors' houses, the one resembling our old French mansions, the others modern and charming, all possessing gardens, flowers, noble or laughing prospects. The oldest, under the portraits of the predecessors, contain every modern comfort. I compared them to those of our scholars, resembling cages, to the third-floor in a great city, to the dismal lodgings of the Sorbonne, and I thought of the aspect, so gloomy and confined, of our College of France. Poor Frenchmen, so poor, and who live encamped. We are of yesterday, and ruined from father to son by Louis XIV., by Louis XV., by the Revolution, by the Empire. We have demolished, everything has required to be rebuilt anew. Here the generation following does not break with the preceding one; reforms are superimposed on institutions, and the present, based upon the past, perpetuates it.

XI.

VILLAGES AND FARMHOUSES.

SHORT excursions and sojourns at thirty or forty miles from London. It is necessary to endeavour to see the district, the parish; one does not comprehend the social net-work till after one has studied in detail three or four meshes. Moreover, this time again, the courtesy and hospitality of the people are perfect.

Always the same landscapes; meadows divided by hedges, where large trees stand up here and there. The country is all verdure; the eyes are satiated, glutted with it; that is the strongest sensible impression which I brought back from England. From the top of a great height which we cross is a view, it is said, for forty miles in every direction; nothing but green, no forests, some clumps of scattered trees, beetroot, clover, hops, fields of peas, bushy parks, hollows in which swollen yellow streams meander along, moist meadows, wherein heavy cows browse and ruminate. Fresh plants, continually removed, multiply and superabound; hence the store of meat, milk. Contrast that with the bread, the wine, the vegetables, which form the principal nourishment of our peasants; by this trait, as by many others, the Englishman much more resembles a Dutchman than a Frenchman. A Paul Potter, a Ruysdael, would find here subjects for pictures. Beauty is not absent from this curtained sky, full of greyish and almost black clouds, which creep over a background of motionless vapour. Far off on the horizon the view is obscured by a downpour, and all these tints are soft, delicately blended, melancholy.

We skirt deserted, wild commons, where, at intervals a horse feeds amid the solitude. This was the primitive soil, filled with heaths; generation after generation it has diminished; civilisation, like a rising tide, has eaten into it and left fragments only. How much labour was required to cover this with herbage and vegetables, how much patience and effort to fit it for man! They have succeeded in doing this, and, at each century of their history, have converted into enclosed meadows thousands of acres of uncertain pasturage. It was more beautiful in its first state; its thorny or rude plants, its dull or blackish tints, the tone of its flowers better suited the aspect of the sky. At present this civilised nature bears too visibly the imprint of industry; it has too many ordered rows; its colours are false or discordant; the turnip leaves have a violet or harsh green; the light plants shine in the sun with a display too dazzling and too slight; one feels that their presence has been commanded, and that their life is artificial. The country resembles a large manufactory of fodder, the vestibule of a dairy or a slaughterhouse; from picturesque ideas, one descends to utilitarian ideas. It must be said, however, that the latter are equal to the former; after all, man lives on chops, and the spectacle of a niggard land transformed into a good nurse is still a fine one.

A walk in the country and in the villages; every

two hours there is a shower. This recalls the English saying, "When it does not rain take your umbrella; when it rains do as you please." But in the sunshine the effect of this humidity is charming; this grass has a delicious freshness and novelty. The drops of running water shine like pearls; beneath a ray of the sun a meadow instantly glistens, and its trains of yellow and white flowers appear laden with light. However the sky continues spotted with vapour; here and there the clouds turn to slate, become violet, blend at a quarter of a league. The interchange is perpetual between the moist sky and the moist earth, and the contrast is curious between the splendid colours of the soil and the mixed tones of the air. The eyes follow the changing tints and the vague movements of the universal exhalation which drags and is torn along the hedges like muslin. A feeble breeze inclines and balances the foliage of the great trees, and one hears the slight noise of the drops which descend upon their pyramid.

Several cottages are very poor, being of clay covered with laths, a thatched roof, the rooms are too low and too narrow, the windows too small, the partitions too thin. Think, of a large family huddled in winter in two of these rooms, with clothes drying, the swaddling clothes of infants, and the chimney roaring; during the long days of rain and snow, they must live in an unwholesome air, amid their own vapour. Many of the mothers have a lean face, marked with pimples, a worn-out pinched air; they have too many children and too much toil. The occupant of one of these thatched huts is a day-labourer, married, the father of six children, who earns twelve shillings a week, being generally employed by the year or by the half year; a cottage like his costs from three to four pounds sterling yearly; his features are delicate, drawn, his physiognomy is sad and humble. I was introduced to all these people with consideration and courtesy; they were asked with apologies to permit a French gentleman to enter. They instantly consented with civility and a pleasant smile. I remarked that I have seen in France many thatched huts much worse furnished; whereupon my companion replied that was some consolation. The poor day-labourer did not appear to be of that opinion.

However, his little house is clean; the blue patterned plates are ranged in good order above a dresser; the fireplace is of iron and is well constructed. I had previously seen other cottages elsewhere of this stamp; nearly always, at least in one room, an old carpet covers the floor; often there is a coloured paper, chairs of polished wood, small framed engravings, always a Bible, sometimes other volumes, religious books, new novels, the art of rearing rabbits, &c., in short, more useful objects than in our very poor thatched huts. In addition, the care taken is greater; there are no doors off their hinges, hanging shutters, broken panes, stagnant pools, scattered dunghills; the pavement of the soil is well swept, nothing lies about at random. Probably confusion and uncleanliness are more unhealthy in this climate than in ours, and man is bound to be orderly, prudent, regular as in Holland.

The village contains but four hundred souls; yet the little inn is decent, shining with cleanliness; one would sleep there readily, and one would be comfortable. We visit a carpenter, then a carter's; they are seated at table by themselves and take tea with butter. Their houses are of brick and covered with red tiles; one of them is flanked with a pretty large garden filled with vegetables, well cultivated, garnished with fine strawberries, with some bee-hives in a corner; both of them have a small flower-garden, roses, ivy, some creeping plants, and adornment. The rooms are rather low, but are not wanting in air; the small panes of glass connected by slight triangles of lead allow plenty of light to enter; one goes along a passage of bricks carefully washed to enter the outhouse; the retiring place, half open, is as well kept as in a middle-class house; on the first-floor are two bedrooms. Some books, the "Whole Duty of Man," one of Murray's guides, the family Bible, five or six volumes of history. Not a particle of dust on the windows, not a speck of mud on the floors, not a hole in the garments. Many other persons of the same condition pass along the streets, and their clothes are the same; it is true that to-day is Sunday. But, on the whole, my impression is that they are better provided and more careful than the peasants of France. The glory, the foolish vanity, and the superiority of ours consist in possessing land; they prefer being abstinent, stinting themselves, and having their acre in the sun; in order to acquire it they save out of their comfort. But this acquisition is a fund; in case of sickness or scarcity, they have a sure resource at hand. On the contrary, here every one tells me that a countryman is as much a spendthrift as a workman, as improvident, as exacting as far as comfort is concerned. Let an accident occur, and he instantly becomes a burden upon the parish.

I visit a farmer who cultivates one hundred acres. Here the cleanliness is altogether Dutch; I never saw anything superior in the environs of Utrecht and of Amsterdam. The farmer's wife says that every year the walls are whitewashed inside, that every week the paving stones are washed with a sponge; one is ashamed to walk upon them and dirty them. Another farmer, who also tills one hundred acres; pays the landlord £100, and rates and taxes in addition; the same cleanliness and the same condition. A third has three hundred acres, and also pays a pound an acre: but this is because his land is bad; his neighbour on the other side of the hill pays £800 for four hundred acres. The interior is as comfortable and agreeable as that of the largest and the finest farms of the department of the Beauce and of the environs of Paris. His house is old, with a porch in front forming a vestibule; here and there, in the courtyard, are fine pines, ornamental trees; a pretty green garden borders one of the wings; in the large hall is antique furniture. The staircase, of massive wood, and a sideboard date from the sixteenth century. An immense fireplace, capable of containing an entire trunk, a real yule log, with a double wooden screen, which, in summer, closes the opening, and, in winter, is a protection from draughts. Some pretty good engravings, and a rather large number of books, besides the great family Bible. The farmer has twelve huge and superb horses, and a steam threshing machine; among his profits, he sells eighty fat pigs yearly. A determined face, intelligent, serious, and calm; he is neither slovenly nor boastful; his wife seems an orderly and understanding house-keeper. It would be necessary to belong to the country, and live a year here, in order to know what there is in these heads. George Eliot, in "Adam Bede," has depicted a farmer and his wife, who are types in high relief, and minute in detail;

my friend tells me that these are excellent in all points and strikingly correct.

We go and see the last farm; six hundred acres, about £600 rent; I was thunderstruck. We were shown into a large, fresh, and plain drawing-room; large curtains, supported by gilded poles, two elegant and well-framed mirrors, tasteful armchairs; in the middle a table, covered with pretty volumes; in short, the country-house drawing-room of a Parisian who has an income of one thousand a-year. Immediately adjoining is a sort of hot-house, a glazed conservatory, filled with flowers, looking upon the most pleasant landscape, on sloping meadows and distant woods. The farmer's wife entered; she is a woman of thirty, who looked like twenty-six, in a dress of small-striped grey silk, with one or two rings on her fingers, perfectly white hands, pink and cared-for nails, an admirable waist, tall and lithe as a Diana, extremely beautiful, full of gaiety and vivacity, without any embarrassment, and who kept up the conversation very well. I learned later that she rode on horseback, played on the piano, and is none the less a good housekeeper; she goes to the kitchen every morning, orders, superintends, and sometimes makes a little pastry; once, having visitors, and the cook being absent, she set to herself, and prepared the dinner. Excepting some shades in manners and talk, she is a lady; she is wholly so in heart. My guide praised her greatly, but he added that in other cases, which are numerous, this education, these tastes, put a person out of humour with their condition, that at present many farmers' daughters are elegant, profuse, indolent, out of their sphere, and unhappy.

"Since you have begun," B—— said to me, "continue to the end." And, twelve miles from thence, we came to a model farm. No large central court; the farm is a mass of fifteen or twenty low brick buildings, constructed economically; as it was intended to furnish a model, it would not do to present a costly edifice as an example. Oxen, pigs, sheep, each in its stall, well-ventilated and well-cleaned; we were shown a set of stables in which the flooring was open; animals being fattened remain there six months, without moving. Selected and expensive breeds; a bull and his progeny are Indian, and recall the Buddhist sculptures. Steam machines for all the agricultural operations, and a small railroad for conveying the food to the animals; they eat sliced turnips, bruised beans, oil-cake; culture, thus understood, is a complicated industry, based on theory and experience, constantly improved, and worked with perfected tools. But I am not competent, and I amuse myself with observing the farmer's face, his red hair, his clear complexion, veined with scarlet like a vine-leaf scorched by the autumn sun, his cold and reflecting physiognomy; in a black hat and black riding-coat, upright, in a court, he gives orders in a dull tone, with few words, without making a gesture, without moving a muscle of his countenance. An admirable thing is that the establishment yields a return, and the great lord who has founded it in the public interest, finds it to his personal profit. I seemed to see in the farmer's attitude, in his apparently positive, applied, well-balanced mind, the explanation of the miracle.

We returned home, and all around us over the country, night fell. The indistinct trees disappeared in a grey smoke; strange yellow tones spread over the meadows, the dim air became thicker; it enveloped even the hedges of the road, and bathed everything in its soft covering. In this twilight, which resembles a picture by Rembrandt, I turned over the things which had struck me the most; in the foreground stand forth the children's faces, so fresh, so healthy, so vigorous, so chubby, even in the poorest thatched cottages. One of them, in its cradle, slept, stretching forth an arm; the little turned-up nose was almost transparent in the light; its mouth seemed a cherry, and the cheeks two full roses; the dimpled flesh yielded under the finger which touched it; the petals of a flower, moistened with dew, had not more softness and lustre. To my taste this leaves the types of the south far behind; there man, almost from infancy, is made, finished, stable, set in a fixed design and in a definitive shape; here one feels, as with Rubens, the continual growth of life, its fragility, its delicacy. and, at the same time, its sap, the inexhaustible and spontaneous replenishment of the human substance. A little boy of four, leaning against a wall, astonished, mute, cast down his great bashful eyes, held one finger in his mouth, and suffered himself to be caressed without uttering a word; an instant afterwards he ventured to raise his eyebrows, and gazed upon us as curious animals; then instantly repenting, covered his cherub face with his two hands. One sees the emotions pass over these complexions, as one sees the colours change upon their meadows.

My friends tell me that this village is a good specimen, that the interior of these farmers' and peasants abodes exhibits with sufficient exactitude the average of comfort among the class; that, however, in several districts—for example, on the side of Norfolk and Lincoln—I shall find finer farms. Since then, and judging from official documents, I have seen that this view was not correct; the evil is greater, and the poor become more and more poverty-stricken. The large property increases, and the small one diminishes. At the close of the last century, Arthur Young wrote: "I do not know a single cottage to which a piece of land is not attached." Moreover, the poor villagers had some fowls, and a pig on the common. But, by the Enclosure Acts, the commons are being constantly reduced in size; hence the peasant has no longer the resource of fowls and pigs; having sold his bit of land, he can count upon his arms alone, and he lets them for hire. In the purely agricultural districts it appears that the wages are from seven to eight shillings a week, and not twelve, as I have found them here. To add to this, the villager lets for hire the arms of his wife and of his children; one sees bands of them hoeing root-plants, of which the culture extends itself unceasingly. Agriculture being conducted on a large scale, and having become a scientific form of industry, has had the counter-effect of introducing into the country districts the rule, the monotony, the miseries of manufacture. The children wither, remain ignorant, become vicious; in a district of Lincolnshire, out of four hundred cottages, two hundred have but a single room wherein the whole family sleep promiscuously.

I saw one of these days a picture in *Punch* on this head. A landed proprietor takes Mr. Punch into his stables, which are admirable "Yes, Mr. Punch," says he, "pretty clean stalls—airy, plenty of light, drainage, perfect ventilation, the best water, and the best possible food, good treatment, that is my plan." One passes to the cottage. A single chamber, almost bare; three chipped plates on a board; a bad kettle, two pieces of linen drying; the distress and the stench are terrible. A wretched man in rags, with a battered hat, warms himself with a gloomy air before a small fire o. brushwood; the wife, hollow-eyed, lies with two infants on a pallet; on another pallet are a little girl and a little boy; on a mattress in the corner is a young man; they are all emaciated, wild, and Mr. Punch says to the proprietor: "The arrangement of your stables is excellent. Suppose you tried something of the same sort here? What think you of that?" Here the disease and the remedy are exhibited together. On the contrary, I can venture to say that, among our four millions of peasant proprietors, the state of comfort, especially during the last twenty years, is increasing; the vice of our organisation is displayed in other ills, on the side of politics, by the instability of the Government and by the absence of lasting freedom. But each State has its hereditary scrofula; one can only verify the sore, show that it is connected with the organisation, apply a temporary palliative to some parts; the great surgical operations, which many persons recommend, have seldom any other result than that of still more reducing the patient.

After a renewed investigation, it seems to me certain that, in this country, the class of agricultural labourers having no land of their own to farm is the most unfortunate and the most brutalised. A learned man said to me: "As regards intelligence and ideas, the distance is as great between them and mechanics as between mechanics and men like myself." Two persons who have lived in France add that the French peasant is much superior; they especially praise his frugality, his custom of depending upon himself, his ardour in working, his passion for land. According to them, the English peasant is quite different, improvident, wasteful, always a burden to the parish or the charitable rich. Even were he to possess, like ours, a bit of land, he would not know how to make it yield wherewithal to live—in the first place for lack of economy, because he is heavy, incapable of setting his wits to work; next, because the English soil, being of very mediocre quality, requires much manuring, capital, and is suited only for cultivation on a large scale, for pasturage, for rearing cattle. According to a clergyman, who has lived in Devonshire and in other counties, the wages of a villager are from eight to nine shillings a week; sometimes he earns ten shillings; but he requires to be very strong and skilful to earn twelve. Now he has often six children besides; it is impossible for eight persons, and even for five or six persons, to live upon that sum; he cannot then dispense with public or private help. Besides, a female peasant, and in general every woman of the lower class in England, is lacking in address; she has not, like a Frenchwoman, the talent for keeping house, the spirit of order, the habit of bargaining, the art of making a little go a long way, and of producing something out of nothing; she does not know how to mend and turn a garment, make one dish serve; very often she cannot work. One of our friends, a member of the board of guardians in his district, got a grant of fifteen shillings a week for a family in which there were fourteen children: neither the wife nor the eldest daughter knew how to make soup, a roast, a dish of any sort; they went to the tradespeople and bought new bread, butter, tea, ham, and always at the highest prices; every one in this family could hoe a field, not one could cook a chop. Add that, since agriculture has been transformed, the tastes of the stomach have altered. Fifty years ago, meat was a luxury among the peasants; they ate it but once a week; in winter, they had salt meat only. Now they require fresh meat every day; and England, which produces so much of it, is obliged, in addition, to procure it from abroad, from Denmark and from Holland; in 1861, there entered every week, by the Thames alone, three thousand head of living cattle. The conclusion of the whole matter is, that day labourers in the country live partly on alms, and the poor-rates, though they are so heavy, and private charity, though it is so liberal barely suffice to maintain them.

XII.

LANDED PROPRIETORS AND ENGLISH GENTLEMEN.

LET us now see the good which is the counterpart of this evil. I have already made two excursions like these to places at forty or fifty miles from London, and there, as here, the number of parks is astonishing. One never ceases to see them along the road; in certain localities they form a line which continues as far as London. In fact, not only are the old estates maintained in virtue of the law which gives the real property to the eldest son, but also nearly all the men, who by their talent or by their industry have grown wealthy, have an ambition to acquire an estate, to fix their family on it, and to enter the local aristocracy. It is chiefly in this direction that the hundred millions of annual savings, accumulated in England, flow; they serve less to solace the poor than to enrich the rich. As compensation, these rich men are natural, benevolent, and recognised chiefs. In the circle of acquaintances of B———, two score families are counted as forming the society and leading the locality—a marquis, whose park is seven hundred acres, four baronets, a lord, and several members of the House of Commons. The clergyman with whom I took a walk told me that they were " almost fathers of the people."

B—— himself is the near relation, the heir, of a great lord whose lands he administers; one day he will have an income of £40,000; meantime, and for the sake of his relative, he supervises, directs, builds healthy cottages for the labourers, subscribes to enterprises of public utility, and, while improving the property, renders a service to the country.

It would be difficult to find one of these landlords who does not give up a portion of his money and of his time to the general good. They are municipal magistrates, overseers, justices of the peace, chairmen of committees and of useful societies. One of them, possessing £1,600,000, and whose brother is equally rich, has a share of £40,000 in an undertaking formed to bring potable water to London; there are forty shares each of the like amount. As a relaxation from Parliament and from business, he has built a church, which we visited, very pretty, in an elaborated Gothic style, with stained-glass windows, wainscoting, a sculptured pulpit—in short, a little gem, bound in evergreen laurels: he has endowed it, and secured an income for the chaplain. Immediately adjoining, he has founded a free school; among other things, singing is taught there, he has placed a piano in it, little concerts are given; he amuses himself by making the children sing. As he believes in the good effect of music, he frequently sends the master right and left in the district to further its adoption. In another village which I passed through, the gentry have hired a two-storied cottage, to be used by the villagers as a kind of evening club; out of the fund subscribed, the rent, the books, the newspapers, fire, light, and a woman to keep the house, are paid for. But it is arranged so that this club shall be self-supporting in the end by means of the contributions of its frequenters. Man is thus made, that he does not appreciate a pure gift; it is necessary that he should bear a fraction of the expense and co-operate freely for his own welfare. In the first room are books and newspapers; in the second one plays at draughts and chess, one chats, and one smokes. The aim of the founders is to compete with the tavern. They understand human nature, they know that they must find an outlet for instinct, a food for wants. The instinct and the wants always satisfy themselves; strive in order that their satisfaction should be innocent, and, if possible, beneficent. For example, the villagers do not work on Sunday; when it is cold, dirty, and dark, they naturally proceed to the place where they find fire, light, amusement, and this place, twelve months out of the year, is the tavern. Give them a tavern, less dear, where, instead of gin, they drink tea; they will thus occupy their leisure hours, and will not return home drunk. For the same reason, one of my friends in London is a member of the society for secularising Sunday; its object is to procure the opening of museums, the authorisation of concerts, public lectures; thus it is that drunkenness is battled with, and more efficaciously than by sermons.

To this intelligent beneficence join a quantity of respects and attentions. A peer has lent his park for the last archery meeting, and presides over the festival; his little harangue, grave and bantering, his respectful gallantry, were excellent for flattering and gratifying the ladies. We enter the park of Sir John ———; it is traversed by a public road open to pedestrians; it may be visited without leave. I have seen that of the Duke of Marlborough at Blenheim;

over the entrance gate is the following inscription:—
"The Duke of Marlborough begs the persons who may walk through the park to keep to the high road, and not to walk on the grass." The gate of this park is open; the first comer, an inhabitant of the village, may go and take the air in it with his wife. Sir W. B—— is master of the hunt in the district, and many gentlemen of low position and farmers follow the chase. The mistress of the house in which I am staying knows all the good women in the locality; she graciously recognises them, and shakes hands when she enters their cottages with me; they respond with a cordial and even affectionate air; it is easy to see that there is no distrust or hostility betwixt the two classes. The inferior is not envious; it does not enter his head to long for the place of the wealthy gentleman; he is rather prone to consider him as his protector, to be proud of him, especially if the family be an old one, and, for several generations, settled in the locality; in that case it has a place, like the fine trees, among the ornaments and the glories of the country. Lately, in a railway carriage, I chatted with some of the Life Guards, true giants and good fellows; they said with pride, "all our officers are noblemen." After some questions about their pay, which is two shillings daily, they said that among them about one-third were married men. "Have the widows a claim for pensions?" "No; but private subscriptions provide for them." All that is the remains of the good feudal spirit. The chieftain provided for the wants of his vassal, and the vassal was proud of his chieftain.

This spirit is all the more powerful as the population in England is distributed, even at the present day, in feudal fashion. Everywhere, in the midst of cottages, are one or more country seats, modern, comely houses, which replace the olden castles, and wherein the master plays, under new forms, the part of the olden baron. In every parish, even the most distant, one finds two, three, five, six families who have their hereditary seat there, the favourite place of abode, and whose patronage is accepted, efficient; this is the ancient patronage of the mailed chieftain, but transferred from physical to moral matters, applied to things of peace and no more to those of war, exercised by intelligence and no more by the sword, authorised by superiority of education and no more by superiority of armour. In fact, it is no longer a concern to set men in battle against the enemy, but to diminish ignorance, misery, and vice; for this object as for the other, it is necessary to have local chiefs, proved, accepted, capable, and these chiefs are the gentlemen proprietors of the parish or of the district. Poggio, in his travels, wrote three centuries ago, this sentence so full of truths and of consequences: "Among the English, the nobles think it shameful to sojourn in cities; they inhabit retired parts of the country among woods and pastures; they consider him the most noble who has the largest revenue; they addict themselves to field affairs, sell their wool and their cattle, and do not consider rural profits disgraceful."

The contrast was great for Poggio between this country life of the English nobility and the city life of the Italian nobility. It is not less for a Frenchman, and, although among us the Revolution has sent many nobles to their estates, it continues still. The town is not in England, as among us, the chosen abode. Excepting the great manufacturing cities, the country towns, York, for example, are scarcely inhabited by any one but shopkeepers; the select few and the cream of the nation are elsewhere, in the country. London itself is but a great gathering place for business; people come there during three or four months in summer, to converse and get relaxation, to see their friends again, provide for their interests, pass their acquaintances in review. But they are rooted in their country seats; that is their true country, the loved domestic circle, the family centre, the place where they hunt, where they receive long visits from guests, where they act effectively, where they find at each step the memorial of their good deeds or of the good deeds of their ancestors, where the familiar faces at a street corner, the accustomed contours of an eminence at the end of a road, leave in the mind the friendly impression of being at home. There one takes an interest in parish affairs, desires to discharge the minor functions. When one obtains them, one exercises them with zeal, conscientiously and with pleasure; during the season, the Saturday evening train transports from London a number of landed proprietors who proceed to a distance of forty, eighty, one hundred miles to deliver a lecture, hold a meeting, fill the unpaid office of magistrate or overseer of the parish or the church. Moreover, they are bound to be first in opening their purses, as the feudal baron was bound to go first into the fight. B—— says that he gives the tenth of his income in subscriptions, and that his neighbours do likewise. Count again the poor-rates which here are three shillings in the pound of the estimated territorial return, and which in certain districts are seven shillings. Voluntarily, or in accordance with the law, the propertied classes lend a shoulder with true courage to sustain the heavy burden of public poverty.

Naturally, such a circle is closed, and strictly maintains its limits; the aristocratic institution has its drawbacks like others. Thackeray, in all his writings, has described and bitterly rallied this system of social enclosures, the effort of the inferiors to break in, and of the superiors to keep them out. For example, a person like the elegant and intelligent farmer's wife of whom I 'spoke above is not in society; she is not invited to archery meetings; several ladies whom B—— mentioned to me, and whose conduct in this respect he disapproves, refrain from bowing to her, in order to put a stop to the beginning of possible familiarities. Doubtless the English who have lived abroad, and whose mind is open, are superior to this miserable pride; they frankly acknowledge its folly and excess. But beneath much reticence, it is discernible in the others. At the bottom of their hearts, and perhaps without realising it to themselves, they believe or are tempted to believe that a manufacturer, a merchant, a monied man, obliged to think all day about gain and the details of gain, is not a gentleman, and cannot belong to the world of fashion. He has not the requisite education, the ideas, the language. "What can a tradesman or farmer speak about, except the objects of his trade?" According to them the sentiments lose something also; the monied man and the man of business is inclined to selfishness; he has not the disinterestedness, the large and generous views which suit a chief of the country; he does not know how to sink self, and think of the public. This title alone gives the right to rule; thus, till the contrary be proved, he is kept apart, and his family cannot be received among the governing families. The latter are at home, and it is they who make the first advance in adopting a newcomer. When a rich man has bought an estate, it is not necessary that he should trouble himself nor inform any one; if, in mind, in character, and in manners, he is a gentleman, this will be known at the end of a fortnight, and the neighbouring families will of their own accord come and call upon him. But, even when adopted, he will not yet enjoy all the privileges of the others; he will not succeed in being returned to represent them in Parliament; if he become a candidate, the public will say, "He is too little known, he does not belong to the county yet." He is implanted, but he has not taken root. Perhaps his son or his grandson will be elected, but not he. To represent a district one must be connected with all its interests, its customs, be deeply imbued with them for generations through every fibre. The first condition of acknowledged command is long residence, and every strong aristocracy is local. In like manner, in France, if, during the Revolution, La Vendée alone followed the lead of its gentlemen, it is because, alone in France, the gentlemen of La Vendée, country folks and sportsmen, lived and remained in intimate intercourse with the peasants.

I endeavour rightly to comprehend the epithet so essential, "a gentleman;" it constantly recurs, and comprises a mass of ideas wholly English. The vital question in the case of a man is always put thus: "Is he a gentleman?" Similarly in the case of a woman: "Is she a lady?" In these two cases, one means to say that the person in question is of the superior class; this class is recognised in fact; a workman, a peasant, a shopkeeper does not try to step over the line of demarcation. But how is it recognised that a person belongs to the superior class? In France we have not the word because we have not the thing, and these three syllables, as used across the Channel, summarise the history of English society. The gentlemen, the squires, the barons, the feudal chieftains have not become, as under Louis XV., simply privileged persons, ornamental parasites, hurtful in the end, unpopular, odious, outlaws, then, badly reinstated, with antiquated minds, being henceforth without influence, and maintained in the State rather as a tolerated memorial than as an effective moving power. They have continued in communication with the people, they have opened their ranks to men of talent, they have taken recruits from among the cream of the untitled, they have continued commanding or directing personages, or at least influential in the parish and the State. For that purpose they have accommodated themselves to their age and their part; they have been administrators, patrons, promoters of reforms, good managers of public affairs, diligent, instructed, capable men, the most enlightened, the most independent, the most useful citizens of the country. After this pattern has been formed the idea of a gentleman, quite different from that of the French *gentilhomme*. *Gentilhomme* awakens ideas of elegance, delicacy, tact, exquisite politeness, tender honour, cavalier turn, prodigal liberality, brilliant valour; these were the salient traits of the superior class in France. In like manner "gentleman" includes the distinctive traits of the superior class in England; in the first place, the most apparent, those which strike dull eyes, are, for example, an independent fortune, the style of the house, a certain exterior appearance, habits of luxury and ease; very often, in the eyes of the common people, especially in the eyes of lackeys, these externals suffice. Add to them for more cultivated minds, a liberal education, travel, instruction, good manners, knowledge of the world. But, for real judges, the essential part of the personage is the heart. When speaking to me of a great lord, a diplomatist, B—— said to me, "He is no gentleman." Dr. Arnold, when travelling in France, wrote to his friends, "What strikes me here is the total absence of gentlemen, and of all persons having the education and the sentiments of a real gentleman. . . . . . there are very few persons here who have the appearance and manners of one. . . . . . A real English Christian gentleman, of manly heart, enlightened mind, is more, I think, than Guizot or Simondi could be able to comprehend; no other country could, I think, furnish so fine a specimen of human nature." Strip off these exaggerations of national self-love, instructive testimony will remain. For them, a real gentleman is a real noble, a man worthy of commanding, upright, disinterested, capable of exposing himself and even of sacrificing himself for those whom he leads, not only an honourable man, but a conscientious man, in whom generous instincts have been confirmed by straightforward reflection, and who, acting naturally well, acts still better upon principle. In this ideal portrait, you recognise the accomplished chief; add to it the English varieties, empire over self, continuous coolness, perseverance in adversity, natural seriousness, dignity of manner, the shunning of all affectation or boasting; you will have the model superior who, copied closely or vaguely discerned, here rallies all who aspire or who will serve. A novelist has depicted him under the name of "John Halifax, Gentleman;" the subject is a poor abandoned child who ends by becoming the respected leader of his district. A single phrase will show the tone of the book: when, after great misadventures, John attains independence, buys a house and keeps his carriage, his son exclaims, "Father, we are gentlefolks now!" "We always were, my son."

XIII.

MANSIONS, PARKS, AND GARDENS.

LET us look, however, at the outsides; they are indexes. B——, my entertainer, who has been married a year, wished to have a cottage. This cottage is charming, even elegant, furnished with all the refinements of neatness, of comfort and luxury, it is of brown brick, with several turrets, slanting roof, being nearly altogether enveloped in ivy. Around is a little park with the velvet lawn rolled daily, two or three superb clumps of flowering rhododendrons, ten feet high, thirty in length and breadth; on the grass are garlands of exotic flowers of vivid hues, groups of trees well arranged, a covered hedgerow forming a lovers' walk for a young newly-married pair; then, beyond the hedges, a horizon of large trees and glimpses of views over the everlasting verdure. A real nest for a married couple : within, pink and white paper-hangings, light painting, in lilac or light yellow; delicate tiled floors and many lozenge-paned windows which recall the Middle Ages. In the drawing-room, an excellent piano, and several fine books which are wedding gifts, Tennyson, a Prayer-Book, and others bound in blue velvet, in wood with carving, in gilded morocco, illustrated with care, with the neatness of pencil which is peculiar to English artists, some ornamented on each page with paintings and coloured arabesques. Not an object which does not denote an exquisite and even fastidious taste. Everywhere are flower-stands filled with rare flowers; without, within, flowers abound; this is the fullest detail of luxury, and they understand it as those who really delight in it.

This understanding and this care are manifested in everything. There is not an object which fails to exhibit forethought and calculated comfort. There are carpets and long oilcloths from top to bottom of the house: the carpet serves for warmth; the oilcloth on which one treads may be washed and kept as clean as a carpet. In my bedroom is a table of rosewood; upon this table a slab of marble, on the marble a round straw mat; all this to bear an ornamented water-bottle covered with a tumbler. One does not simply place one's book upon the table; upon the table is a small stand for holding it. One does not have a plain candlestick, which one blows out before going to sleep; the candle is enclosed in a glass cylinder, and is furnished with a self-acting extinguisher. Other details are still more striking; a moment's reflection is required in order to comprehend their use. Sometimes all this apparatus hampers; it involves too much trouble for the sake of comfort. In like manner, on a journey, I have seen Englishmen supplied with so many glasses, opera-glasses and telescopes; with so many umbrellas, canes, and iron-tipped sticks; with so many overcoats, comforters, waterproofs, and wrappers; with so many dressing-cases, flasks, books, and newspapers, that were I in their place I should have stayed at home. From England to France, and from France to Italy, wants and preparations go on diminishing

Life is more simple, and, if I may say so, more naked, more given up to chance, less encumbered with incommodious commodities.

Fifteen hundred pounds of income, three to four horses, two carriages, six servants, a gardener. The same style of living would require nearly the same outlay in France.

We have visited five or six parks, large or of the average size, nearly all are beautiful, two or three being admirable. The intact and well-kept meadows sparkle in the sun, abounding with daisies and buttercups. The oaks are old, often enormous. At the bottom of the valleys, rivulets, properly disposed, form little lakes in which swim foreign ducks; here and there, in a zone of glittering water, an islet covered with rhododendrons rears its pink tuft. Along the woods rabbits speed off beneath our feet, and at each winding of the road the undulating plain, strewn with clumps of trees, sets forth its verdure varied, mellowed, as far as the blue distances. What freshness and what silence! One feels in a state of repose; this nature welcomes one with a tender, discreet, intimate caress; she is some one; she has her accent, the affectionate accent of domestic happiness, like a beautiful bride who has adorned herself for her husband, and advances in front of him with a soft smile. Every original work—a garden, like a book or a building—is a secret which unveils deep-seated sentiments. In my opinion this one, more than any other, shows the poetic dream of an English soul. It is not so with their dwellings—huge machines, partly Italian or partly Gothic, without distinctive character. One sees that they are spacious, comfortable, well-kept—nothing more. These are the houses of the rich, who understand comforts, and who, sometimes rather unfortunately, have had architectural fancies; many elegant cottages, covered and encumbered with turrets, seem playthings in glazed pasteboard. All their imagination, all their national and personal invention, have been expended upon their parks.

This one of seven hundred acres contains trees which two or three men could not encircle with their outspread arms—oaks, limes, plane-trees, cypresses, beeches, which have freely developed the amplitude and fulness of their forms. Isolated or in groups upon the mellow and rich meadow, their rich pyramids, their vast domes expand at will, and descend to the grass with a largeness of expansion such as cannot be imagined. They have been tended like rich children; they have always enjoyed perfect liberty and perfect satisfaction; nothing has lessened their luxuriance or hampered their growth; they respire the air and use the soil like great lords to which the soil and the air belong by right. In the centre of so many living emeralds is a still more precious jewel—the garden. Clumps of rhododendrons twenty feet high there display themselves, with all their flowers in bloom; their petals, which are red or of pale violet, shine softly in the sun, beneath the humming hosts of bees. Bushes of azaleas, tufts of full-blown roses, beds of flowers with pearl, azure, velvet, or flesh tints, dainty and winding borders form indistinguishable circles—one walks environed with perfumes and colours. Wise art has regulated the succession of the plants in such a way that those which bloom late replace those which bloom early, and that, from one end of the season to the other, the vast flower-bed is always blooming. At intervals a sycamore of noble port, a foreign beech of copper-coloured foliage, sustain with their grave note or with their sudden resonance this too-long-drawn-out concert of delicious impressions. Verily this is a concert for the eye, and like a magnificent and full-toned symphony, which the sun, that powerful leader of the orchestra, causes to swell in unison beneath the stroke of his bow. As far as the distant places of the park, farther off still, in the woods, on the common, one feels them near at hand. Beautiful plants have climbed over the walls, and suddenly, amidst wild firs, one meets with a pink and smiling rhododendron, like an Angelica of Ariosto in the midst of the forest of the Ardennes. All these distances are agreeable; the land rises and falls under a thick covering of brushwood; here and there ferns, with their vivid and charming green, relieve the uniformity of their tint; in several places ferns abound, and one sees them meandering, twisting about, marking rose-windows on the large russet carpet. At the extremity a line of pines bounds the horizon, and the undulations of the ground are developed by insensible stages in the pale warmish mist, transpierced with light.

The house is a large mansion, rather commonplace, solid in appearance, arranged in modern style; the furniture of the ground floor and of the first floor, recently renewed, cost four thousand pounds. Three rooms or drawing-rooms, sixty feet long, twenty high, are furnished with large mirrors, good pictures, excellent engravings, with bookcases. In front is a glazed conservatory, where one passes the afternoon when the weather is bad, and where, even in winter, one can fancy that it is spring. Bedrooms for the young ladies who come as visitors; fresh, clear, virginal, papered in blue and white, with an assortment of pretty feminine objects and fine engravings, they are well fitted for their amiable occupants. As for the rest, the picturesque sentiment of decoration and of the arrangement of the whole is less keen than among us; for example, the objects and the tones are rather placed in juxtaposition than in accord. But there is grandiosity and simplicity; no fondness for crowding and for old curiosities. They readily submit to large bare plane surfaces, empty spaces; the eye is at ease, one breathes freely, one can walk about, one has no fear of knocking against the furniture. Attention is given to comfort, notably to what relates to the details of sleeping and dressing. In my bedroom, the entire floor is carpeted, a strip of oilcloth is in front of the washing-stand, matting along the walls. There are two dressing-tables, each having two drawers, the first is provided with a swing looking-glass, the second is furnished with one large jug, one small one, a medium one for hot water, two porcelain basins, a dish for tooth-brushes, two soap-dishes, a water-bottle with its tumbler, a finger-glass with its glass. Underneath is a very low table, a sponge, another basin, a large shallow zinc bath for morning bathing. In a cupboard is a towel-horse with four towels of different kinds, one of them thick and rough. Another indispensable cabinet in the room is a marvel. Napkins are under all the vessels and utensils; to provide for such a service, when the house is occupied, it is necessary that washing should be always going on. Three pairs of candles, one of them fixed in a small portable table. Wax-matches, paper spills in pretty little holders, pin-cushions, porcelain extinguishers, metal extinguishers. Whiteness, perfection, softest tissues in every part of the bed. The servant comes four times a day into the room; in the morning to draw the blinds and the curtains, open the inner blinds, carry off the boots and clothes, bring a large can of hot water with a fluffy towel on which to place the feet; at midday, and at seven in the evening, to bring water and the rest, in order that the visitor may wash before luncheon and dinner; at night to shut the window, arrange the bed, get the bath ready, renew the linen; all this with silence, gravity, and respect. Pardon these trifling details; but they must be handled in order to figure to oneself the wants of an Englishman in the direction of his luxury; what he expends in being waited upon and comfort is enormous, and one may laughingly say that he spends the fifth of his life in his tub.

Several of these mansions are historical; they must be seen in order to understand what inheritance in a large family can bring together in the form of treasures. One was mentioned to me where, by a clause in the conditions, the possessor is bound to invest every year several thousand sterling in silver plate; after having crowded the sideboards, in the end, a staircase was made of massive silver. We had the opportunity of seeing in the retrospective exhibition an entire collection of precious curiosities and works of art sent by Lord Hereford. In 1848, he said to one of his French friends, greatly disquieted and a little put out, " I have a mansion in Wales which I have never seen, but which I am told is very fine. Every day dinner for twelve is served there, and the carriage drawn up at the door in case I should arrive. The butler eats the dinner. Go thither, make yourself at home; you see that it will not cost you a farthing." Naturally, fine things accumulate in these wealthy hands. Baroness

Burdett Coutts, Lord Ellesmere, the Marquis of Westminster possess picture-galleries which would do honour to a minor State. Lord Ellesmere has in three rooms, as lofty as the gallery of the Louvre, a number of Poussins, the best Flemish painters, above all three Titians of medium size, "Diana and Acteon," "Diana and Calypso," "Venus leaving the Waters," of a warm amber colour, of the richest and most lively beauty. The Marquis of Westminster has, in two galleries and four enormous rooms, an hundred and eighty-three pictures, with an accompaniment of busts, statues, bronzes, enamels, malachite vases, six large Rubens, three Titians, one Raffaelle, two Rembrandts, a number of Claudes, chosen from among the finest. These palatial mansions are but samples, and it would require too much space to mention them all. In another tour, I saw Blenheim Palace, near Woodstock, belonging to the Duke of Marlborough. This is a sort of Louvre, formerly presented by the nation to the great captain, built in the style of the period, much ornamented. Several rooms are as lofty as the nave of a church, the library is an hundred feet long, an inner chapel contains the monument of the founder, one gallery displays the family portraits, another contains porcelain, several others paintings. The park is two miles in circumference, magnificent trees, a large stream of water, crossed by an ornamental bridge, a column bearing the statue of the first duke, a private cabinet containing, under Titian's name, twelve copies, being the loves of the gods, voluptuous figures of life-size, presented by the princes of Italy to the conqueror of Louis XIV.; in the apartments are works by Reynolds, five or six large portraits by Vandyck, a Madonna by Raffaelle, two Rubens, where sensuality, passion, audacity, genius, overflow like a river in splendours and enormities. Two are bacchanals; one gigantic female fawn is lying on the ground, curved upon her pendent breasts, and her two little ones, turned on their backs, fastened to the udder, suck eagerly in a mass of quivering flesh above; the torso of a dark Silenus forms a contrast to the dazzling whiteness of a wanton and twining nymph; close by, another copper-coloured, huge Silenus, heartily dances, with a drunken laugh which shakes his paunch, whilst a beautiful young woman, bent upon the hip, sets forth the soft undulations of her side and throat. I dare not describe the third picture, the most pungent of all, of a sublime crudity, all the sap and all the flower of an indomitable temperament, all the poetry of abandoned wickedness, and of bestial gourmandising, " Lot and his two Daughters." But I have forgotten myself, these memories return upon me like a hot gust. All that I wish to say in conclusion is, that these large hereditary fortunes are conservatories prepared to be stocked with all fine things. At the end of several generations a mansion, a park become a jewel case.

Several consequences flow from this, some, which are evil, affect the individual; others, which are good, concern the State.

According to S———, who is cosmopolitan and well connected here, the law of primogeniture, especially in the case of noblemen, has many unpleasant results. Very often the eldest son, having his head turned from his college days with servility and flattery, is a foolish spendthrift or lunatic; he travels without learning anything, brings back with him the worst of Continental customs, or wearies. If the aristocracy were not recruited by men of talent among commoners, its members would soon become useless, narrow-minded, and even pernicious, as frequently happens elsewhere. Moreover, the inequality of the children leads to bitter contrasts. Here I speak less of noblemen who can procure the advancement of their younger sons in the army, the Church, or the administration, than of the simply rich men; in these families the younger son bitterly experiences the constraint which casts him naked or supplied with a trifling patrimony among the chances and the battles of life, which sends him abroad, postpones his marriage, condemns him during ten or twenty years to subordination, striving, to privations, whilst his brother, independent and rich from birth, has but to occupy the mansion and park prepared for him. However, this notion distresses him less than we should imagine; he is accustomed to it from childhood; as the usage is old, legal, and national, he submits to it, and even accepts it on the same footing as a natural necessity. Besides, by temperament, he does not dread hardship, and pride whispers to him that it is best to shift for himself by working.

That being admitted, let us trace the advantages. An Englishman has nearly always many children, the rich as well as the poor. The Queen has nine, and sets the example. Let us run over the families we are acquainted with: Lord ―― has six children; the Marquis of ――, twelve; Sir W――, nine; Mr. S――, a judge, twenty-four, of whom twenty-two are living; several clergymen five, six, and up to ten and twelve; a certain Church dignitary has only four sons, but he expends in keeping up his position and in charities his two thousand pounds of salary. The Bishops, many of the high officials or landed proprietors, act likewise. In general one saves little here; a medical man, a lawyer, a landlord has too many public or private claims upon him, taxes, subscriptions, the education and travels of his children, hospitality, horses, servants, comforts. One knows not how to keep within bounds, one wishes to have every enjoyment, to make a figure; one prefers to add to the task rather than diminish the style of living; in place of retrenching, one scatters abroad, at the close of the year the utmost is to make both ends meet. Too much toil and too great outlay, that is admitted by my English friends to be the English shortcoming. Now consider these younger sons, well brought up, well trained by a general education and by a special education, informed from their earliest years that they must count upon themselves; accustomed to comfort, followed by the memory of the paternal country-seat; can there be a sharper spur? They have a stimulus to work. Not to reascend to their father's position is to fall lower; they feel bound to rival the fortune of their eldest brother. In this fashion the law of primogeniture, combined with the experience of what is comfortable, is a system of emulation; they rush to the Indies, to China, to Australia, take the cream off the world, and return to found a family. In London there is a quarter called the Australian, inhabited by people who have made fortunes in Victoria, in Melbourne. The weak succumb under this system; but the spirit of enterprise, initiative, energy, all the forces of human nature are brought into full play. The individual is braced by the struggle, the select few of the nation is renewed, and gold flows in torrents over the country.

Another advantage, but which appears to be one only in the eyes of a philosopher and of an artist; however, it is an advantage. Without an aristocracy, a civilisation is not complete; it wants large, independent lives, emancipated from all mean care, capable of beauty like a work of art. Some one has said, "War to castles, peace to cottages." I think it would be better to say, "Peace to cottages and to castles." Proudhon wished to see France covered with neat little houses, in each house a half-country half-city family, and round about a small field and a garden, the whole soil being thus parcelled out. From the historian's point of view, this is the desire of a market-gardener; if there were nothing else in it than vegetables, the country would be very ugly. I have no park, and yet my eyes are satisfied with beholding one—only it must be accessible and well-kept. It is the same with the lives of the great; they perform the functions of parks among the garden plots and tilled fields. The one furnishes venerable trees, velvet greenswards, the delicious fairy-land of accumulated flowers and poetic avenues; the other maintains certain elegancies of manners and certain shades of sentiments, renders possible a cosmopolite education, supplies a hotbed for statesmen. One of the first manufacturers in England, a Radical and supporter of Mr. Bright, said to me, with regard to electoral reform, "We do not wish to overthrow the aristocracy; we c nt to their keeping the government and the high o . As members of the middle class we believe that specially-trained men are required for the conduct of affairs—trained from father to son for this end, occupying an independent and commanding station. Besides, their title and their genealogy are a gilt feather; a troop is more easily led when its officer wears a plumed hat. But we absolutely require that they should fill all the places with competent men. Nothing for mediocrities; no nepotism. Let them govern, provided, however, that they have talent." They have profited by their recent experience. They know that during the Crimean campaign the flood of public anger nearly swept them away. They have felt that they must emerge from negligence and disorder; they have yielded to opinion, they have ended by directing reforms. It may be affirmed that during thirty years they have governed, not in the interest of their class, but in the interest of the nation. Since 1832 they have ceased to prey upon the public funds; they are rich or well-to-do persons, who pay the heavier share of the taxes; the principal transformations of the Budget have had the effect of relieving the people. On the whole, England is becoming a Republic, for which the aristocratic institution fabricates the required contingent of ministers, representatives, generals, and diplomatists, as a polytechnic school furnishes the indispensable quota of engineers. Many are incompetent; let them remain out of service, and let them occupy themselves in spending their income. But the necessary staff may be picked out of the mass; and nothing is more precious than a good staff.

XIV.

CHARACTER AND POSITION OF THE CLERGY.

ALONGSIDE of him who conducts affairs, there is another who governs consciences, instituted on the same principle, and leading to the same result—I mean to say the governance exercised by the most worthy, respected, stable, and perfectable. This refers to the clergy; in the first place, however, let us see the sentiments which support them.

It is Sunday; the domestics are excused waiting at table; each guest helps himself; the Sabbath day is respected as much as possible. These biblical traits are encountered at every step; for example, newspapers do not appear on Sundays; one train excepted, the railway traffic ceases; in Scotland, the Duchess of ———, who was going to see her dying mother, could not get the special train on Sunday, for which she would have paid.

We go to church for afternoon service; the parson, a tall, thin man of forty, takes as his text the life of St. John the Baptist in the New Testament, briefly narrates this story, and extracts the fitting applications from it with good sense and calmness. Good pronunciation, gravity, no emphasis; solid and clear argument, developed in a serious tone, is always useful teaching for the public, especially for the village public. Before, and after, he reads the service, and the small congregation sings the psalms, accompanied by the organ. Excellent behaviour and general attention. The music is a grave recitative, rather monotonous, but never clamorous or bellowing, like our church singing. This liturgy, those psalms, translated or arranged from the Hebrew, are truly eloquent, elevated, imposing; the Hebraic style, with its abruptness and sublimity, runs well in English. It has been softened, rendered lucid in the translation; but the English tongue, among all others, is the most capable of sustaining its grandeur and of adapting itself to its jerks; for it can express concentrated and powerful emotions, impassioned and profound veneration. For example, the words "Mon Dieu" are inexpressive and almost devoid of accent in French; the same English words, "My God," are an intense cry, or sigh of aspiration and of solemn anguish. The more I read the "Book of Common Prayer," the more beautiful and appropriate to its purpose do I find it. Whatever be the religion of a country, church is the place to which men come, after six days of mechanical toil, to freshen in themselves the sentiment of the ideal. Such was the Grecian temple under Cymon; such the Gothic cathedral under St. Louis. In accordance with the differences of sentiment, the ceremony and the edifice differ; but the important point is, that the sentiment should be revived and fortified. Now, in my opinion, that occurs here; a lay labourer, a mason, a seamstress who leave this service carry with them noble impressions, suited to the instincts of their race, a vague notion of an august, I know not what, of a superior order, of invisible justice. Moreover, a cultivated man can seat himself beside them; he is not repelled by too base superstitions. No petty decorations, painted images, childish parade, posturings, set marches, and antiquated ceremonies, whereof the congregation have forgotten the meaning. The walls are nearly bare; the hymns and words are in the vulgar tongue; the officiating clergyman does not make genuflexions; his bearing is that of a magistrate; except the surplice, he has the garb of one, and, according to the saying of Joseph de Maistre, he may be defined as a gentleman charged with holding forth worthy discourses to you. The ceremony is a moral gathering, where the chairman speaks in a pulpit, in place of speaking from a platform. Besides, in his discourses as in his worship, dogma is always put in the background; before everything else, the art and will to live rightly are considered. Religion itself, with its emotions and its great vistas, is scarcely anything but the poetry, and the far beyond, of morality; the prolongation into the infinite of a luminous and sublime idea—that of justice. A reflecting mind can accept the whole, at least in guise of symbol. In this fashion, and without renouncing his personal interpretation, he remains in communication and in communion with the simple who are near him. On the fundamental point, which is the moral emotion, all are agreed, and, in consequence, all reunite to surround with assiduous respect, visible and unanimous, the Church and the pastor.

Thus he possesses authority. Note, moreover, that he is a gentleman, frequently by his birth and by his fortune, nearly always by his education. The Bishop of London has £10,000 a year; one of the two Archbishops, £15,000; a certain dignitary of Cambridge, £7,000; the Dean of St. Paul's, £2,000; that of Westminster, £3,000. Literature and science are passports to these high offices; one attains a bishopric through Greek; as was the case of Dr. Thirlwall, author of a very good history of Greece. The average of all the salaries put together and divided by the number of incumbents is £140; generally a cure or living is worth £200 or £300 a year, the smallest are £80; one is said to be worth £10,000. The Lord Chancellor has seven hundred in his gift, the others are in the gift of private persons, inheritors or founders. In addition, and not unfrequently, the incumbents have fortunes of their own. Several good families have a son in holy orders; he brings with him his share in the estate, sometimes a large income, or the fortune of his wife; many pious and well-born girls like to marry a clergyman. In fine, the ecclesiastical profession is a career very similar to that of the magistracy among us, comprising marriage, a serious life, moral pre-occupations, select education, elevated sentiments, but not an ascetic system, a solitary hearth, and passive obedience.

The majority have been at Oxford or Cambridge; those of my acquaintance all read French, and possess a solid foundation of appropriate study, Greek, Latin, mathematics, general instruction. They have read Shakespeare and Tennyson; they are not unacquainted with the different points of view of interpretation, with the history of this Church. One of them gave me particulars about the successive versions of the Prayer-Book, and said that it would have been better to have retained the first. Another was tolerant in the matter of Dissenters, and only blamed the haughty disposition which leads each to form a doctrine for himself. On this subject, witness the tone of their orthodox reviews: it is firm, but not violent. An entire fraction of the Church holds broad views.

Liberals, like Milman, independent investigators, bold commentators, like Stanley, have been thought worthy of the highest posts, Deans in the capital. All that denotes a rather lofty average of education and spirit, very lofty, if we compare it with the corresponding grade in France. As to their manners and externals, they are those of a gentleman, of a gentleman of independent means, if the living be large enough, or if the incumbent have private fortune; besides, a wife always imparts comfort and enjoyment to the house which she manages. Many of them keep horses, a carriage, several servants. In the case of one, his cottage, the small park, the style of the house, were as well looked after as in that of Mr. B——, my entertainer. In that of a second, six miles from this place, the style is not inferior. I know not whether it be accidental or not, but it has never seemed to me that they are prudish in their tone or their manners. Lately, at Venice, I dined at table with a gentleman, his four daughters, and his wife; he was not serious, like most Englishmen; on the third day he told me he was a clergyman, and we went to the theatre together to see *Mary Stuart*. Thus by their ideas, their conduct, their education, their manners, sometimes too by their fortune and their birth, they can mingle with the local aristocracy. They are not peasants with the rust badly rubbed off at college, fed upon antiquated theology, set apart from the world by their profession, their celibacy, their deficiency in experience, but are relatives, equals, men of the same sphere. The clergyman at table alongside the landlord is the director of morals, alongside of the political leader, both of them allied together, are visibly the superiors of those they lead, being accepted by them as such, and are generally worthy of being so accepted

When I walk to the village with the clergyman, he enters the houses, pats the little ones on the head, gets information about their progress, admonishes the bad boys, speaks against drunkenness, chats with the people about their concerns; he is their natural counsellor. His wife teaches the poor children; the indigents come to the parsonage to seek help, a bottle of good wine, some delicacies for a sick person. Another clergyman whom I knew in London, recently took the ragged-school children into the country. There were two thousand of them; it was at once a festival and an autumn procession, with flags, music, &c. They remained away from seven in the morning till the evening; they ate and drank; the cost of the whole was about two hundred pounds, supplied by voluntary contributions. The object was to give a day's pleasure in the open air to these poor little ones who dwell in dirty holes or on the pavement. Spiritual guides and temporal guides; on both sides the superior class fulfils its task; and in local life as in general life, its ascendency is merited and undisputed.

XV.

THE GOVERNING CLASSES AND THE GOVERNMENT.

RETURN to London: I have vainly striven to procure precise information, some figures about the fortunes and number of the persons who compose this disseminated and local aristocracy. In 1841, according to Porter, in England and Wales there were 123,000 males and 322,000 females enjoying an independent fortune, the population was 16,000,000; now, in 1861, it is 20,000,000, and wealth has largely increased. In 1849, the number of persons keeping riding and carriage horses was 140,000, of whom the half kept two horses and upwards. In 1841 the number of persons having male servants was 120,000, of whom the half had two men servants and upwards. Now, my friends tell me, that to keep a horse and a man servant denotes an outlay of £800 to £1,000 a year. I suppose that, in accordance with these figures, the number of rich or well-to-do families of the country may be estimated at about one hundred and twenty thousand.

Observe the supports of such a constitution; it is based on the number, the distribution, the fortune, the antiquity, the capacity, the residence, the probity, the utility, the authority of the entire upper class, one hundred thousand families. All the rest is secondary. For eighty years our publicists have reasoned themselves blind concerning constitutions; 1 know one among the most eminent who would transport that of England or the United States to France, and asks two years only for rendering the nation accustomed to it. One of them said to me, "It is the locomotive; it is enough to bring it across the water, and instantly it will replace the diligence." In fact, nearly all Europe has essayed or adopted the English system—monarchy more or less tempered, Lower House and Upper House, elections, &c. Consider how grotesque the result has been in Greece, lamentable in Spain, fragile in France, uncertain in Austria and in Italy, insufficient in Prussia and in Germany, successful in Holland, in Belgium, and in the Scandinavian States. To import the locomotive is not everything: to make it run, a line is requisite. Or, rather, one ought to put aside all comparisons drawn from mechanical things; the constitution of a State is an organic thing like that of a living body, it pertains to the State alone; another cannot assimilate it, the outside merely can be copied. Underneath institutions, charters, written laws, the official almanack, there are the ideas, the customs, the character, the condition of classes, their respective position, their reciprocal sentiments; in short, a ramified network of deep-seated, invisible roots beneath the visible trunk and foliage. It is they which feed and sustain the tree. Plant the tree without roots, it will languish, and will fall at the first gust. We admire the stability of the English Government; this is due to its being the extremity and natural unfolding of an infinity of living fibres rooted in the soil over all the surface of the country. Suppose a riot like that of Lord Gordon's, but better conducted and fortified by socialistic proclamations; add to this, what is contrary to all probability, a gunpowder plot, the total and sudden destruction of the two Houses and of the Royal Family. Only the peak of the Government would be carried off, the rest would remain intact. In each parish, in each county, there are families around which the others would group themselves; important personages, gentlemen and noblemen, who would take the control and make a beginning, who are followed, who are marked out beforehand by their rank, their fortune, their services, their education, and their influence; born captains and generals who will rally the dispersed soldiers, and instantly re-form the army, quite the opposite of France, where the middle-class citizen and the workman, the noble and the peasant, are distrustful and at variance, where the blouse and the coat rub shoulders with rancour and fear, where the sole chiefs are unknown functionaries, movable, provisional, to whom exterior obedience is paid but not close deference, and who are submitted to without being accepted.

Thus their Government is stable, because they possess natural representatives. It is necessary to reflect in order to feel all the weight of this last word, so simple. What is a representative? To represent a person or a society, great or small, it matters not of what kind, is to *render it present* in a place where it is not, to decide, to order, to do in its stead and for it, that which through absence, ignorance, insufficiency, or any other hindrance, it cannot do except by substituting for its own incompetent will the competent will of its representative. He is like a manager, a proxy, like a captain entrusted with the guidance of a ship, or an engineer employed to construct a bridge. Thus, in public affairs as in private affairs, my true representative is he whose decisions are based on my firm support. Whether that support be manifested or not by a vote matters little; votes, counted suffrages, are simple signs. The essential thing is that the support exists and subsists, written or not, noisy or silent. It is a constant mental state, being an energetic and persistent disposition of the mind and of the heart; here, as in all the moral sciences, it is the *interior* that must be regarded. Now observe that the legal indexes by which this is thought to be determined are not infallible; universal suffrage or any other electoral combination may concentrate on a list or a name the majority of votes, this majority does not prove firm support. Compelled to choose between two lists or two names, about which he has not a decided and personal opinion, an ignorant person has not really made a choice, and nearly all the nation is composed of ignorant persons. The twenty thousand peasants, workmen, members of the lower middle-class, who are led to each urn, go thither like a flock; they do not know the candidates except by hearsay, scarcely by sight. We are acquainted with some who vote at random, and say, "The one's as good as the other." In every case their preference is faint, consequently weak and vacillating. They may abandon, leave the person of their choice, whom they prefer so slightly, in the lurch; hence their government, whatever it may be, wants root. A current of opinion, a street riot may overthrow it, setting up another in its place. The thing done, many will repeat again, "The one's as good as the other." This waning affection is most frequently merely commonplace toleration, and never stiffens into a settled choice. Thus all our establishments, Republic, Empire, Monarchy, are provisional, resembling the great drop-scenes which in turn fill an empty stage, disappearing or reappearing on occasion. We see them descend, reascend, with a sort of indifference. We are inconvenienced on account of the noise, of the dust, of the disagreeable countenances of the hired applauders, but we resign ourselves; for what can we do in the matter? Whoever happen to be our official representatives, in whatever fashion chance or election gives them to us, the public will does not unite itself in a lasting way to their will. They are not our effective and true representatives, and our society does not allow of better ones; let us retain these, lest we meet with worse. The upper class does not supply them, since among us levelling envy accepts but sulkily the rich and the noble. As for the imitation of America and the installation of an intelligent democracy where a mason, a peasant, shall possess an amount of instruction and of political views which are now possessed by a country schoolmaster, a notary, to arrive at that point, will require a century and upwards. Meantime, and as a preparation, one might try the double vote, the first for the Commune, the second for the chief place of the arrondissement; yet these are but distant experiments and dubious expedients.

On the contrary, in a country like this one, the representatives, being natural, are effectives; the support which maintains them is not slippery, but firm. They are really the persons which the public desire to have at the head of affairs, and not others; and it desires them without hesitation, determinately, with a resolution which lasts. Each parish or district is acquainted with those of its choice, a day-labourer distinguishes them as easily as a cultivated man would do. They are like to the five or six large trees of the locality, recognisable by their bearing and circumference; everybody, down to the children, has reclined under their shadow and benefited by their presence. In default of enlightenment and nice discernment, interest, custom, deference, and sometimes gratitude, will suffice to ensure votes for them; for these are holds as tenacious as those of tradition, of sentiment, and of instinct; attachment is the strongest fastening. They are thus marked out for government, and in this respect the written vote or the raised hand does nothing but confirm the tacit assent. Even in the days of rotten boroughs, Parliament then represented the public will. It represents it to-day, although the number of electors is small. It will still represent it ten years hence, should the Reform Bill extend the suffrage.* In my opinion these legislative changes do nothing but perfect details without touching what is fundamental. The important point is always the assent of the public. Now, voters or non-voters, the day-labourer and the shopkeeper wish as a leader a man of the better class. Whether they have or have not the legal means for expressing this approval, and of giving effect to it in the case of this or that individual, it is gained for the class. The leader once elected, whether by them or by others, they faithfully follow him, and by this silent support he becomes their member by a more solid title than among us where their voices are counted.

By a more solid title and also by a better title. For it does not suffice to be appointed leader in order to know how to lead; the election which confers the power does not in any wise confer capacity. A long preparation, special education and studies are required to be a lawyer or an engineer; they are

* This was written before the passing of the last Reform Bill.

required for a stronger reason to constitute a statesman, to vote with discernment upon great public interests, to sift the opportune and the possible, to contemplate the whole from afar, to have a reasoned and valid opinion as to the degree of extension which it is fitting to accord at a given moment to the suffrage, about the transformation which is suited for tenant-right and property in Ireland, about India, about the United States, about the various powers of Europe, about the chances and the future of commerce, of industry, of the finances, and the rest. Success is not attained in these matters by abstract principles, by newspaper phrases, by vague notions brought from college or from a school of law, which among us constitute the ordinary luggage of a politician. Such optical instruments are of no avail, or are deceptive. The advocate's education, the routine of the head of a department, limited, local, and technical experience, add nothing to their reach. It is not thus that extended views are obtained. They are not procured save at great cost. One is bound, in order to procure them, to travel, to know languages, to meet abroad learned men and make political acquaintances, to acquire terms of comparison among foreigners, to mark on the spot foreign manners, institutions, governments, public life, and private life. Many members of Parliament make no other use of their holidays than to proceed to the Continent and institute an inquiry for a fortnight or for six weeks. They come to France, to Spain, to Italy, to Germany, in order to refresh, rectify, deepen their previous impressions, not once, but five, six, and ten times. They wish to keep themselves abreast of what is going on, follow the fluctuations of public opinion. In this manner, their judgment is never behind-hand, and its chances of being correct are increased. Let a black spot form in Denmark, in Poland, at Rome, in the United States; almost immediately they are there, and bring back precise information. Abroad, they get introduced to eminent or special men, invite them to their residences, turn them over and read them like volumes, frequently noting all the details of their conversation, and on their return communicating the manuscript to the persons of their circle. I have read such manuscripts; nothing more instructive. To this information they add inspection of things. One of them goes to our farms, examines the manure, the implements, the cattle, makes a collection of statistics, and, on his return, prints or delivers a series of lectures on the state of agriculture in France. Another one surveys the Paris manufactories, whilst his wife visits the professional schools. Below the statesman, nearly all the rich or merely well-off people do likewise. I know one who, having several children, and making some £500 a year, annually deducts from this moderate income £40 for an excursion. Not one young man of good family does not make the round of the Continent; every complete education includes travels and a residence abroad for a longer or shorter time. During the vacation, barristers, lawyers, professors visit Germany in hundreds. Many observe but the outsides of things; a vessel cannot hold more than its capacity; yet all bring back with them some ideas, or, at the least, notions less false, and prejudices less gross. All this information combined forms a more enlightened public opinion on great subjects, less incompetent in political matters, more sensible, nearer the truth, more open to good counsel. As a consequence, the statesman who has discerned the right path is sustained, encouraged. The crew elects the captain by acclamation; frequently, indeed, opinion seeks him out, and leads him to the helm.

A thing more essential still is that such an education is the surest means for forming him. Spread over the whole upper class, it inevitably descends upon the great spirits as upon the minor spirits of the class. If one of them be well endowed, he does not miscarry for lack of sufficient and appropriate culture; he receives that which develops it, and his talent or his genius attains its full growth. As, moreover, his situation, his fortune, and his connections exempt him from too lengthened an apprenticeship and the petty troubles about money, he can yield his fruits at an early period. Thus it was with the second Pitt, Canning, Sir Robert Peel, Lord Palmerston; at the present day with Mr. Gladstone and Lord Derby. Doubtless it is unfortunate that hereditary riches and premature importance should serve unjustly to crown an entire class, and, in consequence, some rascals, several brutes, and a quantity of mediocrities. But it is at this price that a select few can be formed. The institution resembles a stud; out of one hundred animals you get six good racers; out of a thousand, a racer of the first class. Consider that, without competent chiefs, a State cannot prosper, and that there are cases where, for want of a great man, a State falls; can you pay too dearly for a certain contingent of competent chiefs, and the frequent chance of a great statesman?

XVI.

RAGGED SCHOOLS, HOSPITALS, WORKHOUSES, AND THE VOLUNTEERS.

LET us see the machine at work. The *Edinburgh Review* for July, 1861, says: " It is a distinctive trait of this country, and a trait of which we are proud, that we manage our affairs ourselves, and without the intervention of the State." For example, in twenty-one years, out of £13,200,000 expended in national education, the State has contributed only £4,200,000; the rest has been supplied by subscription. Private societies abound: societies for saving lives from drowning, for the conversion of the Jews, for the propagation of the Gospel, for the advancement of science, for the protection of animals, for the repression of vice, for rendering working men possessors of freeholds, for building good dwellings for them, for producing funds for their savings-banks, for emigration, for the propagation of economic and social knowledge, for the right observance of Sunday, against drunkenness, for founding a school for female teachers, &c. It is sufficient to walk through the streets and turn over the newspapers or reviews, to divine the number and the importance of these institutions. My friends tell me that they are nearly all conducted seriously and conscientiously. The

Englishman does not sever himself from public affairs; they are his affairs; he desires to share in their management. He does not live apart; he considers himself bound to contribute in one way or other to the common good. In like manner, among us an ordinary honest man considers himself bound to go regularly to his office or his counter, there to inspect matters or to labour; he would lose all esteem for himself, he would regard himself as an odd fish, or, what is more, a fool, if he entrusted this to another, if he suffered himself to be put in a bad way, to be duped, to be robbed by a representative.

C—— took me to a meeting for the education and the reform of young vagabonds. The association maintains about one hundred youths from thirteen to twenty, some having been convicted, the others introduced by very poor parents, who place them in charge to prevent them keeping company with rascals, and to hinder them from becoming thieves. They are lodged, they are clothed, they are fed, they are taught a trade (shoemaking, printing, toy and furniture-making, &c.). Those in the second category have the privilege of belonging to a brass band, which plays in the court before the proceedings begin. Their faces are dull, and not very pleasing; they have a special uniform, grey and blue; a penitentiary, even a private one, even well-kept, is never a place of pleasure. The establishment was founded by Mr. Bowyer, a sort of lay St. Vincent de Paul; it bears this name, "Preventive and Reformatory Institution." Contributions are asked from those who enter, and a little pamphlet is handed to them. I there read that "the cost of maintaining each youth in the establishment is on an average about £17 a year, whilst the cost for maintaining each criminal in Holloway Prison is equivalent to a curate's salary (£75), and that the thefts of a London pickpocket are not estimated at anything less than £300 a year." Conclusion: it is more economical to pay here for a young vagabond, than to let him grow up outside. English charity justifies itself by figures.

Fifteen of them leave to-day for Australia, of their own choice; their passage is paid; to-day's meeting is on account of their departure.

They are in the middle of the audience, on three benches, and they listen. Lord ———, member of the Upper House, and a wealthy landed proprietor, is chairman, and opens the meeting. Timid air, small shrill voice, large pointed collar sticking up from a badly-made coat; he has rather the mien of a retired shopkeeper than of a great lord. After some halting phrases, he reads several very proper letters from the youths who have left the institution. One of them, a woodcutter in the virgin forest, thought at first that it would be impossible for him to become used to the solitude; now he labours, without being weary, from the rising to the going down of the sun. Yet he can speak to no one, save for a quarter of an hour to the woman who brings him his food daily.

Another speech, that of an oratorical Bishop, and who makes similar ones every day: "You have been supported here, sheltered from temptations, like plants under glass; this was in order to allow your good instincts time to take root. Now you are about to be transplanted into the open air, left to yourselves; it is necessary that your roots should implant themselves and live. For that do not have confidence in yourselves, but in Jesus Christ, who is your only friend, who will be your help in solitude, amid temptations."

Good delivery, paternal and grave, without emphasis or book phrases; he adapted his language to the listening minds. Besides, the Protestant religion is efficacious in such a case; the Bible of Robinson Crusoe is the companion of the squatter alone amidst desert woods.

Third speech by Mr. S——, a member of the House of Commons, who especially addressed himself to the audience. During an experience of twenty-five years he has verified the extreme usefulness of transplantation; in the first place, because it removes the youths from the contagion of bad example; next, and above all, because it induces the development of English qualities—energy, habits of self-reliance, fondness for striving, all the inclinations which, having no outlets on the London pavement, are turned at home against society and in favour of evil. Good reasoning, very pertinent, free from rhetoric; that is rare in France. He ended by proposing thanks to the Bishop, and the whole audience, the ladies and the young girls too, raised their hands to vote the thanks.

Thence we went to visit a ragged-school. This is a large brick building, in which the rooms are very airy and well-kept; I silently contrasted them with the narrow chambers of a corresponding school in Paris. Unfortunately they were empty; the children had a holiday to-day, and the friend who brought me was obliged to go away. He said, "That does not matter; there is another ragged-school close by, in Brook Street; go and see it." "All alone, without introduction?" "Certainly, and they will be very polite." I went thither, and, in fact, a gentleman who was about to leave, made me enter, introduced me to the master, and conducted me through the whole establishment, which is very complete, and, in addition to the school, includes a nursery, an asylum, workshops, &c.; on the upper floor, dormitories for the elder ones. During the day, the beds are turned against the wall; during the night, by means of machinery it would take too long to explain, they can be isolated and carefully watched.

In the shops, the young boys worked at basket-making, at preparing small wooden models for drawing-schools; they were made to sing, close up, march before me. Assuredly it is right to occupy and instruct them in this way; for their faces are disquieting, and resemble those of young prisoners. The large room for the very young children was nearly full, and yet had no bad smell. Nearly all had shoes, and they were not too ragged. Several little girls held a suckling in their arms. The most skilful and docile of the band are monitors over the others; they receive a few pence weekly. Every one is taught to read, to write, to reckon, to sing, to go through drill. The mistress teaches sewing to the girls; she is a young and pretty person, full of spirit, good humoured, whose joyous mien and cordial manners are excellent in such a place; she earns twelve shillings a week, and the master twenty-five. In my opinion, an establishment like this, especially in a poor neighbourhood, is a moral disinfecting apparatus; indeed, documents show that in London the numbers of the youthful delinquents, which were 10,194 in 1856, had fallen to 7,850 in 1866. It is calculated there are twenty-five thousand children in the London ragged-schools, three hundred thousand in those of all England. Three among them alone are aided by the Government; all the others are entirely supported by private persons. They feel that the school, like the police, and better than the police, contributes to the security of the streets.

Conversations in the evening about various analogous societies; too many were named to me, I can but mention some of them. An establishment has been founded, a sort of club, where governesses, ladies of good character, having good certificates vouching for them, can find, when they come to London to make purchases or to give lessons, a dinner, fire, a library, tea, persons of their acquaintance. Another private establishment contains about eighty poor young women; this is to remove them from temptations; they are furnished with work, and, besides, living in common is less expensive. The cost for each of them is about ten pounds a year. There is a society for selling Bibles; they are sold instead of being distributed, because, if given away, they would not be valued. The ladies of the association, being too far apart from the people, had no hold over them; they devised as intermediaries poor, honest, zealous women who act as their representatives, carry the Bible into the worst neighbourhoods, make friends with the working men's wives, assemble them in a room at night, teach them sewing, housekeeping, &c. At this moment, an hundred of these Bible-women are on duty; one of them, last year, sold 419 Bibles and 501 New Testaments. Temperance associations; there are some throughout all England. I recently saw, in the street, young wives who belonged to these societies; there were ten carriages; they were going to a meeting. They pledge themselves never to drink spirits; some of them through scruples have refused to take the potion prescribed by the doctor, or even the sacramental wine. A placard intimates that the "Total Abstinence Association" will hold its meeting at a certain place, and gives the programme of the proceedings: several bands of music, tea at four o'clock, walking in the park, exhibition of a collection of carpets, divine service in a pretty church, speeches by the principal members, admission at reduced prices for the members of all the temperance associations. This absurd mixture of purposes and opposite attractions is truly English. Many of these societies correspond or act in concert; for example, most of the mechanics' institutes and the ragged-schools are in combination with a savings-bank; this is to teach saving and its advantages to children and young people. When one of these societies is important, it has its journal, its review, magazine, its special publications: that is the case in the Wesleyan Association, the Ragged-Schools Union, the Society for the Diffusion of Social Science, the large society which multiplies and distributes Bibles, &c. I do not speak of the leagues which have for object some legal reform, which are transitory like their object; the most celebrated of these was the Anti-Corn Law League, of which Cobden was the chief. Details concerning it will be found in the works of our Bastiat: enormous subscriptions, meetings, itinerant lecturers, public lectures, small popular tracts, big learned works, a universal and incessant propaganda; the machine is admirable for rousing and altering opinion. Here, let a man have a good idea; he communicates it to his friends; many of them think it good. Together they find the money, publish it, solicit support and subscriptions. Sympathy and subscriptions flow in, publicity increases. The snow-ball goes on increasing, strikes against the door of Parliament, pushes it partly open, and ends by opening or breaking through it. Such is the mechanism of reforms; it is thus that one performs one's work oneself, and it must be said that over all the soil of England there are pellets of snow on the way to become balls. Many break the one against the other, or melt by the way; but new ones are always being formed out of their fragments, and to see the human ant-heaps determined to push them along is a fine spectacle.

To explain this zeal, we find the following reasons: 1. The Englishman has need of action; when he has done his own business, a surplus of energy remains which is expended in public affairs. Besides, many persons being independent, and possessing leisure, have no other outlet; it is the same need of action which produces their travels and a quantity of painful enterprises; for example, Miss Nightingale was neither a devotee nor a mystic after the manner of a Sister of Charity, when she went to organise the hospitals in the Crimea; her whole incentive consisted in the idea of humanity and a very active mind. 2. The Englishman is rich, and, in addition, when he provides for the future, it is in another way than the Frenchman—by his expenses, not by his savings. For instance, he prefers to leave less to his children, and to give them a better education; he consents to work an extra hour daily in order not to forego an excursion. Owing to the same motive, he can give, and he gives willingly, a portion of his time and of his means to consolidate and improve the society which protects him and will protect his property. A man who rightly understands his interests upholds the roofs of the great national mansion as carefully as those of his private house. 3. By tradition, the antiquity of self-government, the diffusion of economic knowledge. The Englishman is accustomed to look far into political and social matters; he knows the inconveniences of an unmended roof, the effect of water coming through, the danger of a rotten beam. Being sensible, reflecting, docile to rational reasoning, he inspects his rafters and tiles every morning, he pays the slater without hesitation. 4. He can, without wearying, perform all wearisome things, attend meetings, examine accounts, &c. He has less need of amusement than a Frenchman.

Visit to St. Bartholomew's Hospital. It has an income of £40,000, in addition to special donations. A number of hospitals bear the inscription "Supported by public subscription." The council meets once a week; the treasurer, so burdened with work, is not paid. Six hundred patients; eight hundred could be accommodated. The edifice is very vast, and includes a library, collections, an anatomical museum. The young doctor who took me over it, and had lived in France, said to me that here a student can see the patients all day, and that among us, if he be not an intern or extern, he cannot visit them after ten o'clock in the morning. The beds are separated by a distance of five or six feet, and are much more roomy than in France. Perfect cleanliness; everything seems to be well appointed and kept; enormous kitchen, where all is cooked by gas; a spacious room is arranged as a larder. In addition to the female attendants, there are nurses who superintend them, who had themselves been female attendants, all of them being generally of mature age and respectable; they do not watch. They get from fifteen to twenty shillings a week; they are not found in food. They may be hired, like our Sisters of Charity; hence the lay conscience can replace religious fervour.

Many fractures, and a quantity of very ingenious apparatus for supporting the limb, for supporting it so that the air circulates, allowing it certain movements without detriment to the formation of callus. But above all, a quantity of coxalgia, nervous affections, scrofula, attributable to impurities in the blood, to bad nourishment, to the impoverishment of the human substance. The pallid, dilapidated, exhausted faces are lamentable. The young doctor admits that an excess of labour and of gin in England enormously multiplies idiots and lunatics. The patients here do not dream of paying in order to escape dissection, which is their great preoccupation among us; the use made of their bodies is concealed from them; besides, they are stupefied, worn out. So is it with the street girls; a French mind is more elastic, and retains its spring longer.

The doctor put me into the hands of a clergyman who was one of his friends, a philanthropist, and an instructed man, who took me to St. Luke's Workhouse. Everybody knows that a workhouse is an asylum a little like a prison: in conjunction with the poor-rates, it forms one of the distinctive traits of the English constitution. It is an English principle that the indigent, by giving up their freedom, have a right to be supported. Society pays the cost, but shuts them up and sets them to work. As this condition is repugnant to them, they avoid the workhouse as much as possible.

This one contains at present five to six hundred old people, children who have been deserted or who have no resources, men and women out of employment. The last class is the least numerous, thirty or forty women and a dozen of men; in winter there will be more of them. In addition, the establishment gives out-door relief and at home; this week it assisted in that way 1,011 persons. Within doors the outlay by the head is three or four shillings a week.

We went over sixty to eighty rooms, chambers, and compartments; washhouse, brewery, bakehouse, shops for carpentering, for shoemaking, for oakum-picking, nursery for all the young infants, school for girls, rooms for the old men, rooms for the old women, rooms for the sick women, rooms for confinements, rooms for sick men, for sick children, for lunatics; dormitories, refectories, parlours, places for taking exercise, &c. All seems sufficiently clean and healthy, but it appears that other workhouses would be much finer specimens. The children sing out of tune, but look very well. As for the lunatics, the sick, the aged, I find them to be, as I always do, more worn-out than in Italy or in France; the human toiler is more pitiable in Holland, in Germany, in England, than in the Latin countries. However, I consider them well enough cared for; three meals a day; meat three times weekly, and daily for the sick; excellent bread; the kitchen and the provisions have a comfortable appearance. The sheets are changed every fortnight. The rooms are airy, and there is a fire in each of them. The old people get tea, sugar, some newspapers. Here and there one observes a book of natural history, of piety or morality, *Chambers's Journal*, a Bible, and upon the walls, texts out of the Scriptures. Touching detail, on the table is a pot of fresh flowers. But it would require here a specialist who had time to make a stay, and I am only a curious inquirer who passes by. I have seen enough, however, to feel how much this society occupies itself about its poor. With regard to workhouses and useful institutions the public mind is always kept on the alert by collateral associations, by newspapers and reviews, and even by romances, which then become the summaries of inquiries, and the means of popularising them. I have read some about prisons and prison life; all that serves a purpose. For example, last week Pentonville was shown to me, a prison of probation, where the convicts remain nine months before being transported, and, according to the character of their behaviour, obtain a greater or lesser reduction of their punishment. This is an admirable iron hive, so ingeniously constructed and arranged, that it might be placed in an exhibition among model machines.

This afternoon, I received tickets for the review of the volunteers, another spontaneous, free institution, and based upon the love and understanding of the public good. "In the event of invasion, England will not have soldiers enough. Let us supply the soldiers, to wit, ourselves, and soldiers equipped, embodied, drilled." Following this reasoning, they have enrolled, clothed, armed themselves at their own cost, without intervention or help from the central power, and in six months they numbered one hundred and thirty thousand, and they count upon reaching two hundred thousand. A painter and a barrister among my friends are, the one a private, the other a captain. On an average they drill for an hour and a half daily. For some time back, in addition to the morning's hour and a half, they have had three hours' drill in the afternoon as preparation for the grand review. Often they get wet, but they joke about their fatigues. A Crimean officer whom I know says that they are already sufficiently taught to begin a campaign.

Private subscriptions have flowed in; the great help the small; the Duke of —————— has despatched to the review, by special train, two thousand of his miners. Nearly all the rich or well-to-do young men have put their names down; their club bears the title "For Hearth and Home," and the ladies encourage them.

It is in Hyde Park that the evolutions take place. An immense stand surrounds the enclosure; around, the windows of the houses are crowded with spectators, even the roofs are covered; boys have climbed the trees, and hang there in clusters, singing with a sharp voice. The Horse Guards keep the ground, and the Queen in her carriage is welcomed with loud hurrahs. As far as can be seen red uniforms stand out upon the verdure, and at last is seen the grey line of the new militia. As well as I can judge they go through their movements well; at all events, they are equipped in a practical manner, without luxury or frippery, not to make a show, but to do work. What this institution has given rise to in the shape of meetings, discussions, letters published in the newspapers cannot be described; to me it is clear that self-government, among other advantages, has the privilege of bringing into play at every moment all the thinking faculties of the nation.

XVII.

THE CONSTITUTION. THE HOUSES OF PARLIAMENT.

THE better I become informed and the more I reflect, the more it seems to me that the mainspring of this government is not this or that institution, but certain very energetic and very widely diffused sentiments. If it be solid and is upheld, it is because of the universal and profound respect entertained for several things. If it be active and advanced, it is because, these things excepted, all the rest is thrown open to individual discussion, control, and initiative.

One of my friends knew Vincent, a journeyman-printer, whom the trades-unions sent during the elections to harangue the people. Vincent summarised his oratorical experiences thus: "I can utter all that comes into my head, attack it matters not whom or what, except the Queen and Christianity; if I spoke against them my hearers would throw stones at me." In addition to these two inviolable sanctuaries, public respect covers, though in a lesser degree, the two great edifices whereof they are the centre. Christianity is respected, so is the Church, the clergy, the pastor. The Queen is respected, so is the Constitution, the hierarchy, the nobility, the gentry. Doubtless, many working men are secularists, imbued with doc

THE CONSTITUTION.

trines analogous to those of M. Comte, irritated at the monstrous inequality between profits and fortunes. But, on the whole, the nation is conservative, and lends itself to reform without yielding itself to revolution.

Classes are not divided among themselves as in France; there is no unexpected blow to be dreaded, neither from on high, on the part of the throne, nor from beneath on the part of the street; there are no available and spare systems which any one dreams of substituting for the existing system. Every one is agreed about the whole, and before the law each one bows the head. Out of an hundred examples in proof of this, I shall cite two from both ends of the ladder. The Queen and the late Prince Consort confined themselves to their parts as constitutional rulers, and never dreamed of overstepping them; they consented to be merely simple moderators, to follow the bent of Parliament and of opinion. They had no party in Parliament, they never intrigued against a minister, not even against him whose person and whose ideas were distasteful to them, they loyally supported him to the very end. On the other hand, here is a street scene which was narrated to me by one of my friends who came from Manchester. A girl in a rage had thrown a stone through a pane of glass, a policeman arrives, takes her gently by the arm, and persuades her to go with him to the station, "Come along with me, don't resist, you will only be locked up for the night." She refuses, sits down on the pavement, then lies down, saying, "Drag me if you like." A crowd gathers, all her companions come and advise her. "Go then, Mary, my girl, don't be quarrelsome; go with him, you were in the wrong." The policeman calls his companions,

Mary is carried off; neither tumult nor outcries, no one resisted; it was felt reasonable to obey the law. My friend added that here when a man who is arrested begins to argue, the onlookers make inquiries, and that should they find the policeman in the right, they give him their help. It is the same in case of outbreaks, every class supplies volunteer constables. In short, they support their government, and we submit to ours.

An establishment so firmly based can bear attacks: speeches, meetings, leagues, will not overturn it. Consequently, criticism has the right to be continuous, energetic, and even violent. The solidity of the Constitution authorises full freedom of control. Indeed, this control is exercised without ceasing and without sparing; every home or foreign question is probed to the bottom in fifty articles, handled and turned over in every sense, with a force of reasoning and an abundance of evidence which one cannot help admiring.

To estimate this it is necessary to read the principal journals during several months: *The Times, The Saturday Review, The Daily News, The Standard,* and the political or economic section of the great quarterlies. Very often they attain high eloquence : good sense and manly reason, complete information, verified and drawn from the best sources, entire frankness carried to the verge of rudeness, the lofty and hard tone of militant conviction, cold and prolonged irony, the vehemence of concentrated and reflective passion ; indignation and scorn well from the fountain-head in a full stream. A similar polemic among us would infallibly end in duels and in risings. Here, the coolness of the temperament modifies the too hasty impression. It is admitted that invective, even when personal, does not extinguish a politician, and that no one should fight about a sheet of inked paper. It is understood that the clamour and tocsin of the Press never terminate in the taking up of arms, but only in meetings, in protests, and in petitions. The day of my arrival in London, I saw board-men in the streets carrying placards before and behind with the following phrases on them: " Great usurpation of the rights of the people The Lords add four hundred and fifty thousand pounds to the budget without the nation's consent." (They had made this addition by altering the budget voted by the House of Commons.) " Fellow countrymen, petition." Some days afterwards, being in a distant neighbourhood, at Clerkenwell, I read in a local journal the announcement of a meeting on that subject. Nothing more; but this open speaking and these perpetual meetings suffice. It may be said that, by newspapers and by meetings, one great universal Parliament and many minor parliaments disseminated over the country, prepare, control, and complete the task of the two Houses.

We proceed to the Houses of Parliament; as a whole the architecture constantly repeats a rather poor idea and does not show great invention, it has the merit of being neither Grecian nor Southern; it is Gothic, accommodated to the climate, to the requirements of the eye. The palace magnificently mirrors itself in the shining river; in the distance, its clock-tower, its legions of turrets and of carvings are vaguely outlined in the mist. Leaping and twisted lines, complicated mouldings, trefoils and rose-windows diversify the enormous mass which covers four acres, and produces on the mind the idea of a tangled forest. In default of genius, the architects have had good sense;

they have recalled the Flemish town-halls, the lofty chapter rooms, alone capable, by the variety, by the elegance, by the audacity, by the delicacy, and multiplicity of their forms, to satisfy northern minds and modern minds. One of these halls, Westminster Hall, which serves for great State trials, is immense and of the greatest beauty. One hundred and ten feet in height, two hundred and ninety in length, sixty-eight feet in breadth; the rough wooden ceiling which overhangs and sustains the roof, dates, it is said, from the eleventh century. In all the other chambers, carved wainscoting eight feet high covers the walls with its dun facing; above is gilded leather, red and brown hangings, stained glass; from the ceiling descend lamps suspended from lustrous chains. The effect of the whole is rich and grave; for want of sun and light, they have recourse to colour like Rembrandt, to the contrast of light projections and sombre recesses, to the power of red and black tones, to the gleaming of leather and wainscoting, to glass which exaggerates and diversifies the daylight.

The Lords' chamber is fine, comfortable, and well-adapted for its purpose. Seats in red leather, deep and rich wainscoting, Gothic gilding in dull gold; an impression of serious opulence is produced by this. The members present are not numerous; I was told there are sometimes five or six; save on great political occasions they stay away; besides, discussion is frequently useless, each vote being known before hand. The leading members were named to me, and I heard enormous fortunes mentioned, the largest are £300,000 a-year. The Duke of Bedford has an income from landed property of £220,000; the Duke of Richmond has 300,000 acres in one holding; the Marquis of

Westminster, proprietor of a district of London, will have a revenue of £1,000,000 on the expiration of the long leases The Marquis of Breadalbane, it is said, can ride on horseback for thirty leagues in a straight line without quitting his estate; the Duke of Sutherland possesses an entire shire of that name in the north of Scotland. Three Bishops in white surplices occupy their places. But the outsides of the assembly are scarcely imposing. One peer has the face of an old diplomatic machine, another that of an amiable and worn-out librarian; the minister who rises resembles an intelligent attorney. Some young peers are dandies and have their hair parted in the middle; others, hugely bearded, remind one of commercial travellers. Lord C—— alone has the fatigued, penetrating, and fine physiognomy of an artist. Their ways are very simple; they might be called ordinary men at their club; they keep their tall chimney-pot hats on their heads, speak from their places, without fuss, in a conversational tone. This absence of stiffness is excellent; an embroidered uniform like that of our senators or of our peers is a pomp and a superfluity which re-acts within from without and renders the thought as artificial as the appearance. These persons do business and do not make phrases.

In the House of Commons from ten o'clock till midnight. There is still greater freedom from constraint; the House is full, and all have their hats on their heads; some wear them far back and pressed down. Several wear white hats, fancy trousers and coat, are leaning back, half-lying on their seats, one of them is entirely lolling on his, and two or three are rather free and easy. They enter, go out, talk with a wearied and unceremonious air; certainly a club in which one were to behave in this style would be moderately respectable.

The ministers were pointed out to me—Lord Palmerston, Mr. Milner Gibson, Lord John Russell, Sir Charles Wood, Mr. Gladstone. Alongside of us, in the gallery, several members of the Upper House came and seated themselves, one young immensely rich duke, all had bad cravats, and he had a shabby coat. Below us there is silence. The members, tightly packed on their benches, have not even a desk on which to write. They take notes upon their knees, drink a glass of water which they afterwards put on their seat. Each one speaks standing in his place, in a natural tone and with few gestures. Certainly a chamber arranged in this way, and so narrow, is incommodious, and even unhealthy, too warm in summer and for the night sittings; a man must be quickly worn out there. But this simplicity denotes a business-like people, who suppress ceremonial in order to get through their task. On the contrary, a raised tribune, isolated like that of our Legislative Assembly, leads to theatrical eloquence.

The business of the day related to the encroachment of the Lords, who had voted a money bill without the assent of the Commons; the debate, it is said, is one of the most important of the year; the House is full and attentive. After Mr. Seymour, Mr. Horsman rises. Very distinct pronunciation, a perfectly just and convinced tone, energy without emphasis. His thesis is that the Lords are not a body of simple, privileged personages; though not elected, they represent the people. They are country gentlemen, like the others, holding lands and shares like the others, having the same interests, the same education, the same ideas, being as well situated as themselves to decide about the common interests. Election is but one means only for naming the representatives of the nation; there were others, for example the possession of a certain dignity, which is the case of the Bishops, inheritance, which is the case of the Queen and of the lay Lords. Besides, since 1832, the Commons have had a marked preponderance; the control of a second body is required, without which they would fall into pure democracy, &c. Rather long, he repeated himself; however, he made an impression; cries of "hear, hear" arose at nearly every sentence. After him, and in the opposite sense, spoke Mr. Bright, an accomplished orator. But I had seen too many things these days; my nerves are not as strong as those of a member of Parliament, and I left the House.

How do they get admitted to it? B———, who has an important place in the Government, nevertheless avows that the electoral machinery is rude, often foul. The candidate hires an hotel or a tavern, there keeps open table, hangs out flags, pays for drink, brings the electors in carriages, hires musicians, roughs, election agents, tap-room orators who make speeches in his behalf, sometimes prize-fighters who use their fists and throw apples at his opponent. The scene is tumultuous, often brutal; the popular bull feels himself half loosened. It is admitted that an election is costly; Parliament allows certain expenses, and does not think there has been corruption so long as these are below a certain figure—four or five hundred pounds. For this purpose a party can raise funds; the Duke of Buccleuch was cited to me as having once sent forty thousand pounds sterling for the election expenses of his party. But, beyond the authorised expenses, there are others greater still. It is estimated that an election costs often four, five, six thousand pounds sterling and upwards. To induce the elector to trouble himself by coming to vote, something of a positive kind must be given him—a place, the promise of a place, several good dinners, unlimited ale and wine, sometimes cash down. The result of an inquiry was to show that Mr. X——, at Z——, had paid £30 for one vote, and £40 for another; a third elector, desiring to cloak his doings, sold to him a hair-brush for £40, which was worth 3s. The legal expenses of this election were £461, and the secret ones £3,700. At another election, the electoral agent, seated in one room, received the electors, agreed as to the price, made them go into another room, where a second agent paid them the sum agreed upon; the bargain and the payment being thus separated, each agent could declare that he had never performed the twofold operation called bribery. But painters alone know how to give the life-like details; on this subject read the account of two elections, the one by Thackeray in the "Newcomes," the other by George Eliot in "Felix Holt the Radical." On the whole, local influence is the great prime-mover, and is chiefly based upon the ownership of the soil and upon wealth, upon antiquity of residence and of the family, upon the extent of the patronage exercised, upon the notoriety and the social position of the candidate. After all I have seen of the upper class, it seems to me that these roots are good, healthy, living, despite the mud and worms among which they spread themselves like every human plant, although it will still require much drainage to purify the mud, much supervision to destroy the worms.

The machine works well. It does not break down,

nor does it threaten to break down. It operates, and, in addition, it accommodates itself to the times, renewing its wheels. More than that, by the way in which it operates, one feels that it is capable of thorough renovation. It will perhaps be able later to permit of the indefinite extension of the suffrage, the diminution of the prerogatives of the Lords, the suppression of the monopoly of the Church; all that without outbreak or dislocation, by a gradual, careful adaptation of the ancient parts to new uses. The governing classes are becoming informed, they take soundings at every moment to measure and ascertain the direction of the popular currents, they have an exact notion of what is necessary and possible. I was present lately at a sitting of a committee of the House; the business was to decide whether the British Museum, which is at once a library, a museum, and a collection of natural history, should continue as it is, or whether a portion of it should be removed to another locality. Seven or eight members were before a table in a lofty room which was open to the public. They questioned men of special knowledge; the first the secretary of a natural history society, then the Crown Architect, then the Director of the South Kensington Museum, and others besides; meanwhile they took notes. The tone was simple, moderate, sometimes there were smiles; the proceedings might be called an instructive conversation; in fact, it was nothing else. The questions were exceedingly minute and precise, relating to the way of arranging collections of animals, to the number of specimens possessed, to the advantage of exhibiting together the male, the female and the young, to the number of visitors, to their age and condition, to the days when they were most numerous, to the number of square feet contained in the building, to the interior arrangements, &c. This is how one obtains information, by inquiry and counter-inquiry, with figures, details, certainty, acquisition of positive and applicable evidence. Recently Lord Derby made a speech about India, conceived in the like spirit, wholly founded upon the statements and decisions of generals and administrators of the country, textually cited, so that this speech summarised the experience of thirty or forty eminent and competent lives. What a guide and what a corrective is experience! How much good sense is needed to trust to it alone! How much art and care are wanted to face it, repeat it, limit it, rectify it, rightly apply it! And how far off are we from this good political education!

XVIII.

THE CLUBS, THE BRITISH MUSEUM, THE CRYSTAL PALACE.

I HAVE been elected member of the Athenæum Club for a month. This club is a select and central place of meeting, where one can dine and study. It is almost a palace, and is surrounded by similar palaces, reminding one of our Place Louis XV. It has a peristyle, looks upon a garden, and has very spacious rooms. The servants in livery are numerous, attentive, quiet. Every modern and desirable luxury is found there. The library contains 40,000 volumes; the reading-room is splendid, containing all the reviews, in all languages; every new publication; easy-chairs, as comfortable in summer as in winter. At night, sun-burners in the ceiling diffuse a subdued light over the sombre woodwork. Every want is provided for; all the senses are soothed by a multitude of trifling attentions due to skilful, comprehensive, and perfect forethought. Close at hand is another place—the Travellers' Club—of a similar character. How well they know how to organise comfort! Yesterday evening I read in the Athenæum Club an essay by Macaulay, who names Galileo, Locke, and Bentham, as the three originators of the greatest modern ideas; instead of great, put fruitful, and the paradox becomes a manifest truth. It is by recourse to experience, it is by the liking for fact and minute observation, it is by the advent and reign of induction, that man has been able to become master of Nature, to reform society, to ameliorate his condition, to adjust things to his wants, to establish a society, the institutions, the masterpieces of good arrangement and of ordered comfort, such as I enjoy at this moment.

I have letters of introduction and a ticket of admission to the British Museum. About the Grecian marbles, the original Italian drawings, about the National Gallery, the Hampton Court galleries, the pictures at Buckingham Palace and Windsor Castle, and the private collections, I shall say nothing. Still, what marvels and what historical tokens are all these things, five or six specimens of high civilisation manifested in a perfect art, all differing greatly from that which I now examine, and so well adapted for bringing into relief the good and the evil. To do that would fill a volume by itself. The Museum library contains six hundred thousand volumes; the reading-room is vast, circular in form, and covered with a cupola, so that no one is far from the central office, and no one has the light in his eyes. All the lower stage of shelves is filled with works of reference—dictionaries, collections of biographies, classics of all sorts—which can be consulted on the spot, and are excellently arranged. Moreover, a small plan placed on each table indicates where they are placed and the order in which they stand. Each seat is isolated; there is nothing in front but the woodwork of the desk, so that no one is annoyed by the presence of his neighbour. The seats and the tables are covered with leather, and are very clean; there are two pens to each desk, the one being a steel, the other a quill pen;

there is also a small stand at the side, upon which a second volume, or the volume from which extracts are being copied, may be placed. To procure a book, the title is written on a form, which is handed to the central office; the attendant brings the book to you himself, and does so without delay: I have made trial of this, even in the case of works seldom asked for. The holder of the book is responsible till he has received back the form filled up when he applied for it. For ladies a place is reserved, which is a delicate piece of attention. What a contrast if we compare this with our great library at the Louvre, with its long room, with half of the readers dazzled by the light in their eyes, the readers being packed together at a common table, the titles of the books being called out in loud tones, the long time spent in waiting at the central office. The French Library has been reformed according to the English model, yet without being rendered as convenient. Nevertheless, ours is the more liberally conducted; its doors are open to all comers. Here one must be a "respectable" person; no one is admitted unless vouched for by two householders. This is said to be enough; as it is, those gain admission who are worse than shabby—men in working clothes, and some without shoes; they have been introduced by clergymen. The grant for buying new books is seven or eight times larger than ours. When shall we learn to spend our money in a sensible way?

In other matters they are not so successful, such as the Crystal Palace at Sydenham, for instance, which formed the building for the Great Exhibition, and which is now a sort of museum of curiosities. It is gigantic, like London itself, and like so many things in London, but how can I pourtray the gigantic? All the ordinary sensations produced by size are intensified several times here. It is two miles in circumference and has three stories of prodigious height; it would easily hold five or six buildings like our Palace of Industry, and it is of glass; it consists first of an immense rectangular structure rising towards the centre in a semicircle like a hothouse, and flanked by two Chinese towers; then, on either side, long buildings descend at right angles, enclosing the garden with its fountains, statues, summer-houses, strips of turf, groups of large trees, exotic plants, and beds of flowers. The acres of glass sparkle in the sunlight; at the horizon an undulating line of green eminences is bathed in the luminous vapour which softens all colours and spreads an expression of tender beauty over an entire landscape. Always the same English method of decoration—on the one side a park and natural embellishments, which it must be granted are beautiful and adapted to the climate; on the other the building, which is a monstrous jumble, wanting in style, and bearing witness not to taste but to English power. The interior consists of a museum of antiquities, composed of plaster facsimiles of all the Grecian and Roman statues scattered over Europe; of a museum of the Middle Ages; of a Revival museum; of an Egyptian museum; of a Nineveh museum; of an Indian museum; of a reproduction of a Pompeian house; of a reproduction of the Alhambra. The ornaments of the Alhambra have been moulded, and these moulds are preserved in an adjoining room as proofs of authenticity. In order to omit nothing, copies have been made of the most notable Italian paintings, and these are daubs worthy of a country fair. There is a huge tropical hot-house, wherein are fountains swimming turtles, large aquatic plants in flower, the Sphinx and Egyptian statues sixty feet high, specimens of colossal or rare trees, among others the bark of a Sequoia California 450 feet in height and measuring 116 feet in circumference. The bark is arranged and fastened to an inner framework in such a manner as to give an idea of the tree itself. There is a circular concert room, with tiers of benches as in a Coliseum. Lastly, in the gardens are to be seen life-size reproductions of antediluvian monsters, megatheriums, deinotheriums, and others. In these gardens Blondin does his tricks at the height of a hundred feet. I pass over half the things; but does not this conglomeration of odds and ends carrry back one's thoughts to the Rome of Cæsar and the Antonines? At that period, also, pleasure-palaces were erected for the sovereign people; circuses, theatres, baths wherein were collected statues, paintings, animals, musicians, acrobats, all the treasures and all the oddities of the world; pantheons of opulence and curiosity; genuine bazaars where the liking for what was novel, heterogeneous, and fantastic ousted the feeling of appreciation for simple beauty. In truth, Rome enriched herself with these things by conquest, England by industry. Thus it is that at Rome the paintings, the statues, were stolen originals, and the monsters, whether rhinoceroses or lions, were perfectly alive and tore human beings to pieces; whereas here the statues are made of plaster and the monsters of goldbeater's skin. The spectacle is one of the second class, but of the same kind. A Greek would not have regarded it with satisfaction; he would have considered it appropriate to powerful barbarians who, trying to become refined, had utterly failed.

XIX.

STREET PREACHERS AND RELIGIOUS SENTIMENTS.

LAST Sunday and the preceding Sunday open-air preachers, with their Bibles and umbrellas, were plying their mission in Hyde Park; these were laymen who felt impelled to communicate their religious impressions to the public. On another Sunday I saw two men in frock coats and black hats singing psalms on the green of a village forty miles from London. I was told this was no uncommon sight, especially when the afternoon sermon had been good, as the hearers brought away with them overplus of fervour which required vent. They had long lean bodies, nasal voices, upturned eyes; they were surrounded by twenty persons improving themselves by the performance. Zeal is very keen, particularly among the Dissenters; their youths have duties assigned to them; one occupies himself on Sunday in distributing tracts at an appointed corner; another holds a meeting of bargemen on Thursday, and expounds the Bible to them. Even at the present day female Methodist preachers may be heard; it is said that one of the most notable authoresses of the age began life in this vocation. In Paris itself we sometimes experience the operation of this eccentric form of piety. For instance, the Rev. Reginald ——

advertised his sermons with the invitation printed in large type, "Come to Jesus." Indeed, the maxim of this sect is that the most hardened sinner may be instantaneously converted by an act of grace. The Rev. Reginald —— ascended the pulpit, gave out his text, and then presented one of his flock, a healthy and stout young man, as an example and visible token of success. The latter opened his lips and said, "Yes, my brethren, I have been a vile sinner; but the grace of God has touched me," &c., &c. This is a truly English method of procedure; it consists in producing the document, the tangible proof, the living specimen, after the fashion of a zoologist, to uphold a spiritual doctrine.

Another Sunday, at eight o'clock in the evening, in a University town, I saw two gentlemen and a member of the middle class preaching in the public highway. They do this every Sunday. The first, a young man of twenty, is openly affected, tries to conquer his bashfulness, uses much gesticulation. He says, "Jesus Christ came for sinners like us, he took pity upon us, miserable sinners," &c. After this beginning the second opens his Bible and reads a passage about the inhabitants of Jerusalem besieged and famished by the King of Assyria; the latter being terrified by the Angel of the Lord, precipitately retreats; two lepers who were the first to venture without the walls, find the tents filled with provisions, and eat and drink with delight. This is typical of the Christian who has but to rid himself of sin to find entire satisfaction in the Lord. Christ is our consolation, our asylum, our protector. In relation to this a story was told of a sailor going to sea, who replied to a gentleman speaking about the risk he ran, "It is true that my father was drowned, that my brother was drowned, and that my grandfather was drowned also." "Then, why do you go to sea?" "Sir, where did your father die?" "In his bed." "And your grandfather?" "In his bed." "And your other relations?" "In their beds." "Yet you are not afraid to lie down in bed, and with good reason. For a Christian, whether on sea or land, the only assurance is to know Christ." The last of the three—a thin young man, lantern-jawed, and with a grating voice —appeared moved by the spirit; but, as his theme was the same, I went off at the end of a quarter of an hour. The audience consisted of about fifty persons, men and women, well-dressed for the most part; at intervals some of them whispered and smiled ironically, but the majority of the men and all the women listened attentively, and appeared to be edified. I heartily approve of these proceedings. In the first place they provide a vent for a consuming passion, for an intense conviction which for lack of an outlet would degenerate into madness, melancholy, or sedition. In the second, they are moralising and may do much good to many consciences. In the third, they keep alive among the public the belief that there are noble ideas, genuine convictions, perfectly zealous souls; for man is only too ready to fancy that indifference and amusement are the end of life.

These are relics of the old Puritan spirit, the stunted remains of a grand fauna which has become fossilised. Yet the essence is altogether religious. According to G———, who has finished his studies here, most of the young men, including those whose intellects are active, have never had a twinge of infidelity; that which is the rule with us being the exception with them; they throw their whole soul into the service at church. Three-fourths of the newspapers and books denounce, with an air of conviction, "French scepticism and German infidelity," that is to say, the heresy which denies, and the heresy which affirms. As for grown-up men, they believe, though lukewarmedly, in God, in the Trinity, in Hell. The Protestant dogma chimes in with the serious, poetic, and moral instincts of the race; they require no effort to retain hold of it; they could not reject it without much effort. An Englishman would be exceedingly mortified if he had no faith in another life; in his eyes it is the natural complement of the present one; in every important crisis his thoughts grow solemn, and turn towards the vista beyond the grave. In order to image to himself the mysterious country which attracts the aspirations of his soul, he has a sort of antique map, which is Christianity explained by a highly revered body of geographers, who are the clergy. The map admits of many explanations, and the official geographers permit a certain latitude to individual views. Being unfettered, he is not dissatisfied; never dreams of distrusting either his geographers or his map. On the contrary, he would be displeased with the meddlers who should endeavour to unsettle the opinions he holds on this head. They are formed, fixed, rooted; they constitute a part of his education, of his traditions, of the great public body whereof he forms a unit. He accepts Protestantism and the Church as wholes, along with the English Constitution. He sees in Protestantism a rule of conduct, a command to do justice, an appeal to internal self-government. The Church he regards as an auxiliary of the State, an institution of moral hygiene, a good government for souls. All these reasons combine to make respect for Christianity alike a duty and a matter of propriety. It is very reluctantly admitted that an unbeliever can be a good Englishman and an honest man. Censure is passed upon those who, having become sceptics themselves, try to shake the faith of others. " Intellectual poltroonery," says the *Edinburgh Review* for April, 1848, " is the only species of cowardice which is common in this country, but it prevails to a lamentable extent. Most of our writers have scruples and fears about the tendency of their works. The social penalties attached to unorthodox opinions are so severe and unmercifully inflicted, that among us philosophical criticism and science itself mysteriously hint at matters which ought to be proclaimed from the house-tops." Not only are the lofty flights of the intelligence impeded, but in many cases an extreme strait-lacedness checks conversations and even actions. M. Guizot relates in his " Memoirs," that having said in company, " Hell is paved with good intentions," he was taken to task by a lady, who told him that the word " Hell " was too serious a one to be introduced into general conversation. Particular oaths, such as " Dieu me damne," are odious, and nothing is accepted as an excuse for employing them. A young Frenchman of my acquaintance here, when rowing some persons in a boat, made a false move, whereby he fell backwards, letting slip the forbidden oath. The ladies of the party were astounded, and gazed intently upon the water ; one of the gentlemen laughed outright, while the two others blushed like young girls. This religious prudery often leads to hypocrisy. I am acquainted with a London merchant who visits Paris twice yearly on business ; when he is there he is very jovial, and amuses himself on Sunday as freely as any one else. His Paris host, who visited him at his house in London, where he was made thoroughly welcome, going down-stairs on Sunday to the room where there was a miniature billiard-table pushed the balls about on it. The merchant in alarm begged him to stop at once, saying, "The neighbours will be scandalised should they hear this." When next he visited Paris he took his wife and daughters with him; this time there was no more gaiety, good fellowship, or pleasure-trips on Sunday; he was stiff, starched, a perfect pattern of propriety. His religion was a court dress. Such is the cant which disgusted Lord Byron. During the past twenty years it has diminished; Comte's philosophy, German exegesis, the conclusions of geology and the natural sciences, make their way slowly but continuously; free inquiry re-assumes its sway, and opens the doors without breaking the windows.

XX.

ARISTOCRATIC ASCENDENCY.

AS observations multiply they converge. There is **no** greater pleasure when travelling than to see the new facts fit in to those already collected, and group themselves like the traits where the tones of a painting begin. The following are those of this week with regard to the aristocratic ascendency and the sentiments it inspires.

A middle-class lady, but polished and distinguished in appearance, entered a cheesemonger's shop in Brighton. The shopkeeper asks her, in his soft, obsequious tone, "What kind of cheese, ma'am, do you patronise?" It is honourable for merchandise to obtain aristocratic approval. In proof of this one sees on tins of biscuits and pots of pomade the inscription, "Adopted by the nobility and gentry."

B—— came to France during the Exposition, and was surprised at the familiarities of the soldiers with their officers. When a captain of the Guides was looking at a picture in a shop window, two soldiers standing behind him bent forward, and looked over his shoulder. B—— said to me, "Such conduct would not be tolerated with us; we have distinctions of rank." Dr. Arnold, in the notes of his trip made in 1839, made a similar remark at Calais : " I observe here a mixture of classes which may be good, but that I cannot tell. Well-dressed men converse familiarly with persons who certainly belong to the lowest class." For my own part, as a Frenchman, I cannot help feeling slightly surprised when hearing, as I did yesterday, a gentleman of forty years of age, a man of worth and position, saying " My lord " to a little boy of ten, a dunce and a fool, but the son of a marquis.

I dined recently in the great hall of Trinity College, Cambridge. Three hundred persons were at table—everything was served on silver. There was a small side table for the undergraduates, who are noblemen, who wear a distinctive costume. At the universities, and even the public schools, the young nobles are surrounded by tuft-hunters, students of low birth, who strive by their services and their servility to make their fortunes. A nobleman has always a living or a situation in his gift, and this he afterwards presents to his toady as a piece of charity.

It is customary to confer baronetcies on three or four of the most distinguished medical men of the country. During the last reign there was a medical man of exceptional distinction whom it was desired to elevate to the peerage, but who declined the honour. An Englishman who told me this added, " He was right; no man who has held out his hand for guineas could take his place among peers of the realm." As a Frenchman, I am of the contrary opinion ; yet the fact and its commentary are none the less characteristic.

A novelist who was a good observer, and whose writings I have just been reading, says that " in England the people are far too much inclined to adopt the opinions of those above them, and to be governed by them." It is exactly the opposite in France.

I had a conversation with Thackeray, whose name I mention because he is dead, and because his ideas and his conversation are to be found in his books. He confirmed orally all that he had written about the snobbish spirit. I told him a trivial circumstance of which I was eye-witness. At a charity meeting the speaker set forth to the audience the importance of the work undertaken by remarking that the Marquis of ———, "a person in such a situation," had kindly consented to take the chair. Thackeray assured me that platitudes like these are common; he said that he admired our equality greatly, and that great people are so habituated to see people on their knees before them, that they are shocked when they meet a man of independent demeanour. "I myself," he added, "am now regarded as a suspicious character."

Stendhal wrote that, "talent and wit lose twenty-five per cent. in value on reaching England." In truth, the aristocracy of birth or fortune has secured the leading place; artists and authors remain in the second rank, with the exception of five or six of note who are admitted into the drawing-rooms of the nobility, but only as lions and curiosities. A few, on account of the moral or political nature of their writings, are more highly esteemed and considered; such men are of the class represented by Stuart Mill, Macaulay, Carlyle, Dickens, Thackeray, Tennyson, and who all contribute to exercise an influence over the most important of all works, that which concerns the guidance of national affairs or popular sentiments. But, according to what my friends tell me, the position of the others is lower than with us. The able journalists who write masterly leading articles three or four times monthly do not sign their articles, and are unknown to the public. Properly speaking, they are literary hacks. Their article is read at breakfast, as one swallows the bread and butter which is eaten with tea. One no more asks who wrote the article than one asks who made the butter. If next month the article and the butter are of inferior quality, one changes one's newspaper and butterman. No journalist becomes Member of Parliament or rises to be a Minister of State, as in France after 1830. Yet in this matter, as in religion, an insensible change is in progress, the end of which will be that the leading place will belong to intellect.

XXI.

SOCIETY AS DEPICTED BY "PUNCH."

TURN over the pages of the volumes of *Punch*, which is the first of English satirical journals, and compare it with the French journals of the same sort; the contrast is most instructive.

Punch has not a single picture of the lorettes, who form the subject of innumerable pictures in our journals, this being one of our errors; far better is it not to make a parade of vermin. Gavarni said, "I hate the harlot because I love woman," and yet he drew hundreds of sketches of girls of loose character, all of whom, however, he made to look charming. Though his raillery only causes a smile, yet, when one sees such pictures in the shop windows during several years one unconsciously retains an unhealthy impression. I pray the reader to pardon this moral phrase; my excuse is that it is true. Every spectacle, every emotion, leaves a lasting trace on us, and these trifling impressions multiplied together compose that distinct impression which we call our character. At the end of ten, twenty, or thirty years, we possess, so far as gallantry is concerned, a fund of weakness, of curiosity, or at least of tolerance, and a vague belief that it is in the nature of things that there should be spots on the sun.

In *Punch* not a single sketch is to be found of unfaithful wives or husbands. We all know how commonly these subjects were treated in France fifteen years ago; at present there is a diminution, but they are dealt with still. Here, on the contrary, marriage is held in honour; its pleasures, charms, and inner poetry are depicted. Take, for instance, *Punch's* picture, "Saturday Evening: arrival of the Husbands' Boat." The pier is covered with wives, young for the most part, whose faces are radiant with happiness; the children dance for joy. What a welcome! Turn, by way of contrast, to the same subject treated by a French artist, the husbands' train arriving at Tréport or Trouville. The husbands are there represented as repulsive tradesmen, as snarlers and cuckolds. In the conjugal scenes the same sentiment predominates. Augustus, during the honeymoon, is shown trying to make the tea. The scene is laid at the sea-coast in a pretty cottage; he and his young wife, half-embracing each other, go to the window to admire the calmness of the sky and the beauty of the evening. Meantime, the tea-urn explodes, the dog howls, and the frightened servant rushes to see the cause of the noise. Then follows a gentle scolding—the artist evidently envies the cares of the happy couple he represents.

In place of illicit love, permissible love-making remains to be dealt with. This opens up a wide field which our artists never cultivate. Numbers of *Punch's* pictures represent situations wherein parts are filled by a girl and young man who half understand each other's views on the marriage question. We have no such sketches in France, because we have no such subjects. At the sea-side Theodore and Emily, sheltered behind the harbour crane, think themselves out of sight, and

Theodore, on his knees, flattens his tender and snubby nose upon the white hand which is yielded to him. They are both unaware that the mirror of a cameraobscura, which has been directed towards them for ten minutes, reproduces the scene for the amusement of spectators. In another picture, Edwin and Angelina have appointed to meet each other at the end of the pier, but the one has taken the right and the other the left branch of it. Arrived at the end, they find themselves an hundred feet apart, and have to walk three miles before they can meet. Another represents a young lady, a good horsewoman, who has leaped hedges and ditches, and left her rival lagging far behind. "Now, I hope I am rid of Miss Georgina, and I am in the same field with Augustus." Indeed, a horseman is seen in the background. Two lovers on horseback are exhibited on the Brighton sands; the air there is far superior to the fogs of London—"At least, that is their opinion." The irony is well intentioned; it is clear the artist said to himself, "Would that I were in their place." Thus he makes his personages as elegant, well-dressed, well-bred as possible. The young girls are especially fascinating; *Punch* depicts himself as a lover looking in rapture upon their fair hair falling freely over their shoulders; his heart beats; he is overcome, he thinks them too charming. Here is a covey, eighteen in all, in a cove on the sea-coast, in various attitudes, some leaning over their sketches, others doing embroidery, others picking up specimens, all smiling; it is the "Sirens' grotto." Remark that they are all innocent of evil, and that the drawing is as much so as themselves; during the rides on horseback, during the gusts of wind on the pier, there is no exposure; if the wind strikes their petticoats it is to keep them down. For a like reason the gallantry is respectful, the lover holds his sweetheart's skein of worsted, gives his pocket-handkerchief to her little brother; he is not a conqueror, but is under subjection; he submits himself to his fate. Sometimes the girls make the first advance; in this the "Fast Girls" furnish scope for satire; one of them is exhibited at croquet stepping aside to speak to the object of her admiration; another contrives to get a private talk over a game of chess. If need be, Mater-familias begins negotiations. A worthy matron is shown fishing in ecclesiastical waters, surrounded by her three daughters; she casts the line towards a young clergyman, rich and of good family, who is on a visit. She says, "I am very happy, dear Mr. Cecil Newton, to find that you are orthodox; I need hardly tell you that I hope you will not lapse into the sad heresy which enjoins the celibacy of the clergy." As for him, with his embarrassed manner, his edifying and sentimental grin, and his side-glance at the three pretty baits, he presents a most comical appearance. In every case, in these pictures as in the novels, at the end of the road, upon the horizon, marriage is always to be beheld; no one would suspect that there were any intermediate stations; now, to use Shakespeare's words —"All's well that ends well."

Here are the married folks: look at the domestic scenes. They are not unpleasing, bitterly satirical; no broken-down husbands or wretched, bad-tempered and spoilt children, like those which M. Daumier represents so frequently and with so open a hatred, are to be met with here. The artists here nearly always regard infancy as something charming and beautiful. There is a noise in the nursery caused by two processions, each composed of four little boys and girls, who march to the sound of a trumpet; all their cheeks are rosy, and they are all enjoying themselves heartily. Two little girls in the garden gravely come and ask grandmamma to play with the skipping-rope. Another has found the scissors, and is solemnly engaged in cutting her little brother's hair, because he wishes to be bald like grandpapa. On Christmas night there is dancing in a large room decorated with holly, where grandpapa smilingly acts as *vis-à-vis* to his little granddaughter of six, who holds her frock and makes her curtsey with an air of gaiety and coquetry. These are the incidents, sometimes the accidents; but always there predominates the quiet and lasting felicity of family life.

It is true that the father has quite enough to do with his six, eight, or ten children who sometimes come in annual succession; he is fifty years old, his head is getting bald, his proportions are becoming aldermanic, and his youngest has just been weaned. They are as plentiful as rabbits. Another is coming, which may not be the last, nevertheless a host of aunts invades the crowded house. Paterfamilias, turned out of the room, takes his dinner on the stairs. A Frenchman would have perspired at the very prospect; so much happiness would be a misfortune. And, then, the trouble of such a flock! The father must take it to the sea-side, lodge it, provide everything, food, clothing, education, health, amusement, and, above all, must maintain discipline and peace. Indeed, such a family, including servants, constitutes a small nation, of which the father is bound to be the head, the magistrate, and the despotic ruler. I know a family which, living in the country six miles from any town, consists of thirty persons in all. Add to this fifteen or twenty tenants whose houses are close at hand, twelve horses in the stables, a farm adjoining, the meat consumed being produced by animals reared and killed on the property; under such conditions as these a modern gentleman does not differ greatly from his ancestor, the ancient feudal baron. It is true this is a rare case; yet in the families of the middle class in London the father exhibits traces of the same authority. He is neither weak nor is he reduced to the second place, as in our French illustrated books. He feels that he is responsible; he directs; he governs. For instance, he has resolved to introduce hydropathy: one by one the poor children are shown approaching the cold shower-bath in their long shirts and oil-skin caps, shivering and sorrowful, whilst their father brandishes the flesh-brush. Winter has arrived; it is ordered that the family shall be shod in cheap boots, and the shoemaker is represented under the father's eye fitting huge stout boots on his daughter's small feet. Paterfamilias has resolved upon spending a week at the seaside; disliking to go to a hotel, the caricature represents him installed on the sands; two bathing-machines serve as bedrooms, while the dinner is cooked in the open air with the assistance of the aunts, mamma, and the children, all of whom do something, the eldest son, cigar in mouth, being set to prepare the vegetables. Paterfamilias, standing up with a sarcastic and satisfied air, supervises and controls; to look at him, it is clear that no opposition will be made to his will; his broad shoulders, his expression, his hands crossed behind his back, or stuck in his pockets, his gravity, his coolness, the scantiness of his gestures and his words, all manifest that he is inspired by the sentiment of a legitimate and unchallenged authority. I grant you that this is an exaggeration, that it is a fiction, that it is a caricature; yet the document is none the less instructive; it furnishes a glance at one side of the life of an English family. From it one divines why they have and how they control half or a whole dozen of children.

Then come the sketches of servants. As this class is a large one, and an English well-to-do family has several servants, the artist represents them frequently. On the one hand, he pourtrays their troubles. In an aristocratic society their place is a low one, and they are made to do strange duties. A solemn and imposing old lady walking in the park, accompanied by her dog, and followed by her footman, says, "John Thomas." "Yes, my lady." "Carry Beauty; poor thing, she is getting tired." A similar scene between a girl of sixteen and her maid. The latter is already carrying two dogs, one under each arm, yet the little patrician exclaims, "O, Parker, you ought to carry Puppet, too, he will get his feet wet." It is raining in torrents; a miserly nobleman, well sheltered in his carriage, says to his servants, who are dripping wet on the box, "Good heavens, have you umbrellas there?" "No, my lord." "Then hand me your new hats in here." Judging from many of these trifling circumstances, I should think that they have fewer comforts in France, but that they are treated more considerately. At all events, they are not kept at arm's length; the human being is more perceptible, and does not altogether disappear under the livery. The fundamental difference between an aristocratic and a democratic country always making its influence felt. On the other hand, the artist pourtrays their affectations. As a consequence of aristocratic institutions, every class in society sees one which it regards as superior, keeps the boundary line clearly drawn, and never mixes with that below it. Thackeray has sharply depicted this caprice; it was that of the Court when Louis XIV. was king. Here it is in as lively operation among the flunkeys as among the gentlemen; now, nothing is more ludicrous than a valet's pride. One man-servant gives his master warning because he has seen his lordship on the knife-board of an omnibus. Another consents to carry the coal-scuttle to the nursery, "if his mistress asks it as a favour, but hopes that his mistress will not mistake him for a housemaid." They consider themselves gentlemen because they are fine-looking, well-clothed, well-fed, and have plenty of leisure. They are fastidious, are vain of their appearance, and strive to ape good manners. One of them consults his betting book in the carriage. Another, who has been asked to mount behind, languidly stretches himself and refuses, "If my lady does not find it too hot for her, I find it too hot for me." A young married lady says to her maid, "Jane, I was surprised that none of you rose when I entered the kitchen." The maid, tossing her head, replies with an impertinent air, "Indeed, ma'am, we were certainly surprised at your entering the kitchen when we were at dinner." But the faces, the gestures themselves, must be seen; when I seek for words other than English ones wherewith to translate them, I entirely fail. The language of the country alone seems to interpret the things of the country; for example, the puckered face of the servant who has remained single on account of her ugliness, the self-satisfaction, the gravity, the majesty, and the servility of the footman, who knows himself to be a fine-looking fellow.

XXII.

SPORTING, POLITICAL, AND SOCIAL CARICATURES IN "PUNCH."

NEARLY all the amusements are of an athletic cast It is sufficient to turn over the pages of the volumes of *Punch* to see how thoroughly national is the liking for horses and for rough sports. Every number out of three contains representations of equestrian mishaps and adventures. Nervous or unskilful horsemen are continuously jeered at; jokes are cracked about distinguished foreigners who shrink from a leap, or who fear to break their necks. Little boys and girls mounted on ponies join in the fox-hunts which take place during the chilling fogs of winter. The young girls, tall, slim, firmly seated in their saddles, leap hedges, ditches, five-barred gates, dash through the underwood, gallop over the marshes, and come in at the finish with a rush, carrying their horses over every obstacle, putting inexperienced fox-hunters to the blush. Heavy, broad-shouldered matrons trot along with the party under the care of the riding-master. Entire families, from the grandfather of seventy to the maiden of six, ride along the sands like a band of centaurs. Miss Alice, who is eight years old, mounts her father's horse and offers her pony to her mamma, who is slightly nervous. It is clear that they are all the better for vigorous open-air exercise. In a journey among the mountains old and young ladies, wrapped in their waterproofs, sit on the outside of the coach alongside of the gentlemen, the inside being considered fitted only for the dogs, who take their ease there. At the seaside both sexes promenade on the pier during a gale, the wind which whistles in their hair, the torrents of rain which deluge them, seeming to delight them; this betrays a primitive instinct like that of the greyhound and the racehorse; they need muscular exertion and the rigours of the open air to put their blood in circulation. At Paris I have seen young Englishmen every night leaving their windows open during the entire night in winter. This enables us to comprehend their fondness for open-air sports, for cricket, for fishing and shooting. The rain pours down in torrents and the whole country is like a lake; an old gentleman in his waterproof actively handles his fishing-rod. When the river is frozen over, he may be seen letting down his line in the hope of catching a fish through a hole in the ice made by a labourer with a pick. No obstacles, expense, or danger stop them; they make a journey of two hundred miles to the Highlands in order to fish for salmon, shoot grouse or deer; amateurs start from London for the meet, taking their horses with them in the train. B—— tells me that a pheasant carefully watched and fed during the winter costs its owner from thirty shillings to two pounds. One out of every three sportsmen has a limb broken before he dies. The jokes on this head are endless. A gentleman on horseback informs a neighbour that his animal is rather restive "Oh, the animal is well known, it has been the means of breaking more collar-bones than any other in England." A little swell going stag-hunting says to a robust friend on arriving at the railway station, " Will you take a single or a return ticket?" The latter replies, " I mean to take a return because I know all about the horse I shall mount; but I advise you to take a single ticket and an insurance one as well." The prospect seems unpleasant. But it is not always so. For persons of a particular temperament, difficulty, trouble, and danger are incentives. Many English take delight in exerting, hardening, or forcing themselves to surmount obstacles; the Alpine Club and other associations are proofs of this. The qualities of the athlete and the equestrian contribute in their eyes to constitute manliness. Thus general opinion upholds instinct, and affectation is the complement of nature. In India, Jacquemont saw them fill themselves with meat and spirituous liquors, then gallop for two hours under a broiling sun, and do this out of bravado, as a matter of habit or of fashion, in order not to let it be thought that they were effeminate or cowardly, even hazarding their lives in the attempt and losing them.

Most of the youths have the same dispositions. The artist depicts them as being precocious in a manner different from ours, showing not the precocity of forwardness or malice, the precocity of the senses, but that of hardihood and daring. The small and puny street boys are not allied to the Parisian Gavroche; they are more handy with their fists than with their tongues; a good joke pleases them less than a display of skill. Two of these manikins are shown in winter trying to block up a doorway with a snow-ball twice as large as themselves, and though half-frozen are contented and happy. Nor are the rich less venturesome and hardy than the poor. Witness two boys unmooring a boat in order to go to sea by themselves. Their pleasures are rough and boisterous; they wade about bare-legged in the pools of water, they fish for jelly-fish, which they bring into the drawing-room on a stick. While mere urchins they learn to box, and they box with gloves in presence of their mamma. When their father visits the school and asks how they are getting on, he is told, "Oh, pretty well; there are three fellows whom I can lick, and Fred, here, can lick six, including me." Another seated on a pony as large as a Newfoundland dog, prepares to leap a brook, and replies to the servant making objections, "Both my horse and myself can swim." B—— assured me that, from childhood upwards, they are told, "You must be a man." They are trained to think that they ought never to cry or show any signs of weakness, and that they ought to be brave, enterprising, and protectors of the weaker sex. A little boy says to a big lady, frightened at a herd of cattle, "Don't be afraid, shelter yourself behind me." Another, aged six, seated on his shaggy Shetland pony, cries to his grown-up sisters on the balcony, "Halloa, girls, if any of you wish to take a ride along the sands, I'm your man." On the other hand, gluttony is the vice of these boys, which the artist satirises most cordially. Emily has tried to amuse one of them in every possible way; she has given him her paint-box, has played on the piano, has shown him picture-books, yet he is discontented. "I don't call that amusement. I want figs and ginger-bread, or a large bit of toffy. That's what I call amusement." As a matter of course, the draughtsman conforms the physical type to the moral tendency. He does not represent them as refined, but sturdy and robust.

Moreover, he even loves to exaggerate their natural courage. Two children on a donkey wish to leap a ditch before which a gentleman on horseback hesitates. A youngster of five, his hands in his pockets, says to his uncle, a stout gentleman well muffled up, who is going out at night, and who is apprehensive about robbers, "I say, Uncle Charles, if you are afraid to go home alone, I'll escort you to your door." Separate from these caricatures the salient and exaggerated points, the residue is what the English themselves see or believe to be essential. This granted, and subject to the necessary rectifications and modifications, one can perceive the fact as it actually exists.

The proofs which demonstrate the temperament, the race, and the dispositions, are of all grades. The common people, particularly the peasants, the sailors, the farmers, and even the squires of this country, are either jolly fellows or hulking monsters; their outer man bears testimony to their brute force. It is apparent that they glory in guzzling. An old country gentleman has the air of a fat pig, who has a recollection of his grandfather the wild boar. Close at hand is the portrait of an English juryman; he is about to go to court stuffed to the throat, bloated out, having fed like an ogre, and, in addition, his wife fills his pockets with eatables. This is due to the rule that juries are not allowed to separate till they are agreed; hunger makes them unanimous in the end; for such a stomach as this, nothing is more terrible than a vacuum. There is a holiday in the coal districts, at which fisticuffs are the principal attraction; a daughter is represented leading away her father, whose arm has been broken, and telling her lover, a country lout, to go and take part in the fight. Two sailors at Balaclava, imposing and vigorous fighting animals, square-shouldered, and well filled-out, approach their commanding officer, and deferentially say, "Beg your pardon, sir, but may not John Grampus and me have a day on shore to go to the trenches and do some firing with the soldiers?" Yet the most noteworthy personage of all is John Bull, the typical Englishman, such as he is depicted in political caricatures; he is the representative whom they themselves have chosen. In this portrait, which they regard as an abridgment, are shown the essence and foundation of the national character. When young he resembles one of those jovial blades of Rubens, or rather of Jordaens, who, in addition, has the gruffness of a watch-dog. He is adult and resembles a butcher; he is fifty years old, is broad-shouldered; his stomach is prominent under his open-breasted waistcoat; he wears top-boots, a low-crowned hat, and carries a cudgel in his hand. But years have not lessened his energy; he is capable of standing his ground against the most vigorous adversary even when it comes to blows. Picture a type of distinction and then the exact opposite; the latter impression is that which he makes; his neck is short, his chin large; his jaws are solid; the entire masticating machinery is perfectly developed; a stiff collar rises half way above his shaven chin, and his whiskers are of the mutton-chop pattern: thus the lower part of his face resembles that of M. Prudhomme. But his twinkling or angry eyes, his beetle-brows, the entire expression of his countenance, betray marked animal characteristics and the choleric temperament. His forehead is small, his intellect barren; his ideas are few and petty, those which he possesses being the ideas of a tradesman or a farmer. By way of compensation, he is gifted with good sense and energy, a fund of good temper, loyalty, perseverance, and determination; that firmness of character, in short, by means of which a man gets on in the world, and renders himself, if not lovable, at least useful. There is something superior to this in England, yet we shall not err greatly in taking this type and its counterparts to represent the aptitudes and the inclinations of the average of the nation.

At the opposite pole the artistic type is beheld. We all know how in French sketches the artist is raised above the citizen; here, oddly enough, the reverse occurs. Musicians are represented as salaried monkeys, who come to make a noise in a drawing-room. Painters are bearded artisans, unkempt, shabbily-dressed, badly-educated, conceited, hardly one degree raised above photographers. These are workmen who cannot speak English, and who merely form food for ridicule. Thackeray frequently struggled against the common opinion with respect to artists; Clive Newcome, one of his personages, who is a painter and the son of a colonel, remarks with surprise that in Paris artists are on a par with the leaders of society, and that Delaroche and Horace Vernet are invited to dine at Court. A French moralist would never have occasion to demonstrate that the painter's art is as liberal a profession as that of medicine or law. Probably, in the eyes of the burly John Bull, whom I have just described, a painter cannot be a gentleman, seeing that he works with his hands. He is not "respectable" because he has no fixed income; besides, it is said that his studio is always in disorder. He is a journeyman who wants method; he ranks with his neighbour, the mechanic, who works at home, and is the oracle of the pot-house.

The political caricatures appear to have been **drawn**

by John Bull himself; the drawing is stiff, correct, without ease or grace, the pleasantry being harsh and hard; the humour is that of a dog. Moreover, everything is subordinated to a practical object; the intention is to liken an affair of state, a war, a change in the Ministry, a political situation, to a familiar incident of daily life, so that the most obtuse head may understand what is meant. In the sketches of manners the types are well chosen, clearly defined, and they powerfully express the moral trait by the physique. In all these respects the artists are Hogarth's successors. On the contrary, in the frontispieces and the borderings of each Almanack, the play of fancy, the spirit of burlesque, the odd and interminable wealth of imagination, the mountebank scenes, the ludicrous processions, the fascinating shapes, or the monstrosities, the originality, the sentiment, the comicality of invention, abound to an extent as to remind us of Dickens, and sometimes even of Shakespeare.

In order to complete our examination of this collection, let us note two tragical caricatures: the subject is pauperism, whereof the traces, at least, are everywhere visible in England.

The agricultural labourer has been competing for a prize. The miserable wretch in rags, with clasped hands, half-starved, deferential, is kneeling, and is crowned with roses. Behind him stand his wife and six children in a row, looking as wretched as himself. The stout and well-dressed President of the Association solemnly hands him his prize, consisting of a hammer and a stone. He is free to break the stone and distribute the fragments to his famishing children. The spectators smile; the gentlemen and fine ladies who are present gaze with a frigid curiosity, as if he were an animal of an inferior and unknown species, upon the pitiable brute who produces their bread.

Another subject is cheap clothing. Twenty skeletons are sewing on a table; their employer, a stout middle-class citizen, stern-eyed and heavy-jowled, watches them while smoking a cigar.

These two pictures produce the same effect when seen among the others as the sight of one of the squalid lanes near Oxford Street when beheld after a long walk amidst the palaces, the hotels, and the comfortable mansions of the West-end and the City.

XXIII.

INNS OF COURT, BARRISTERS, AND JUDGES.

I HAVE been introduced to John H——, a young and very obliging barrister. He lives in the Temple, a sort of nest of lawyers and law students, in which the multitude of chambers remind one of a Quartier Latin and of a law corporation. The institution is composed of four Inns of Court, each of which possesses a Hall wherein the members dine, the student's chief duty being to eat six dinners here every term for three years. A year's attendance in a barrister's chambers entitles the students to be called to the bar without attending lectures. The professors are six in number, and attendance at a final examination is optional. There is no resemblance between this and an important Law School like ours, founded to teach the theory in the first instance. In like manner there is no Polytechnic school here; he who wishes to become an engineer enters an engineer's office, where he learns by practice, like a painter's assistant. This deficiency in high-class and systematised instruction, this omission in the matter of preliminary lectures on the theory of a profession, is very noteworthy, and is thoroughly English. Besides, it would be no easy thing to deliver a course of lectures on English law. The law is not codified, as in France, upon accepted philosophical principles, but consists of a mass of statutes and precedents, more or less incongruous, and sometimes contradictory, which the future jurist must himself digest after long study. On the other hand, there is no historical school, as in Germany, characterised by delicate tact and comprehensive views, and capable of explaining, first, the gradual adaptation of law to custom, and, secondly, its origin, its bearing, and its limits. The compensation for the lack of philosophical theories and historical treatment is found in practice, and frequently in routine. Some of these lawyers, barristers, solicitors, or attorneys, have incomes of £20,000 a year; one was named to me whose income was from £30,000 to £35,000.

Let us attend a sitting of the Courts at Westminster. In civil as in criminal causes a jury is employed, its duty always consisting in settling questions of fact, as distinguished from points of law. But a jury is employed in civil causes only at the request of the parties, who have to pay the jurymen certain fees. We were present at three trials. One was a divorce case, in which the wife was the petitioner; this right has ceased to be an aristocratic and most costly privilege; it can now be exercised for the sum of £25 or £30, and is thus brought within reach of the humblest purse. Moreover, the reports of these divorce cases, which frequently appear in the newspapers, deserve to be read, because they unveil one of the failings of English households—the tyranny and brutality of the husbands. The duty of counsel is very noteworthy, and is very different from that of French advocates. They examine witnesses as well as plead. At the hearing, the plaintiff, the defendant, and each witness are examined and cross-examined by counsel. The two counsel turn their man inside out in succession, try to trip him up, to disconcert him, to make him contradict himself. Certainly it is not at all pleasant to be a witness in England, the quarter of an hour passed in the box being most trying. As a consequence, the burden of the trial is borne by the counsel, the judge's function consisting merely in supervising, forbidding certain questions, tempering the ardour of the champions in court, as the Queen tempers the ardour of parties in Parliament. Such an active and varied part as that played by counsel largely contributes to heighten their importance and sharpen their wits. Among us they are too often phrase-spinners who plunge into rhetoric, and whom the judge has to silence; here, they are qualified, like our "Juges d'Instruction," to fathom and control men's minds. Three or four of them, with their piercing eyes, clear and thrilling accents, rapid and decided gestures, appeared to me to be first-rate foxes, into whose clutches I should not like to fall. The wife whom I saw under examination stood in a little railed box at the side, but was visible to every one; my guide told me that her condition was low, her language vulgar, and her clothes hired for the occasion. Yet her replies were marked by that concentration and indomitable energy which I have so often noticed in this country. Every minute she had a desire to weep, and restrained her tears. She was asked if she had not beaten her husband with the tongs—if she had not sometimes begun the quarrel? She did not pour forth a torrent of negatives, as a southern woman would have done, but she bent down her head, reflected for half a minute, and then, assured that her memory served her faithfully, after consideration and with confidence she replied, "No; never." She spoke with an accent of conviction, the word "never" being firmly uttered.

The reports of criminal trials must be perused in order to understand to what a degree the judge's part is dignified and honourably filled. Never can there be detected in him any traces of the spirit of persecution, the sentiments of a policeman, the desire to inflict vengeance on behalf of society, the instincts of a hunter warmed with the chase, and intent upon securing his prey. A passage which I translate says "that the principle of English law is, that a man must be held to be innocent till he has been proved to be guilty; the burden of proof rests altogether upon the prosecution." Contrary to the French rule, the prisoner may keep his mouth closed; he is not bound to incriminate himself; no officer of justice of whatever degree is entitled to extract his secret from him under any pretext whatever.

Conformably to this rule of law, when the judge pronounces sentence, he does so with the authority and with the impartiality of a mind thoroughly convinced. He neither declaims nor indulges in invective. He neither conceals the weak points of the evidence nor exaggerates the points beyond dispute. He weighs his words, translating his carefully-formed opinion into clear language, and when he adds moral condemnation to the legal sentence, the gravity and nobleness of his tones are worthy of all praise. More than once I have thought that if Justice herself had a voice, she would speak thus. The man himself is transformed into the simple organ of truth and of rectitude. The prisoner at the bar cannot help bowing before such a power as this, and assenting to the justice of his sentence. I know no other spectacle which can as solemnly imprint in men's hearts veneration for the law. Yet in this, as in other cases, the bad and the good commingle. I am told that the result of the English form of legal procedure is to protect the individual at the expense of society, that it is too difficult to obtain legal proof, and that many guilty persons go unpunished.

XXIV.

THE THEATRES. LIVING IN LONDON.

GOOD society does not go to the theatres, with the exception of the two opera houses, which are the exotic and hot-house plants of luxury, and in which the prices of admission are enormous and evening dress is imperative. As to the others, the audience is recruited from among the lower middle class. There is no longer a national comedy in England: playwrights translate or adapt French pieces. This is very extraordinary, for they have still living manners fitted for representation on the stage. In addition, their novels prove how well they can depict characters. Satiric humour they have always had in abundance; during the last century they had excellent comic dramatists and performers. How comes it, then, that in London there is no comedy, and that in Paris there is one? Is it because there is a scarcity of droll personages in England? It appears to me that they abound more than elsewhere, seeing that types are there more sharply defined and are developed even to excess. Is it because prudery of manners taboos laughter? There is no hindrance to decent merriment, improper joking being alone forbidden. Is it because English reserve has suppressed immoderate gesticulation, spontaneous and free expression of feelings? But the source of interest lies in the situation, and grave personages can play a part in the most exciting performance. The whole matter is a puzzle, especially for the reader who has just turned over the pages of a novel by Dickens or of an album by John Leech.

This evening I went to the Olympic, a small house, corresponding in some measure to our Palais Royal. The opening piece was a burlesque on the *Merchant of Venice*, filled with puns and jokes; but to enjoy such tomfooleries one must be a native of the country. The other piece, *Dearest Mamma*, is based on *La Belle-Mère et le Gendre*. Addison, one of the actors, plays the part of an old uncle with surprising spirit and fidelity. Imagine to yourself a large, bald, and hearty gentleman, rotund, with his coat closely buttoned, thoroughly enjoying life, well pleased to be a widower and unattached, uniformly good-tempered, wholly concerned in preserving " his equilibrium ;" who eats his six repasts and takes his three constitutionals daily, who hums tunes on all occasions, who winds up his sentences with a whistle like that of an old blackbird, who drops off to sleep in every easy-chair, and who, hardened by the tempests of wedded life, wags his head, and ends by snoring comfortably when he is being soundly rated. The type is complete, both morally and physically; it is original and sympathetic, very comical and very natural, and is perfectly rendered.

Shakespeare is played at intervals; I have seen Mr Macready in *Macbeth*, in which he showed himself powerful and dramatic, especially in the scene where Banquo's ghost appears, and where, breathless with fear, and with a hoarse cry, he casts himself on the ground like a maddened bull. The public still laughs when Hamlet says in the churchyard that the noble dust of Alexander might now be used to stop a bung-hole. Our eyes have been too much changed by habit; we have lost the inexperience of the sixteenth century; the illusion is destroyed by the too frequent shifting of the scenery; we cannot now believe in armies represented by six combatants, and in battles fought upon the stage. Even in England educated persons would be disgusted to witness Cornwall publicly plucking out Gloucester's eyes. To my mind the effect of reading Shakespeare's works is far greater now than that made by representing them; at least I do not realise his personages so well when they are placed before me through the medium of an actor.

When one is satisfied with the necessaries of life, living in London is not excessively dear. A young engineer with whom I am acquainted spends 8s. 4d. daily; his dinner, consisting of roast beef, potatoes, asparagus, sweets, and cheese, and beer, costs him 2s.; his lodging, which is very clean, consists of a bedroom and sitting-room. B———, who has come here to read Arabic manuscripts, has a fine room close to the British Museum, for which he pays a guinea a week, breakfast and attendance included. Both of them would pay more in Paris. One may rent an entire house in the neighbourhood of Regent's Park for £100 a year. On the other hand, the expense of luxurious living is prodigious. Four Frenchmen occupying a first-class hotel for three days had to pay a bill amounting to £72. In another hotel, situated in a fashionable locality, a sitting-room, bedroom, and dressing-room, candles, and attendance, cost eighteen guineas a week. Lord S——— smiled with incredulity on hearing my friend Louis

T——, a Frenchman, relate that during the preceding year he had killed thirty-six deer in a park of which the rent was £80. Here all the pleasures of luxury, the opera, sporting, entertaining, are reserved for the possessors of large fortunes, and this constitutes a new line of demarcation between the poor and the rich.

My linen was not sent home on the appointed day, nor till three days after, when it came at last, but unwashed, the reason given by the washerwoman being that two consecutive holidays had fallen in that week, and that all the workpeople had been intoxicated for eight days.

Since my arrival I have seen three drunken women in broad daylight; two of them, whom I saw in a fine street near Hyde Park, were evidently low characters; they had tattered shawls, boots down at the heels, an idiotic smile, tottering legs, and loosened tongues. The third, respectably dressed, and about fifty years of age, staggered in the midst of a crowd, saying with a curious smile that she was drunk, and that the reason was that she had taken too much at the Exhibition. I believe that among well-educated women this vice is exceedingly rare, yet it may sometimes be occasioned by extreme lassitude or grief. George Eliot has depicted it in "Janet's Repentance." The following advertisement in *The Times* for 23rd November, 1870, furnishes material for curious speculations: "A lady in the vicinity of London, who takes great interest in the recovery of ladies from habits of intemperance, continues to receive into her family one lady from the higher classes, requiring help in this respect. A vacancy now occurs. Address, Hon. Sec. of the Ladies' Total Abstinence Association, &c."

Among the people, however, the vice is frightful During three days I have twice visited Chelsea, and each time I have seen men lying in the gutters dead-drunk. My friend, who lives in this neighbourhood, often sees working men in this state and position. A philanthropic clergyman tells me that out of ten workmen eight are drunkards. They get high wages in London, as much as from one to two pounds sterling a week; when once they have paid for their provisions they have a drinking bout of three or four days' duration, imbibing gin, brandy-and-water, and other strong liquors. The intoxication produced by these spirits stupefies a man, rendering him melancholy and often mad. Hence the prevalence of *delirium tremens* and other alcoholic maladies. According to a number of the *Ragged Schools Magazine*, London had in 1848 eleven thousand sellers of spirits and only four thousand butchers and bakers. Thirty thousand persons are arrested during every year on the charge of being drunk and incapable. It has been calculated that 260,000 persons enter the fourteen principal gin palaces every week. In Glasgow there is one whisky shop to every ten houses. Statistics show that in Manchester the working class expends nearly a million sterling every year in drinks; as regards Glasgow, the amount is about the same; in Newcastle it is £400,000; in Dundee £250,000. One hundred and forty-one workmen having been watched at Preston, it was found that the average proportion of their outlay for spirits was 22 per cent. of their earnings—a little more than £11 10s. yearly; that forty-one expended from 25 to 75 per cent. of their earnings, and that twelve were teetotallers, and abstained from strong drink. Such is the effect of the remedy, and one understands alike the energy of the propaganda and the utility of these associations. In many streets I saw illustrations published by them, where the drunkard is represented prone and helpless, surrounded by little demons, who remove his heart and brain piece by piece, whilst the Devil himself looks on, holding a bottle of gin, with the punning inscription, "My best spirits"

XXV.

MANUFACTURES AND ARTISANS.

STARTED for Manchester. During the journey I read various newspapers and reviews, and among others three or four articles upon France, directed against its despotic Government, which does not permit private individuals to take any part in public affairs. The writer argues as if Frenchmen were Englishmen; he unconsciously pictures himself in France; he supposes how uncomfortable he would be there, how his feelings would be shocked, how our administrative system would hamper his actions. Yet these shackles, which appear so serious to him, are trifles in our eyes; the majority of the citizens would be much more sensitive to the opposite system. To take part in public affairs is to increase one's toils; to be member of five or six committees; to prepare or hear reports; to listen to a dozen speeches every fortnight on the same subject; to digest statistics, and make investigations, are all wearisome occupations. We hand over these matters to the Government; if it be a despot, it is also a steward. It trammels us in many respects, but it saves us from much worry. We permit it to cut and carve like a steward possessed of full powers, openly criticising its doings, and privately whispering that should it become unbearable, we have always the option of turning it out of doors. The truth is, however, that this calculation is faulty; for after years of quiet and indifference we suddenly find that we are ruined, and have concluded bad bargains. Besides, the forcible expulsion always leads to rioting. Moreover, as the master cannot get on without a steward, he is compelled, after each disturbance, to select the first comer, the misfortune being that he is often worse than his predecessor.

For the first hundred miles the landscape is flat and tame; after this the hills begin, and the country acquires an expression. The undulating hill-tops are bathed in mist; sometimes, when the sun shines forth, a feeble light rests, like a smile, on the pale green; this fleeting smile, amid the general mourning of sodden fields, is most affecting and sad.

We now enter the coal and iron country; everywhere are marks of manufacturing life; the cinder heaps form mountains; the earth is seamed with excavations; tall furnaces belch forth flames. We are nearing Manchester. In the bronzed sky at sunset a strangely-shaped cloud hangs over the plain; under this motionless covering are hundreds of bristling chimneys, as tall as obelisks; a huge and black mass is next distinguishable, then endless rows of buildings, and we enter the Babel of bricks.

Walked through the city; seen close at hand, it is still more dismal. The air and the soil appear charged with fog and soot. Manufactories with their blackened bricks, their naked fronts, their windows destitute of shutters, and resembling huge and cheap penitentiaries, succeed each other in rows. A large bazaar for the sale of low-priced goods, a workhouse to accommodate four hundred thousand persons, a prison for convicts condemned to penal servitude —such are the ideas created by the spectacle. One of these buildings is a rectangle of six stories, in each of which are forty windows; it is there that, lit up by gas, amid the deafening noise of looms, thousands of workpeople, cabined, classified, immovable, mechanically drive their machines every day from morning to night; can any form of existence be more opposed to, and at variance with, the natural instincts of man? About six o'clock a bustling, noisy crowd pours from the mills into the streets; men, women, and children flock along in the open air; their clothes are filthy; many of the children are bare-footed, the faces of all are pinched and gloomy; several halt at the gin-palaces; the others scatter and hasten towards their hovels. We follow them; what wretched streets! Through the half-open window may be seen a miserable room on the ground-floor, sometimes below the level of the damp pavement; at the threshold a group of white, fat, and untidy children breathe the foul air of the street, less foul, however, than that of the room. A strip of carpet may be perceived, and clothes hung up to dry. We continue our walk in the direction of the suburbs; there, in a more open space, rows of small cheap houses have been erected as a speculation. The black street is paved with iron slag; the low red-tiled roofs stand forth in lines against the prevailing grey sky; yet each family dwells apart, and the fog it breathes is not too impure. These are the select, the happy few. And the time is summer, the finest season of the year! One asks oneself what sort of life do they lead in winter, when the fog bathes, chokes, engulfs all nature, and one feels how heavily man is oppressed by this pitiless climate and this industrial system.

Drives and visits in the wealthy quarter. Here and at Liverpool, as at London, the English character is manifested in the buildings. The City man does his utmost to cast his city skin; he strives to have his country seat and country surroundings at the outskirts; he feels the necessity of being by himself—of feeling that he is alone, monarch of his family and his servants, of having around him a piece of park or a garden as a relaxation from the artificial life of town and of business. Hence have been constructed vast silent streets in which there are no shops, and in which each house, surrounded by a patch of green, is detached and is occupied by a single family. In addition, beyond Manchester stretches Bowden—a sort of public villa, with the splendid park which Lord Stamford throws open for the enjoyment of the multitude, and in which there are magnificent trees, fine turf, and herds of tame deer lying amid the ferns. How one must enjoy the charm and the repose of these natural beauties after leaving the mill and the counting-house! For there are no other beauties. Even a walk through the quarter of the rich is depressing. Ten, fifteen, twenty houses in succession have been built in the same style, and they succeed each other with the mechanical regularity of draughts on a draught-board. The trim lawns, the small gates, the painted fronts, the uniformity of the compartments, make one think of painted menageries, of neat play-things. The ornamentation shows bad taste, capitals, Grecian pillars, railings, Gothic roofs, and other forms have been copied from divers ages and places, the whole being fresh and inharmonious, the display is ginger-bread and trumpery, like that of a man who, having suddenly become rich, bedizens, in the belief that he is adorning himself. It is a good thing to work, and it is a good thing to be wealthy; but to work and be rich are not sufficient.

They are powerful, that is their compensation. The life of one of the heads of these manufacturing or commercial houses may be likened to that of a minor prince. They have the funds, the vast designs, the responsibility, the risks, the importance, and, it is said, the pride of a potentate. Like him they have their emissaries and representatives in the four quarters of the globe; they are bound to keep themselves versed daily in the condition and resources of neighbouring and distant countries; they have to control and satisfy a host of workpeople; they have the power to become the benefactors of thousands of men; they are the generals and governors of human industry. A quarter of a million sterling, half a million sterling, these are the phrases one hears used with regard to their enterprises, their sales or purchases, the freights in their ships, the goods in their warehouses. They despatch agents to examine particular districts of the globe; they discover outlets for commerce and markets for purchases in Japan, China, Australia, Egypt, and New Zealand; they experiment about rearing sheep, growing tea, or cultivating cotton in a new and untried country. This style of conducting business brings all the faculties into play. The warehouses of textile fabrics are Babylonian monuments, the front of one being 500 feet long, and the bales being raised by steam-power. A certain cotton mill contains 300,000 spindles. A friend of mine, an engineer, informs me that authentic statistics show the profits of cotton-spinning in the Manchester district to have amounted during two years to £20,000,000 monthly, and that at present the profit is as much as £8,000,000. We visited the establishments of Shaw and Platt, the one a cotton-spinner, the other a manufacturer of spindles. Platt makes 23,000 spindles weekly, and he has made as many as 35,000; he employs 4,800 workpeople, and does a business amounting to a million and a half annually, of which his profits in one year have been estimated at £200,000. On entering these workshops one is struck with amazement—the whole is a gigantic and ordered chaos, a labyrinth of wheels, gearing, revolving leather bands, a living and moving structure, wherein from floor to ceiling and from story to story work goes on at a giddy pace, as if the whole were an unwearied and indefatigable automaton. In a spacious shed, flame eighteen forges, each flanked by two smaller ones; a hive of workmen labours in the gloom interspersed with lurid flames. In Sharp's locomotive factory from seven to eight hundred workmen turn out an hundred locomotives annually, each worth £3,000. One must come here in order to learn the puissance of fire and water; what we see are melting moulds, resembling trunks of trees; slotting machines which tear off shreds of iron; drilling machines which pierce holes through iron plates as thick as one's thumb as easily as through butter; steam-hammers of 500 lbs. weight, which are so completely under control that they will crack a nut without crushing the kernel; monster shears, gigantic forges. Eight men, ranged in a row, push a tree of red-hot iron, and as large as one's body, into one of these flaming furnaces. Here man is but an insect; the host of machines alone attracts attention.

When gazing upon these oddly-shapen creatures of

steel, so laborious and industrious, amid the grindings and thunderings of their headlong speed, one recalls the subterranean dwarfs and giants of Scandinavian mythology, the deformed monsters who in mountain caves forged ornaments and armour for the gods. At the present day they labour for the insect; he is their master, and sometimes, on seeing the disproportion between the labourers and their head, one forgets on what terms he governs them.

XXVI.

MANCHESTER AND LIVERPOOL.

ON examining a geological map, a large space, coloured black, is seen around Manchester; this is the coal district. Towns spring up there like gigantic mushrooms; around Manchester there are seven or eight new ones with populations of from 40,000 to 45,000 persons, such as Oldham, for instance, which I have just visited. My friend, the French engineer, informs me that 1,000 lbs. of coal cost from 5s. to 8s. here; that the same quantity costs 19s. 2d. at Paris; at Bordeaux from 12s. 6d. to 15s; and in the department of the Vosges from 1l. 8s. to 1l. 15s. Around Birmingham and Glasgow there are the same black marks and the same results. In addition there is clay suited for making bricks; and here, as at London, there is a vast estuary, an outlet, the natural port of Liverpool, capable of holding entire fleets. Add to this a persevering and prolific labouring population, and you will realise this astounding collection of products, of human beings, and of buildings. My friend adds two facts which, in his opinion, explain the prosperity of these vast establishments. On the one hand, the gross capital employed is enormous, and, in the industrial rivalry of different nations victory is always on the side of large battalions. On the other, the organisation is excellent, the workman is industrious, and faithfully copies the pattern placed before him; the foreman is attentive, and is always at his post to the minute; the machines are of superior quality, and the amount of work they will perform can be calculated with precision. Workmen, foremen, machines, clerks, representatives, all perform their duties with regularity and constancy, like a well-poised and well-lubricated wheel. The master spends four hours daily in his counting-house and workshop, supervising the whole; that is enough. The discipline and harmonious action of his subordinates suffice for what remains.

We started for Liverpool. Its name denotes an old pond, and, in truth, the flat damp country, bathed in sea-mist and covered with stagnant water, seems less adapted for men than for wild-duck. Now and then the land appears primeval; untilled downs and sandy-bogs are to be seen; the region, unenclosed, terminates at the horizon in a faint streak of pale verdure. Heavy violet-tinted clouds, exhalations of the sea and the soil, as in Holland, fill and dim the space which stretches beneath the low canopy of sky and the limitless plain.

At the entrance to the city there is a huge Grecian building, a sort of temple with gilt panels, and pillars in imitation jasper, and serving as a concert-hall. In it a frightfully harsh-toned organ makes a din. On the opposite side, in front, is a library which cost £50,000, the legacy of a private individual. This is not the place to seek beauty and elegance. Liverpool is a giant, like Manchester; the shops and warehouses are on a vast scale; the streets are vast, and the houses which line them resemble those of London in being overladen with arcades, pillars, and pilasters, the effect produced on the beholder being an impression of crowding and heaviness. The inhabitants number 500,000, and the port is the most frequented after that of London.

Along the docks the cotton warehouses form a kind of cyclopian, endless and monotonous rampart; nearly all the cotton of the world is housed here. But the appearance of the docks themselves effaces everything. The Mersey, as large as an arm of the sea, stretches towards the west, carrying vessels away and bearing them home. For a distance of six miles along its bank these vessels pass through canals into basins lined with stone, resembling watery streets and squares, multiplied and ramified, wherein they are repaired or discharge their cargoes. Their closely-packed masts appear like a forest in winter, extending as far as the eye can reach, and blocking up the entire horizon towards the north. Yet the spacious and numerous docks do not suffice to contain the multitude of ships; they are crowded together in rows and masses at the entrances, awaiting their turn to pass in; at Birkenhead, on the opposite bank, new docks are being built for their accommodation.

I believe this spectacle to be one of the grandest in the world. Some of the vessels are 3,500, others 4,000 tons burden. A steamer is upwards of 300 feet in length. A vessel at anchor, the *Great Britain*, is about to carry 1,200 emigrants to Australia. If one descends the dry docks to the keels of the ships, one perceives that the hull is from forty to fifty feet in height. The swelling and copper-sheathed sides have the fine curves of a sea-bird about to slumber upon the waves.

The view from Birkenhead commands the harbour

and the vast reach of the river; it is rather agitated, and gleams with yellow lustre, amid a slight haze. The steamboats ascend and descend, cross and re-cross, with stiff mechanical movements, like black crabs. Sailing ships, lightly heeling over, skim along like beautiful swans. The *George*, a man-of-war carrying 86 guns, arrives in lordly style, all the others making way for her. On the other side the boundless row of masts and rigging lines the sky, while the huge city is massed behind.

We visit several workshops, among others, the establishment of Messrs. Laird, the builders of iron ships. It is said that within the last thirty years they have built two hundred and fifty; they employ fifteen hundred workpeople, have gigantic furnaces and machines, and have stocks, to which water is brought through canals. At present the hull of a paddle steamer is on the stocks, its length is 350 feet, and it is designed to make the passage between England and Ireland at the speed of twenty miles an hour. It will cost from £80,000 to £100,000, will be completed in six months; the iron compartments which contain the eight boilers are composed of metal beams as large as a man's body.

The same impression is always produced, that of hugeness. Yet do labour and power suffice to render a man happy? M. B——, a leading merchant, sits for three hours after dinner with his guests drinking port wine in silence. Another, whenever he can get away, rushes off to his country seat to brace up his nerves; he is enthusiastic about breeding pigs. When man is dissatisfied with his lot he seeks for compensation in dream-land. I was shown a spot where four or five preachers—Methodists for the most part—come to address a crowd on Sunday in the open air; the idea of the Kingdom of God, of the loving Christ, of the all-powerful and tender friend, is one refuge for distressed minds.

Another refuge is intoxication. The authoress of a "Life for a Life" writes:—"This Liverpool is an awful town for drinking. Other towns may be as bad; statistics prove it; but I know no place where intoxication is so open and shameless. Not only in bye streets and foul courts, where one expects to see it, but everywhere. I never take a short railway journey in the after part of the day but I am liable to meet at least one drunken 'gentleman' snoozing in his first-class carriage; or, in the second class, two or three drunken 'men,' singing, swearing, or pushed stupidly about by pale-faced wives. The sadness of the thing is that the wives do not seem to mind it, that everybody takes it quite as a matter of course. The 'gentleman,' often grey-haired, is but 'merry,' as he is accustomed to be every night of his life; the poor man has only 'had a drop or two,' as all his comrades are in the habit of taking whenever they get the chance; they see no disgrace in it, so they laugh at him a bit, and humour him, and are quite ready to stand up for him against all incomers who may object to such a fellow-passenger. *They* don't; nor do the women belonging to them, who are well-used to tolerate drunken sweethearts, and lead about and pacify drunken husbands."

It is now six o'clock, and we return through the poorer quarter. What a sight! In the vicinity of Leeds Street there are fifteen or twenty streets across which cords are stretched and covered with rags and linen, hung up to dry. Bands of children swarm on every flight of steps, five or six are clustered on each step, the eldest holding the smallest; their faces are pale, their light hair in disorder, their clothes are in tatters, they have neither shoes nor stockings, and they are all shockingly dirty; their faces and hands appearing to be encrusted with dust and soot. Perhaps two hundred children romp and wallow in a single street. On nearer approach one sees one of the mothers and a grown-up sister, with little more covering than their chemises, crouching in the dusky passage. What interiors! They contain a little piece of worn oil-cloth, sometimes a shell ornament, one or two plaster ornaments; in the one corner is seated the idiot grandmother; the wife is busied in mending the wretched rags of clothing, the children push each other about. The smell resembles that of an old rag-shop. The ground-floor of nearly every dwelling is a flagged and damp basement. Can one imagine what life in these cellars must be during winter? Some of the younger children are still fresh and rosy, but their large blue eyes are painful to behold; their good blood will deteriorate; as they grow older they will waste away, the flesh becoming flabby and of an unhealthy pallor; many of their faces are scrofulous, being marked with small sores covered with plaister. As we proceed the crowd is more dense. Tall youths seated or half-crouching at the side of the pavement play with black cards. Old, bearded hags come out of the gin-shops; their legs totter; their dull looks and besotted smile are indescribable: it appears as if their features had been slowly eaten away by vitriol. The rags which they wear are falling to pieces, displaying their filthy skins; these were once the fashionable dresses of fine ladies. A shocking detail is that these streets are built with regularity, and have a modern aspect; probably this is a quarter modernised and rendered more airy by a beneficent municipality; such, then, is the best that can be done for the poor. The uniform row of buildings and pavements borders the two sides of the way, inclosing in its mathematical lines this teeming heap of horrors and human wretchedness. The air is close and oppressive, the light wan and dim; there is not a tint or a shape on which the eye can rest with pleasure; Rembrandt's beggars were far better off in their picturesque holes. And I have not yet seen the Irish quarter! The Irish abound here; it is supposed they number 100,000; their quarter is the lowest circle of Hell. Not so, however; there is a still worse and lower deep, particularly, I am informed, at Belfast, in Ireland, where, in the evening, on leaving the factories, girls without stockings, shoes, or shifts, in their grey working-dress, loiter on the pavement to add a few pence to their day's earnings.

XXVII.

ENGLISH WORKING MEN.

AFTER careful observation, it appears to me that the types of workmen which are most prominent, and round which the largest number of varieties may be grouped, are as follows:—

First, the athletic and well-fed type. The trunk is square-set, the frame is huge, the breech enormous; porter is said to be the agent in thus developing their muscles. These broad backs, brawny chests, massive shoulders, constitute a superb spectacle. Some of the men are giants of six feet and upwards. This type is most frequently met with in the iron manufactories; a placid colossus may be there seen placing and turning monster pieces in the forge. My friends tell me that I shall meet with still finer specimens in Yorkshire.

Secondly, the phlegmatic; this is found everywhere, but chiefly in the cotton mills, and, in truth, nearly all the faces blend into this type. The colour of those belonging to it is pale, their eyes are dull, their expression is cold and fixed, their movements are correct, regular, and under control; they expend no more than the minimum of exertion, and hence it is that they are first-rate workers, being mere machines adapted for guiding machinery.

French manufacturers tell me that in France a workman is very diligent during the first hour, less so during the second, still less so during the third, and so on in diminishing ratio, till he becomes good for nothing during the last. His muscular power gives way, and his attention becomes relaxed. Here, on the contrary, the workman labours as well during the last as during the first hour. Besides, his working day is but ten hours, while that of the French workman is twelve. As a consequence of his more uniform attention, an Englishman can accomplish more work. In Shaw's mill, a man and two children are able to manage 2,400 spindles; in France, two men and three or four—sometimes more—children are required to perform the same task. By way of compensation, the French workman is more neat-handed in some respects; the weavers of the Vosges, for example, produce stuffs far neater and prettier than any produced in this country. The difference between the two races is always the same. The Frenchman appreciates and instinctively discovers harmony and elegance; he has a taste for them. A Parisian ironmonger told me that, after the conclusion of the Treaty of Commerce, a quantity of English tools, such as files, awls, and planes, was imported into France. These tools were of good quality, the handles were solid, the blades excellent, their prices were moderate—nevertheless they were unsaleable. The Parisian workman examined them, handled them, and ended by saying— "These don't please the eye;" he never bought any. An excellence always engenders a defect, and reciprocally. This delicacy of sense and these exigencies of the imagination hinder the French workman from being steady, persevering, unyielding, when the task is monotonous; he does not understand how to tread the appointed round like a cart-horse; he stops now and then, goes on at redoubled pace, becomes sick of his work, is tempted to try a new method, and to follow the bent of his fancy.

How do the English workmen live, and what are their receipts and expenses? On this head I possess recent statistical works—among others the work of Mr. Chadwick, but more especially the information given to me by engineering and manufacturing friends. In iron manufactories, the good workmen earn from 33s. to 36s. weekly; the others from 15s. to 20s. In cotton mills a man earns from 16s. to 28s. a week; a woman, a young girl, or boy, from 7s. to 12s.; thus, a wife and children help to swell the family earnings. It is estimated that the average wage in Lancashire is 20s. for an adult, and that he can live upon 10s.; that if he have a wife and four children, he must expend 30s.; and that in general his receipts and his expenses exactly balance each other. He swims on the top, and with difficulty; it is the skilled and superior workman who can alone command his price. The lot of the others is very hard when an accident, an illness, or a suspension of business occurs. Five causes of misery weigh upon them.

Firstly, as the climate is very bad, they are obliged to expend much in coal, light, spirits, meat, and they have to wash and change their clothes at short intervals. In addition, workmen in general are thriftless, and the English workman in particular. At Oldham he takes four meals a day—tea, coffee, a bottle and a half of ale, butter, cheese, and has meat three times. At Manchester the working classes are notorious for getting the first of the early vegetables. Secondly, as competition is very severe, each one is bound to labour to the utmost of his strength; more exertion is required here than elsewhere to keep one's head above water; at the slightest symptom of exhaustion one sinks to the bottom, and the bottom is truly terrible. Thirdly, they have children in droves—four, five, more frequently six and upwards. One of my friends knows families in which there are fifteen and eighteen. Count the cost of pregnancy, of the confinement, of the baby clothes, of the illnesses of the children and of the mother; besides, a child has to be maintained, and earns nothing up to the age of ten years. If four survive out of the whole number, it is imperative either that the industry of the country should double itself every thirty years, or that one-half of the population should emigrate. Fourthly, under the rule of the industrial system dull seasons are inevitable. Sometimes you are deprived by a rival nation of a market upon which you counted; sometimes it is closed by scarcity, war, or the changes of fashion. Add to this strikes, and hundreds of thousands of working men turned into the streets without work to do or food to eat. Fifthly, they are prone to drunkenness, and of all curses this is the most awful. The climate disposes them to it, because it is really needful for them to warm themselves, to cheer up, and to enjoy themselves, forgetting for the moment the gloom and strain of their lives. I have just read the annual reports made by a clergyman to a charitable society; from this point of view they are tragical.

The effect of these causes combined is that few workmen rise to be independent, becoming fundholders, or small shopkeepers. A person who is in constant association with them, and who has lived here for twenty-six years, calculates that the proportion of these fortunate ones is five in every hundred, or one in twenty. Most of the others die in hospitals, in workhouses, or are maintained in their old age by their children. As a rule, the industrial system deteriorates a population; the population of Manchester, for instance, is more stunted than that of Oldham, a new town. As the majority of English workmen is engaged in manufactures, and as agriculture is here a manufacture also, it is necessary, if we would compare the average of happiness in France with the average of happiness in England, to contrast the life of an English working man with that of a French peasant. The latter is frugal, follows beaten paths, and moves within a narrow sphere; yet he is nearly always the possessor of a piece of land or on the way to acquire it, that is to say, capital in a tangible shape, a secure means of subsistence, which puts his mind at ease and over which he gloats in imagination; moreover, the agricultural system and peasant culture are compatible with the most natural and the least constrained form of existence. By way of compensation, the English workman, especially in the cities, possesses more ideas and notions of all kinds, more intelligence in social, political, and religious matters; in short, his horizon is more extended. He hears important interests discussed and the affairs of different countries; he reads the newspapers, and collects curiosities. Recently an itinerant lecturer delivered two lectures on Macaulay here, the price of admission was 1s. 6d., and the hall was filled with working men. In London gratuitous and public lectures on the utility of geology had to be established. There is another reason for development. A working man who is a unit in a large organisation feels how greatly he is dependent upon others, in consequence of this he associates with his comrades, and thus escapes from a life of isolation. A—— narrated to me the history of twenty-five working men who, having each saved thirty pounds sterling, formed an association some years ago in order to manufacture engines. For several months they had no orders. Taking counsel together they resolved to persevere and reduce the outgoings of each to 3s. 6d. weekly—that is to say, they fasted, they and their families. A customer appeared, became interested in them, bought an engine, and invited the public to come and see it; the engine turned out very well, and their credit was thus secured; they prospered, and, after giving them compensation, they expelled twelve of their number, who were not industrious or skilful enough, reorganising their society on a new basis. At first each one was manager in turn; now, the most capable is chosen to be the permanent manager. He distributes several pounds annually in dividends, but devotes the greater portion of the profits to extend the business. The present value of the business is from £5,000 to £6,000. The labours of the manager are performed gratuitously, all the members work with their hands or superintend the workshops; not one dreams about retiring and living in idleness on his gains.

Visiting Oldham, we found the working men keeping holiday in honour of the society to which they belong. They walked in procession, carrying flags—on one flag, that of the brickmakers, were the portraits of the founders; in the centre was a luminous eye surrounded with mottoes, to the effect that they asked for justice and nothing but justice. The excitement was great, women and children walked alongside, forming an escort. The women were neither pale nor slim; they had fine plump naked arms, broad shoulders, ample bosoms; their trunks were badly set up, but their frames were substantial; even the slender ones had powerful skeletons. They remained congregated outside the doors while their husbands feasted within.

Here, as in all the other manufacturing towns, the aim of the society is to keep wages at a certain level, and to increase them. All these societies are in correspondence, and have their head-office in London. When one of them goes on strike its members are maintained out of the local funds, and by the central funds also, should the central committee consider the object praiseworthy. To meet these expenses each workman subscribes a shilling weekly; in addition he pledges himself not to work for less than a particular wage. As compensation, during illness, or when work is slack, he is paid so much a day out of the common fund. Meetings are held once a week; these meetings, as well as the regulations, are kept secret. The presidents, treasurers, and other officers, are elected; their duties are performed gratuitously; each workman fills one of the posts in turn. Thus constituted, these societies are very powerful; their capital amounts to several millions of francs; they have been able to continue strikes for six months, and even for a year, sometimes with success. Every workman who leaves the union, or refuses to join it, is regarded as a black sheep; he is sent to Coventry, no one speaks to him, no one answers him, he is condemned to moral isolation. The result of investigations recently made has been to show that to these means of intimidation are added violence, sometimes robbery, and even murder; a secret committee, or kind of Vehm Gericht, pronounces and executes the sentence. Associations of this kind naturally lead to the establishment of a dictatorship. It is noteworthy that these societies do not lose sight of their special object. They have no other aim than the increase of wages, they never think of attacking the Government, as they would assuredly do in France. They are not political; they are not even social; they entertain no Utopian schemes, never dream about reconstituting society, suppressing interest, abolishing inheritance, equalising incomes, making the State a joint-stock company, in which every individual is a shareholder. Manufacturers tell me here that in this country there is nothing of that sort: "Our working men do not generalise like yours; besides, they have a smattering of political economy; above all, they have too much common sense to pursue chimeras. A strike is what we have to fear, and not a socialistic movement." I have just read a very fine novel written by a person who lived here, and who was an acute observer, "North and South," by the late Mrs. Gaskell, in which the character of a working man is depicted and the history of a strike is narrated. If the portrait is as faithful as I believe it to be, then the men of that class are possessed of a large store of reason and fairness. They are perpetually at variance with the masters, but the struggle is restricted to the question of supply and demand. In this enclosed field each one is armed with the same weapon, the refusal to give or undertake employment, a refusal as hurtful to the one as to the other. Each one persists in his refusal in proportion to his courage and strength, the working man fasting and the master being ruined; thus the struggle is at once fair and lawful. While awaiting the result the law is respected, and there is no resort to force; opinion is a neutral power which the working man must gain to his side by displaying wisdom and patience. Such is Higden's advice with regard to strikes. B—— tells me that he is acquainted with many working men who follow this line of conduct. They admit that a dispute between master and workman is a matter of private concern; society may remain apart; in any case, society has the right not to be disturbed by the strife, while master and workman have both their rights, the one to dispute about his price, the other to defend his interests in his own fashion. B—— engaged a skilled workman at high wages for his manufactory in France, but did so subject to the condition that his wages would be diminished by one-half should he mention their amount to his new comrades. "I understand, sir," the workman replied, "it is proper that the masters should make their own bargains." According to B——, a French working man would not be able to forget himself in this way, and consider the matter coolly and abstractedly. Transported into an out-of-the-way village, this man has worked very hard; his life is not lively, he does not know a word of French, and is unable to converse with his fellows. But he has his little son, with whom he diverts himself greatly. B—— sends him an English newspaper three times a week, and exchanges a few words with him when inspecting the manufactory. These things suffice for him; he has lived more than a year in this way, silent and respected.

Nevertheless the situation has had its effect, and it cannot be denied that the workman regards his master as his natural enemy. The masters make very great and very praiseworthy efforts with a view to lessen this feeling of hostility. They found or become trustees of savings-banks and of penny banks, in which the workman may deposit his smallest saving. They build and let houses to them on a system which, through the operation of a sinking fund, enables the workmen to become owners of them after the lapse of a certain number of years. They establish ragged schools and mechanics' institutes. When the Queen paid a visit to Manchester, sixty thousand Sunday-school children were ranged before her, and sang "God save the Queen."

The masters are obliged to send to school for two hours daily all the children from twelve to fifteen years of age who work in their factories. The principle involved is at once a question of interest and philanthropy; all these institutions are designed to diminish improvidence, which is said to be the capital vice of the English working man. Here the animal nature is too strong; the reasonable and reasoning faculty can with difficulty come to the surface. Its flame is smothered beneath the thick and heavy smoke of the instincts, nor does it flash forth spontaneously, keenly, lightly, as in the Southern races. It must be fanned, fed with suitable material, before it waxes strong enough to vanquish the gross matter which obscures it. When this occurs it is all-powerful; but nowhere is the civilisation of the human being a matter more urgent and indispensable.

We visited several establishments for instruction and public recreation. We went first to Peel's Park, a sort of large English garden, situated in the heart of the city, where the poor may seat themselves amid trees and flowers. It was founded by means of a private subscription amounting to £35,000, and includes in addition a museum and a library. The museum contains a gallery of first-rate paintings and drawings, which the owners have lent for six months; a room of natural history, containing collections of birds, serpents, butterflies, &c.; a room filled with old or foreign fabrics; a room filled with industrial products, such as cotton, hemp, madder—in short, an array of objects to instruct the mind and please the eye. Our guide, who was a leading merchant, said to us: "All these things address the senses, and do so in an interesting manner; they all attract the working men, and impart ideas to them; it is indeed necessary that they should have something to distract their thoughts; moreover, every hour spent here is so much time abstracted from the public-house." He called our attention to the fact that there were no keepers in the rooms, they being under the protection of public honesty and good sense; not a single article has been stolen, injured, or even handled, and the average number of daily visitors is 2,550.

Thence we proceeded to the free library, also established by private subscription, and chiefly used by working men. It contains 25,000 volumes. The librarian said that there are 10,000 readers a month; newspapers are to be found there also. Whoever is introduced by two respectable persons may borrow books; from 1,200 to 1,400 persons are regular borrowers. I learn from the register that the lives of Nelson and Wellington are chiefly in request, and that even theological works find readers. According to our guide, many of these working men are well informed, and make collections; one was mentioned who knew the names and appearance of 900 species of beetles. Natural history and the natural sciences in general are greatly to their liking; they are fond of facts, and of proofs established by experiment, and are often led far beyond the Bible to the very depths of Positivism; the Secularists get many recruits from among their number. On the other hand, they read treatises on political economy, and newspapers; now English newspapers, even those of a small town, are instructive, filled with correspondence, with circumstantial and accurate information. It seems to me that one of these working men, who does not drink, and who reads for an hour a day, must have a well-filled and healthy head.

Another institution, the Mechanics' Institute, is also founded and maintained by subscription. It has six hundred pupils, both girls and boys, above the age of ten years. There are two sorts of classes: in the one, French, German, drawing, music, and mathematics are taught to pupils who pay a small fee, and who are generally tradesmen's children. The other classes are free; reading, writing, lineal drawing, and arithmetic are taught. Many factory boys and girls, in ragged clothes, attend them, being sent by their employers. The principal object of the instruction given is to impart a knowledge of lineal drawing and of mathematics; in the upper class, where the pupils are from thirteen to sixteen years of age, the sixth book of Euclid is taught; it is necessary that they should understand their machines. Generally, the master appoints one of his class to act as monitor. There is a library adjoining, containing a thousand volumes, and a room containing newspapers and reviews, which the pupils are allowed to read. At present there is one or more of these schools, specially adapted for the working class, in all the manufacturing towns, and the good results yielded by them are highly spoken of. The fundamental maxim on which they have acted is, that unless a nation be educated it will become ungovernable. Religion aids them in this undertaking; a Protestant must learn to read his Bible. Many schools are attached to the churches, more especially to Dissenting chapels; as a general rule the church engenders the school.

I infinitely admire the spirit of all these institutions, the generous initiative and sensible conduct of the private individuals who freely, and at their own cost, bestow a benefit on the public at large, and engage in affairs of State without State aid. Here large sums are usefully bestowed. To act by oneself, with purse or otherwise, to give the impetus and not wait till it has been given, is quite natural to them. Many burdens to which we submit they would deem insupportable; they have a horror of anything savouring of classification and the barrack. For instance, there are no compartments wherein passengers are herded together at the railway stations; they wait for the train on the platform. Luggage is not registered; each one puts his luggage where he pleases, and finds it again if he can. Yesterday an omnibus was turned from its regular line of route into a side street to oblige two ladies who had obtained the consent of the passengers. Moreover, as it rained, the conductor permitted three persons in excess of the number to stand inside. Last Sunday, in a square, a poor fanatical wretch, a sort of bearded Bunyan, with an old hat and shabby surtout, mounted a post, the New Testament in his hand, and began to lecture:—"You see that the Apostles did not venture to bury our Lord, it was Nicodemus, a rich man and a gentleman, who did it, and this was necessary in order that the prophecy of St. John might be fulfilled." Thereupon he read the prophecy. "Then you ought not to trust tradition, but believe in the Scriptures." He ended by offering up a prayer in a contrite tone, his eyes turned to heaven. His audience numbered about thirty; several boys played tricks and threw his hat down, but five or six persons with stern or wasted countenances listened to him with attention One of the hearers said to me that it was wrong to torment the man, that he neither offended nor insulted any one, that he had the right to speak as his conscience dictated. For my own part, what struck me was his seriousness and his courage; he was unmoved by ridicule; he went forward; having something to say, he uttered it, and cared nothing for what might happen. Self-help is always the watchword, and is one little understood in France; from the same interior source issue forth the societies, the institutions which abound here, among others the municipal institutions; Manchester administers her own affairs, pays and appoints her police, governs herself almost without the intervention of the Government. Consequently the social edifice rests upon thousands of independent columns, and not like ours, upon a single one; accidents, catastrophes, like our revolutions of 1830, of 1848, of 1852, are impossible here.

XXVIII.

SCENES IN MANCHESTER.

OUR friend, the merchant, took us to a large workhouse outside the city. There is another in the city containing 1,200 paupers; this one, however, can accommodate 1,900, but at present it contains 350 only. It cost £75,000; the annual expenses of the two amount to £55,000 raised by the poor-rate; the master's salary is £200, the doctor's £170. Each superintendent receives £20, exclusive of board, lodging, and washing; a master shoemaker receives £1 a week for teaching his trade. The guardians give their services gratuitously. The building is spacious, perfectly clean, well kept; it has large courts, gardens are attached to it, looks upon fields and stately trees; it has a chapel, and rooms of which the ceilings are twenty feet high. It is evident that the founders and managers had made it a matter of conscience to produce a work which should be beautiful, correct, and useful. There is no smell anywhere; the beds are almost white, and are furnished with figured coverlets; the most aged and feeble women have white caps and new clothes. Everything has been considered and arranged to maintain a pleasing effect. One room is set apart for the lunatics, another for the female idiots;

the latter do needle work for some hours daily; during the period of recreation they dance together to the sounds of a fiddle. They make strange grimaces, yet they all seem healthy and not at all sad. In another room the children are taught their lessons, one of the elder children acting as monitor. The kitchen is monumental. Eight or ten cauldrons are set in solid masonry, some to cook the oatmeal gruel, which is the principal article of food. The daily ration of each inmate consists of two pounds of this oatmeal and a pound and a half of potatoes; four times a week the allowance is increased by four ounces of pie or of meat without bone. The drink is water, except during illness. We were astounded; this was a palace compared with the kennels in which the poor dwell. One of us seriously asked our friend to reserve a place for him here during his old age. Recollect that a Manchester or Liverpool labourer can scarcely procure meat once a week by working ten hours a day! Here an able-bodied pauper works about six hours, has newspapers, the Bible, and some good books and reviews to read, lives in a wholesome air, and enjoys the sight of trees. Nevertheless there is not an able-bodied inmate of this workhouse at this moment; it is almost empty, and will not be filled till the winter. When a working man out of employment applies for help to the authorities he is commonly told, "Show us that you wish to work by entering the workhouse." Nine out of ten decline. Whence this dislike? To-day at a street-corner I saw an old woman groping with her skinny hands in a heap of rubbish, and pulling out scraps of vegetables; probably she would not give up her drop of spirits. But what of the others? I am informed that they prefer their home and their freedom at any price, that they cannot bear being shut up and subjected to discipline. They prefer to be free and to starve. But the children, these little ones, with their white skulls sprinkled with flaxen hair, crowded in a room around a pale mother; how is their father able to witness such a spectacle? He does support the sight; he will not separate himself from those of his household, abandon his position as head of the family, and be cabined alone in a compartment; he thinks that, if he submitted to this, he would cease to be a man. The workhouse is regarded as a prison; the poor consider it a point of honour not to go there. Perhaps it must be admitted that the system of administration is foolishly despotic and worrying, that is the fault of every administrative system; the human being becomes a machine; he is treated as if he were devoid of feeling, and insulted quite unconsciously. In "Our Mutual Friend," Dickens has depicted the distaste for the workhouse while siding with the poor.

I spent the evening at Bellevue to see the popular amusements. This is a sort of dancing hall, surrounded by a garden, in which there are shows, curiosities, trumpery works of art. The siege of Badajoz was represented on a stage ornamented with the portrait of Wellington, and this patriotic performance was greeted with loud applause. Shortly afterwards there were fireworks. In the gardens bands of working men and small shopkeepers ate and drank, and played at kiss-in-the-ring. Inside, in a spacious room, working men danced with great energy and vigour, but without indecency, and thus compensated themselves for the deprivation of exercise during the week. Many have a rough and surly air; not one of them has an air of roguery and swagger. The athlete, the relation of the bull and the watch-dog, always appears instead of the witty rascal, the relation of the spaniel and the monkey. The price of admission is a shilling; the ball costs sixpence extra. As Bellevue is some little way off, being at the extremity of a quarter of the city, the expense of transport must be added; indeed there were plenty of omnibuses and cabs at the gate. Reckon also the refreshments, and remember that, as the workman generally brings his sweetheart with him, he must pay for two. Now, a spinner's wage is about 23s. weekly Such is a specimen of English extravagance. B—— says that a workman who earns 5s. a day often spends 4s. on food and drink. Some of the men filling subordinate posts in the iron factories can make as much in good years as £150, £200, and even £300. They expend the whole, and put nothing in the savings-bank. B—— maintains that an English workman who is industrious and thrifty, is certain, unless hindered by accident or illness, to prosper, or at least to gain a livelihood. But the people are not thrifty.

From ten o'clock till midnight two policemen, whom our friends introduced to us, led us through the disreputable quarters. There are six hundred policemen in Manchester, and each gets about 1l. weekly. Those who went with us were detectives. One of them had been twenty-six years in Manchester; the other had been employed in several large towns. Both were serious, sensible, prudent men; they made no parade of their talents, they spoke but little, and their answers were to the point. With their impassive countenance and their meditative expression, they inspired confidence and had an air of dignity. They corroborated what we had heard about the aversion of the poor for the workhouse; in their opinion the workhouse itself was good for nothing, and merely encouraged idleness. A family and three children can live upon 30s. a week; and they make this amount. But most of the men marry young, often at eighteen; at thirty they have six children; they drink much and save nothing; the wife becomes a bad housekeeper in becoming a good factory hand. As a rule, when a workman dies he does not leave enough to pay for his funeral.

We inspected the night lodging-houses, where, in a low and unventilated room, four to five hundred beds were occupied. A whole bed costs fivepence, the half twopence-halfpenny. A husband and wife were in one of the beds. The man's face was thin and pitiful—pallid, sallow, and sunken, as if by illness; it had the look of an old mask in wax. In a casino we found five hundred persons, poverty-stricken in appearance, crowded on greasy seats in front of a platform whereon danced two slender girls in pink gauze. Twopence is the price of admission; the company drank gin and smoked; the atmosphere, loaded with human exhalations, was suffocating. We entered a house of ill-fame. The policeman told us that its inmates are chiefly recruited from the factories. They were collected in a low room, and were decently clad; many were thin, and their vulgar faces had a savage cast. Close to an oily mulatto woman, the pretty form of a young, delicate, and intelligent girl was pensively seated before a blazing fire. The season was July, yet a fire in the evenings is necessary. It was the same in the thieves' kitchen. We visited twenty or thirty of these haunts. A huge mass of coal was burning for cooking purposes and for drying clothes. The men smoked and played dominoes, and, without uttering a word, they gazed upon us with their fixed and gleaming wild-animal looking eyes. The effect of the flaring gaslight on these countenances was horrible. I have seen similar quarters and similar dens in Paris, Bordeaux, and Marseilles, but nowhere has the impression made been as strong. It resembles that produced by a nightmare or one of Edgar Poe's tales. The gaslight does not wholly illumine the darkness of the heavy, choking air, impregnated with unknown exhalations; nothing is more startling than this blackness dotted with flickering lights. The symmetrical streets resemble the skeletons of streets mechanically ranged in motionless rows. Unfortunates wearing soiled bonnets drag along their frippery and their smiles; as they pass, one feels inclined to start back as at the approach of a spectre or of a troubled spirit. Every ten minutes we enter a different den: on our exit, the low room, blazing fire, flaring gas, the filthy band of haggard, beseeching, or dangerous faces, made us think about a vent-hole of Hell. Certainly the horrible and the unclean are worse here than elsewhere

XXIX.

CHARACTERISTICS OF THE ENGLISH MIND.

IT seems to me that I begin to understand the form of the English mind, so different from that of the French mind. When I feel a notion of that sort dawning upon me I impart it to two or three English friends who have travelled; I submit it to their judgment, we discuss it together; at the close of the discussion the notion is corrected or developed, and such as it is I commit it to writing on the following day.

The interior of an English head may not unaptly be likened to one of Murray's "Hand-books," which contains many facts and few ideas; a quantity of useful and precise information, short statistical abridgments, numerous figures, correct and detailed maps, brief and dry historical notices, moral and profitable counsels in the guise of a preface, no view of the subject as a whole, none of the literary graces, a simple collection of well-authenticated documents, a convenient memorandum for personal guidance during a journey. A Frenchman requires that everything and every piece of writing should be cast in a pleasing form; an Englishman is satisfied if the substance be useful. A Frenchman loves ideas in and for themselves; an Englishman employs them as instruments of mnemonics or of prevision. I am about to cite two small facts which will serve as specimens. Stephenson, the great engineer, was asked how he had invented his machines, and the locomotive among others. He replied that it was due to a power of imagining and conceiving with the utmost precision the different parts, their forms, sizes, and connections, their possible movements, and the entire series of changes which the alteration of a part, a size, or of a connection would introduce into their combined working. Thus his mind resembled a workshop, in which all the articles were numbered and classified; he took them in turn, arranged them, mentally set them going, and, by dint of trying, he hit upon the practical combination. As a contrast, Léon Foucault told me that, having one day discovered a proposition of speculative mechanics which Huyghens and Lagrange had overlooked, he worked it out to its final consequences, and these led him to the idea of his governor. In general a Frenchman arrives at the comprehension of a thing by means of classifications and by the deductive method, while the Englishman does so by induction, by dint of concentration and remembrance, thanks to the clear and persistent representation of a quantity of separate facts, by the indefinite accumulation of documents, either isolated or placed in juxtaposition.

Bearing upon this point is a letter in Carlyle's "Life of John Sterling," with which I have always been struck. Sterling was at the Island of St. Vincent, in the West Indies, when he wrote it. A hurricane had devastated the island; he and his wife, who was pregnant, had a narrow escape. He relates to his mother the story of what occurred. Note that the narrator is a man of letters, and a poet, that he has received a thorough education, and is a master of his native tongue. Yet in this case, as in all similar cases, the first care of an Englishman is to transmit to another a true, an exact, and a graphic account. His description is a pure statement of facts:—" My dear Mother, ... Nearly all the property, both of Susan and myself—the very house we lived in—was suddenly destroyed by a visitation of Providence far more terrible than any I have ever witnessed. When Susan came from her room to breakfast, at eight o'clock, I pointed out to her the extraordinary height and violence of the surf, and the singular appearance of the clouds of heavy rain sweeping down the valleys before us. . . . . A very few minutes after the closing of the windows I found that the shutters of Tyrrell's room, at the south and commonly the most sheltered end of the house, were giving way. I tried to tie them, and I found in pushing at the leaf of the shutter that the wind resisted more as if it had been a stone wall or a mass of iron than a mere current of air. The rain on my face and hands felt like so much small shot from a gun. There was great exertion necessary to shut the door of the house. About nine o'clock the panes of glass were smashed by the mere force of the gale, without anything having touched them. . . . . The front windows were giving way with successive crashes, and the floor shook as you may have seen a carpet on a gusty day in London. I went into our bedroom, where I found Susan, Tyrrell, and a little coloured girl of seven or eight years old; and I told them that we should probably not be alive in half an hour. The house was under two parallel roofs; and the one next the sea, which sheltered the other, and us who were under the other, went off, I suppose about ten o'clock. After my old plan, I will give you a sketch, from which you may perceive how we were situated." And, in fact, he draws a plan, or rather two geometrical plans, with letters and indications. "In plan No. 1, *a a* are the windows that were first destroyed; *b* went next; my books were between the windows *b* and on the wall opposite to them. The lines *c* and *d* mark the directions of the two roofs; *e* is the room in which we were, and 2 is a plan of it on a larger scale. Look now at 2: *a* is the bed; *c c* the two wardrobes; *b* the corner in which we were. I was sitting in an arm-chair, holding my wife; and Tyrrell and the little black child were close to us. We had given up all notion of surviving, and only waited the fall of the roof to perish together. Before long the roof went. Most of the materials, however, were carried clear away; one of the large couples was caught on the bed-post marked *d*, and held fast by the iron spike, while the end of it hung over our heads; had the beam fallen an inch on either side of the bed-post it must necessarily have crushed us. The walls did not go with the roof; and we remained for half an hour, alternately praying to God, and watching them as they bent, creaked, and shivered before the storm. . . . . The old cook made five attempts to get to us, and four times he was blown down. The fifth time he, and the negro we first saw, reached the house. The space they had to traverse was not above twenty yards of level ground, if so much." The style continues to be the same to the end, correct, plain, and, in appearance, cold. It is the method of Defoe and of Swift; nothing can be less literary or more instructive.

The impression produced is the same if we consider

in turn the journals, the reviews, and the oratory of the two nations. The special correspondent of an English journal is a sort of photographer who forwards proofs taken on the spot; these are published untouched. Sometimes, indeed, there are discrepancies between the arguments in the leading articles and the statements in the letter. The latter are always extremely lengthy and detailed; a Frenchman would abridge and lighten them; they leave on him a feeling of weariness; the whole is a jumble; it is a badly-hewn and unwieldy block. The editor of a French journal is bound to help his correspondent, to select from his materials what is essential, to pick out from the heap the three or four notable anecdotes, and to sum up the whole in a clear idea, embodied in a telling phrase. Nor is the difference less perceptible if their great quarterlies and our reviews are contrasted. An article in ours, even an article on science or political economy, must possess an exordium, a peroration, a plan. Every one in the *Revue des Deux Mondes* commences with an exposition of general ideas. With them facts, figures, and technical details predominate; their articles are exceedingly heavy, excepting in the hands of a Macaulay; they are excellent quarries filled with solid but unshapen stones, requiring additional workmanship in order to fit them for general use. Moreover, in Parliament and public meetings, English eloquence is hampered by documents, while French eloquence evaporates in theories.

English education tends to produce this result. In the principal school in London B—— had as a friend a very distinguished young man who had taken the second place in mathematics, the first in literature, who was thoroughly versed in Latin authors, and in Catullus among the rest. In his eyes Catullus was the most exquisite of poets. He knew every line by heart, was acquainted with the various readings, had studied the commentaries, and was almost qualified for producing an edition of this author. Yet, if asked to give a general view of him, to write a condensed sketch in six pages, he could not possibly do this, and he candidly acknowledged it. At Oxford and Cambridge studious undergraduates read all the Latin authors, even those of the silver age—Statius, Claudian, Manilius, Macrobius, Aulus Gellius; they are thoroughly versed in Greek also; and they have made Greek verses from the time of leaving school. But they are devoid of ideas, they know the dry bones of antiquity, but are unable to feel its spirit; they do not picture to themselves its civilisation as a whole, the special characteristic of a southern and polytheistic spirit, the sentiments of an athlete, of a dialectician, of an artist. Look, for example, at Mr. Gladstone's extraordinary commentaries on Homer. Nor has Mr. Grote, in his great "History of Greece," done anything more than write the history of constitutions and political debates. Twenty years ago the Universities were the nurseries of Greek, Latin, mathematics; were very exclusive, and maintained the exclusiveness very strongly; were extremely indisposed to afford free scope to human intelligence; the natural sciences, and philosophical history, and English composition were all uncultivated. Recently, however, new discoveries and continental methods of education have gained entrance; still, even at this day, the system of education is better fitted for strengthening than for expanding the mind; graduates leave the Universities as they leave a course of gymnastics, bringing away with them no conception whatever of man or the world. Besides, there is one ready made, and very acceptable, which a young man has no difficulty in adopting. In France no fixed limit bounds his thoughts; the Constitution, ten times altered, has no authority; the religion is that of the Middle Ages; the old forms are in discredit, the new are merely chalked out. From the age of sixteen he is assailed by doubt; he oscillates; if he has any brains, his most pressing need is to construct for himself a body of convictions, or at least of opinions. In England the mould is prepared; the religion is almost rational, and the Constitution almost excellent; awakening intelligence there finds the broad lines of future beliefs already traced. The necessity for erecting a complete habitation is not felt; the utmost that appears wanting relates to the enlargement of a Gothic window, the cleansing of a cellar, the repair of a staircase. English intellect, being less unsettled, less excited, is less active, because it has not scepticism for a spur.

To the education of the youth and the young man, add that of the adult and the man of experience. In the first place, all written or spoken literature conspires to furnish the latter with facts rather than theories; I have already indicated the character of English journals, reviews, and oratory; that of the books is like unto it, not of the solid works alone, but also of the novels, so full of details, so circumstantial, so lifelike, these novels being in literature what Dutch art is in painting. It is also necessary to note and place in the foreground the travels which are the complement of education, the occupation of a holiday, a custom, a pleasure, almost an affectation, and, as a consequence, the taste for reading works of travel. Mr. Murray paid Livingstone £9,000 for his travels; judging from the price paid, one can imagine what the sale must have been, and from the sale one can estimate the curiosity of the public. In fine, it is necessary to take into account the experience of business, as it is here understood, the information which each person collects from reports of the proceedings, and from the meetings of the association to which he belongs, the figures, documents, statistics, and comparative tables which he must study and understand in order to act efficaciously and with success in the larger or smaller circle of his private or public interests. Through all these channels, open from infancy to the close of life, exact information flows into an English head as into a reservoir. But the proximity of these waters does not yet suffice to explain their abundance; there is a slope which invites them, an innate disposition peculiar to the race —to wit, the liking for facts, the love of experiment, the instinct of induction, the longing for certitude. Whoever has studied their literature and their philosophy, from Shakespeare and Bacon to the present day, knows that this inclination is hereditary, and appertains to the very character of their minds—that it is bound up with their manner of comprehending truth. According to them the tree must be judged by its fruit, and speculation proved by practice; they do not value a truth unless it evokes useful applications. Beyond practical truths lie only vain chimeras. Such is man's condition; a restricted sphere, capable of enlargement, but always walled in; a sphere within which knowledge must be acquired, not for its own sake, but in order to act—science itself being valuable only to the office which verifies it and for the purpose which it serves.

That being granted, it appears to me that the ordinary furnishing of an English head becomes discernible. As well as I can judge, an educated Englishman possesses a stock of facts three or four times in excess of that possessed by a Frenchman of corresponding position—at least in all that relates to language, geography, political and economical truths, and the personal impressions gained in foreign parts by contact with men and living objects. On the other hand, it frequently happens that the Englishman turns his big trunk to less account than the Frenchman does his little bag. This is perceptible in many books and reviews; the English writer, though very well informed, being limited in his range. Nothing is rarer among them than free and full play of the soaring and expanding intellect. Determined to be prudent, they drag their car along the ground over the beaten track; with two or three exceptions, not one now makes readers think. More than once, when in England, after having conversed with a man, I was surprised at his store of knowledge, alike varied and sound, and also to find him so deficient in ideas. At this moment I can recall five or six who were so largely endowed as to be entitled to take general views. They paused, however, half way, arriving at no definite conclusion. They did not even experience a desire to co-ordinate their knowledge in a sort of system; they possessed only partial and isolated ideas; they did not feel either the inclination or the power to connect them together under a philosophical conception. Their language bears the best witness to this, it being extremely difficult to translate somewhat lofty abstractions into English. Compared with French and, above all, with German, it is what Latin is to Greek. In French nothing is more natural than the formula, "the beautiful, the good, and the true;" if it be literally rendered in English, it has a repulsive and uncouth appearance; if it be expressed in the common terms, the version becomes unfaithful. Their library of words is wanting in an entire row of compartments, namely, the upper ones; they have no ideas wherewith to fill them.

Some drawbacks and several advantages flow from this. General ideas are frames divided into compartments; once they have been formed by the mind it is merely necessary to apply them in order at a glance to grasp a subject as a whole and in its parts. The consequence is that the mental processes are simplified and accelerated, and if the step be taken from speculation to practice, the power of organisation is facilitated. The word to "organise," which dates from the Revolution and the First Empire, exactly summarises the faculties of the French mind, the success of well-ordered and distributive reason, the vast and happy effects of the art which consists in simplifying, classifying, subtracting. Thinkers of the eighteenth century cultivated it in their closets; it was put in practice by their successors in active life who belonged to the Assembly and the Councils of State. Its memorials are the Civil Code, the University, the military, ecclesiastical and judicial organisations, our great administrative systems, the principal parts of our social machinery. Every nation which does not possess it is destitute also of its results. In place of a legal code, it will have a bundle of legal precedents, and, in place of a School of Law, Inns of Court governed by routine.

I have heard the English lament many such deficiencies. Their legislation is so shrouded in obscurity, that before they can purchase a piece of land, they must consult one or two lawyers as a preliminary, who may occupy a month in examining the vendor's title, in order to determine whether the purchase will not give occasion for legal proceedings. C—— tells me that many of the Government Departments, and the Admiralty in particular, are in a sad state. Complaints are made of confusion, sinecures, expenses disproportioned to results, procrastination, and the clashing of authorities. The mechanism is in a muddle, because no principle has been followed in its construction. In all things they advance, and correct defects, only by groping their way; they gain a knowledge of affairs only by dint of attention, of toil, and of businesslike grinding; they are as empirical in their procedure as the Chinese.

On the other hand, when the acquisition of the power of generalising is easy and rapid, the mind runs the risk of becoming sluggish, and this is the case with the French. Frequently on leaving college, nearly always before they are five-and-twenty, they have learned to indulge in generalisations, and as they find them very handy, they apply them to all subjects; thenceforward they cease to learn anything, believing themselves to be sufficiently well stocked with information. They confine themselves to reasoning, and they often reason in a vacuum. They are not informed as to the point at issue, they have acquired no specific and conclusive facts; they are unconscious of their shortcomings, they never seek for what they require, and they retail the phrases of an old newspaper. They forget that it is necessary to be always versed in the things of the hour, to be always adding to the mental heap, so as never to be taken at unawares, and to be always ready for any event. Not only are mediocre minds among us tainted with this defect, but the very highest intellects are not exempt from the reproach; I know but two who, having passed forty, continue their researches, and have succeeded in renewing their intellectual youth. On the contrary, according to C——, the culture of the English is almost unlimited; even in mature years they travel, gain new information, complete and rectify their acquirements; they strive, especially in economic and political matters, to maintain their views on a level with the fluctuations of things. They are pleased with facts as such, are satisfied to note, and are careful to retain them. Accumulated in this wise, they form a continuous deposit at the bottom of the mind of an Englishman, constituting a solid stratum of good sense; for, disjointed and half visible though they be, yet they are there, they make their weight felt, they will influence the resolutions he may take. Even though limited in range and destitute of ideas, he will guard himself, as if by instinct, from committing very serious blunders; he will vaguely feel that what is desirable lies on one side, not on the other. The scattered items of information he has collected about the United States, India, China, the effect of universal suffrage or of commercial freedom, will dispose him beforehand to adopt the wisest course, and free public discussion will end in inclining him towards the most sensible conclusion Thus fortified, he approves of an expedition like that to Abyssinia, while he would never have sanctioned an expedition like that to Mexico; he desires the gradual extension of the suffrage, but would protest against the sudden enfranchisement of the mob. In this way he is protected against casualties and theories; his constitution never falls into the hands of speculators, nor his affairs into the hands of desperadoes. Such are the effects of public good sense, resembling so many rivulets, which fertilise the several fields through which they flow. We have beheld its fountain-head; it is a deep and dark basin, constantly full, and constantly expanding with new additions—I mean of actual facts, which, accumulated and filtered drop by drop, form an inexhaustible reservoir, and spread themselves in an hundred small, salutary streams over the whole domain of action.

When praising the fondness of the English for facts, it must be noted that this applies to ethical as well as physical facts, they are ardent observers of what passes within their minds as well as what passes without. On this head I happen to have in my hand two long letters addressed to a friend by two brides a month after their marriage. I regret that good taste forbids their publication. They both appear to have been written in order to show the innate custom and the inherited talent of accurate observation as applied by the one to material concerns, and by the other to ethical facts. The one minutely describes her husband's person, his figure, the colour of his hair, his complexion, his country seat, the several rooms and their arrangement, the furniture, the park, the carriage drives, adding statistics of his income, the family connections, and the neighbours whom it is right to visit. The other develops as exactly and in detail all her states of feeling from the day when, at an archery meeting, she first met her future husband. Both conclude in almost the same terms:—"And now, I am the happiest woman in the world." The one is commonplace, the other refined; the one can use her eyes, the other can use her heart. But, in the delicate examination of the conscience, as in the heavy descriptive catalogue, there is the same lucidity and absence of fine writing. Nothing is recounted except facts; there are no general reflections; in the psychological narrative and in the statistical exposition, everything is documentary. It is clear to me that their sole desire was to inform their correspondent, the one about her social status, the other about her private feelings, and that any addition or development would have appeared idle talk to both alike. In default of these letters, let the reader peruse the contemporary English novels, which are pervaded by the same spirit. They are compact packets of trivial material and ethical facts, the latter abounding, and often being of great value. No other literature contains examples of sentiments more clearly set forth and elaborated, of the hidden labour whereby character is formed, of the gradual formation of a passion, a vice, or a virtue, of the insensible gradation whereby, year after year, the mind is moulded. The writers of these works have alone understood the infant, and the manner in which the infant becomes a man. In proof of this read the novels of George Eliot. Since the time of Locke, psychology has been indigenous in England; it goes hand in hand with statistics and political economy. The two means for attaining a prevision almost correct, and an almost sure management of human affairs, are perfect acquaintance with all the external marks which betoken man, and an accurate divination of the inner marks which constitute man.

XXX.

FRENCH WIT AND ENGLISH HUMOUR.

ON this rich soil flourish many original varieties of talent, all differing in aspect from what they have among us, the one sort being of larger growth, the other being stunted and distorted. Let me first speak of the variety of talent which is most commonly attributed to the French. I mean wit. This is the art of stating things in a pleasant way. My English friends think that it forms part of the French temperament. Sir Henry Bulwer writes in his "France: Social, Literary, and Political":—"I asked two little village boys, one seven the other eight years old, what they meant to be when they were men? Says one, 'I shall be the doctor of the village;' 'And you, what shall you be?' said I to the other; 'Oh! if brother's a doctor, I'll be *curé*. He shall kill the people, and I'll bury them—so we shall have the whole village between us.'" At Besançon I once heard two soldiers who were lying on a slope talking together; the one rising up said: "Come, it is time to begin work again." His comrade answered, "Pooh, lie quiet, our coppers will come all the same." A German general relates in his memoirs that after a day's skirmish a French hussar, who was brought in prisoner, had a huge slash across his face. The general said, "Have you received a sabre cut, my poor fellow?" "Pooh, I was shaved too closely this morning," was the reply. An ancient writer remarked that the two qualities most in fashion among the Gauls were courage and wit,* and his Latin sentence exactly defines the spirit of conversation, the talent for coining apothegms, the liking for short, sharp, neat, impromptu, and happy phrases, launched with gaiety or malice. Foreigners greatly admire this gift; they say that it is accompanied with taste, and that both of them are universal and developed among us. A little work-girl dresses well, has nice ways, and a pleasing address; a soldier and a workman are wide awake, circumspect, prepossessing in appearance, and they can take and give a joke; this is the Southern "ingegno," spontaneous, easy, brilliant. That of the North is far more hampered and backward. In England a man belonging to the people is a lout, being a sensible lout at the best; while the members of the lower middle class are but guys clad in gaudy apparel, a long course of training being necessary in order to refine them. Civilisation here is not natural, but acquired, and neither elegance, nor beauty is to be found except among the upper class. Among us a trace of it is perceptible in all classes, and that diffuses much pleasure and embellishment over human existence.

So far as I can judge, the English do not know how to amuse themselves by means of conversation. A Frenchman accounts the happiest moment of his life the period after supper in the private society of well-educated and intelligent men. The brains of all pre-

---

* *Duas res industriosissimi persequitur gens Gallorum, rem militarem et argute loqui*

sent are then in a state of agitation and effervescence. They converse and think in unison about the most exalted subjects, skipping from one to another in short, pithy phrases, and their general ideas, briskly launched, flutter like a swarm of insects. In the space of two hours the untrammelled talk has made the tour of the globe. Each one contributes a condensation of his thoughts in a jesting or serious style, with exaggeration, a dash of paradox and play of fancy, without meaning his sallies to be literally interpreted, and seeking anything else than a relaxation for his mind. Philosophy, science, morals, art, literature, all the treasures of the human intellect are there handled, not in heavy ingots, or in large sacks, but in pretty portable golden coins, beautifully engraved, and sparkling and jingling with a cheerful clink, as they are lightly manipulated by delicate fingers. It seems to me that these coins are rare in England, and that, in addition, they are not current. They are regarded as too thin; their alloy gives rise to suspicions. Far more readiness is shown in handling the rough and ponderous metal of which I have already spoken. The conversation indulged in is chiefly instructive; most frequently there is no conversation at all. Several inconveniences arise from this, and tedium is one of them; the mind wants entertainment. In Italy there are the opera and love-making, in Germany philosophy and music, in France the intellectual fireworks just described. Here, nothing is to be found except conscientious labour and useful production, assured and agreeable comfort. Happiness is not complete, however, when one enjoys a fine carriage, a well-appointed house, regular occupation, a seat in Parliament, and the prospect of a seat in Paradise; for amid all these good things, there are times when one yawns and feels depressed. Then the luggage is got ready, one steps on board a steamer, and proceeds in quest of change, of something to distract one's thoughts, of a glimpse of the sun.

As a compensation, the English make better after-dinner speeches than we do. Some of them may be read every week in the newspapers; several are delivered at every dinner where politicians, geographers, political economists, and men of science meet together; at the dinners of the Corporation, at dinners given in honour of distinguished personages or of illustrious foreigners. I can recall one at which, although unworthy of the honour, I was present in company of one of my French friends, a celebrated traveller. After dinner, the chairman first proposed the Queen's health, and then the healths in turn of several persons present, saying, "I have the honour to propose the health of our eminent guest," so and so; then added a few sentences of praise, uttering the whole with grave cordiality, enlivened here and there with humour. For my part, I greatly admired the happy way in which he spoke, and especially the avoidance of what might weary his hearers. After the guest's health had been drunk, he rose and replied, "I thank the gentlemen present and our worthy chairman for the flattering distinction," &c. Then followed some details, varying with the traveller's experience. The explorer of the Nile promised to join the first expedition sent forth to discover the sources of that river. The Arctic traveller said that his capacity for wintering amid ice had been developed by the hardy system of English education, and by early devotion to field-sports. The colonist from Western Australia remarked that the place was well adapted for an English colony. Moreover, each gave vent to a little pæan over the energy of the Saxon race, the spread of English civilisation, the future of humanity, the advance of science. All present applauded by beating the table with their knives or hands; some cries of "hear, hear," were uttered; and one, two, three, four hurrahs were raised; some stood on their chairs and saluted the speaker by raising their glasses; the feeling of good-fellowship became contagious, and the excitement was at its height. To this rather loud orchestra the successive speeches formed appropriate solos; the common-places of which they were composed were not misplaced; they did not repel by their coarseness, weary by their heaviness, nor shock by their solemnity—at least, the English tablecompanions were attuned to the occasion. My friend, the French traveller, would not join in the chorus; he whispered a request in the chairman's ear to be dispensed from making a speech. I asked him, "Why do you shirk your turn?" Because either they would think what I should say was in bad taste, or else I should think so myself." He disliked spun-out sentences; thinking it affectation to indulge in them, especially at dessert; he preferred to launch a neat phrase, to carry on a jesting conversation with his neighbour, smilingly and in an undertone, to shadow forth his ideas. Here one does not hint a thing, but gives a detailed explanation; one likes to have it developed and emphasized; even at table one submits to the labour and burden of this. I suppose that they derive pleasure from having their nerves braced and their wills influenced by a collective excitement; a dinner of this sort is akin to a meeting, and ends more or less formally in resolutions, subscriptions, in a propaganda and in action.

A slashing journal affirms that no one can speak French without lying; the tongue exaggerates, "A thousand thanks," "I am enchanted with it," "A charming man." It is forgotten, however, that the hearer takes off the necessary discount. The truth is, that our speech and our written style are filled with indications, half-expressed meanings, and nice distinctions. It seems to me that Lafontaine, Madame de Sévigné, Voltaire, Montesquieu, and Courier cannot be perfectly translated into English. Their perfume evaporates, their grace fades, their vivacity becomes heavy. A reviewer lately found fault with Renan's "Vie de Jésus" on account of the "beautiful ambiguous sentences which appeared to express a point delicately, and expressed two contradictory things." Many English do not understand these refinements, and they charge our literature with falsity because their literary sense is obtuse. We can reply to them, in turn, that they cannot discuss without threatening one another with their fists. Their literary disputes are conducted with extraordinary virulence; in France the same style of discussion would lead to daily duels. Happily, they consider that duelling is absurd, and that no defamatory piece of writing justifies an appeal to arms. Their debates resemble their boxing-matches; the combatants, having in turn mauled and knocked each other down, shake hands and bear no malice. After several months of reading of this kind, one becomes accustomed to it, and ends by finding that the plainness of the language is fully counterbalanced by the frankness of the accent, by the strength of the conviction, by the solidity of the reasoning, by the sincerity of the indignation, by the manly and sustained tone of the eloquence It matters not if French wit be wanting; they have a form of it for their own use, which is indeed far from agreeable, but is entirely original, is powerful, poignant, and even slightly bitter in taste, like their national beverages. They call it "humour;" generally it is the pleasantry of a man who, though joking, maintains his gravity. It abounds in the writings of Swift, Fielding, Sterne, Dickens, Thackeray, and Sydney Smith; and in this particular the "Book of Snobs" and "Peter Plymley's Letters" are masterpieces. Much of it, more racy of the soil and rougher in quality, is to be found in Carlyle. Sometimes it leads to buffoonery, sometimes to studied sarcasm. It powerfully affects the nerves, and becomes lastingly imprinted on the memory. It is the product of imaginative drollery, or of concentrated indignation. It delights in striking contrasts and in unexpected disguises. It clothes madness in the garments of reason, or reason in the garments of madness. Heinrich Heine, Aristophanes, Rabelais, and Montesquieu, at times, are those out of England who have been most largely endowed with it. Still there is a foreign element which must be abstracted from the three last. French sprightliness, joy, gaiety is a kind of good wine only grown in the lands of the sun. In its insular and pure state it always leaves an after-taste of vinegar. The man who jests here is seldom kindly and is never happy; he feels and forcibly censures the inequalities of life. This yields him no amusement, for he suffers inwardly and is irritated. In order to study oddities carefully, and deliberately sustain a piece of irony, it is necessary to be continuously affected by sadness and indignation. Perfect examples of this style must be sought for in the works of great writers, yet it is so indigenous that it is daily met with in ordinary conversation, in literature, in political discussions, and it is the current coin of *Punch*. The following is a specimen taken at random from an old number. It is a "Letter from the Secretary of the Treasury to a member of Parliament." "House of Commons Library—Dear Sir,—Lord P. has handed me the letter in which you inform him that the session is drawing to a close, that you have given to his lordship's policy a support alike judicious and unceasing, and that your services merit a recompense in the shape of a place. In reply to your letter, I beg leave to remark that your first proposition is the only one about which her Majesty's Government has the pleasure to agree with you; and for my own part, I have the honour to be, dear sir, your very faithful and obedient servant."

Do you like ale? Drink it, your palate will become habituated to it; as a beverage it is wholesome, and, on the whole, strengthening. So is English humour.

XXXI.

ENGLISH PAINTINGS AND ENGLISH PAINTERS.

VISITED the Kensington Museum, the National Gallery, and afterwards the Exhibition. All English art, both ancient and modern, is collected there; moreover, I have seen two exhibitions at Paris of contemporary English paintings. No evidence is more abundant and instructive for exhibiting the tastes of the English mind as regards physical beauty, the following being the most conspicuous traits:

Examples of high art painting, of nude figures, or of those draped in the classical or Italian style, are few and feeble; there are some very artificial sacred pictures, and some large sentimental and historical, but unsubstantial productions, such as "Edith and the Monks finding the Body of Harold," by Hilton, and the "Death of General Wolfe," by West. The great and noble classical school of painting, the sentiment of a fine form as understood and loved, after the manner of the Revival, the correct and learned Paganism which David and M. Ingres have perpetuated in France, have never taken root among them. Their school is a branch of the Flemish School, a gnarled and stunted branch, which ends by dropping off, but in an entirely original manner.

They descend from Vandyck, through Lely and

Kneller. In the eighteenth century many of them, like Gainsborough and Reynolds, preserved a vivid sentiment of Flemish colouring and flesh in their great portraits and in their landscapes. They are men of the North who, following the Antwerp masters, persist in understanding the man, nature, and physical poetry of a humid country. Among Gainsborough's works are "Nancy Parsons," "Lady Dunstanville," the "Blue Boy," and other portraits, the "Watering Place," the "Market Cart," and sea pieces; in these the carnations are soft and clear, the tones of the blue or pale yellow silk are smooth and blended, the whites of the creased collars harmonise with those of the face, the distances melt into indistinct vapour, relief is given to objects, not by precision of contour but by gradation of tint; they gradually stand forth from the murky air. The artist is endued with all the riches, all the sadnesses, all the refined sensualities, all the penetrating and studied charms of colour. Among the works of Reynolds are "Miss Price," "Lady Elizabeth Forster," "Miss Boothby," "Georgina Spenser," "Duchess of Marlborough," "Marquis of Hastings," "Marquis of Rockingham," "Mrs. Stanhope," "Lord Heathfield," the "Banished Lord," the "Holy Family," the "Graces;" he belongs to the same school, and also in part to that of Rembrandt, only modernised. The excellent engravings in black style, wherein so many portraits of the seventeenth and eighteenth centuries have been reproduced, also exhibit the Dutch sentiment of light and shade combined by masses of vague darks. There is something of Flemish colouring in Hogarth's pictures, less harsh and matter of fact than his engravings, and the traces of it may also be found in Constable, Wilkie, Lawrence, and Turner.

But, from its very origin, the English vigour penetrated the Flemish surface, and made known its presence by effects more or less marked. The painter ceased to be a painter merely; the soul, the thought, the invisible interior received as much of his attention as the living body itself; he soon gave the former the preference, and exhibited sometimes the moral tendency, sometimes the shade of melancholy, sometimes profound pensive reverie, sometimes the distinction of aristocratic haughtiness. Gainsborough's "Blue Boy" already possesses the expressive and wholly modern physiognomy by which a work falling within the painter's province oversteps the limits of painting. His "Musidora" has such delicate feet and so intelligent a head that she is no simple girl bathing, but a lady. In the same way Reynolds is a descendant, though a remote one, of Vandyck, but he is so much refined and spiritualised as to appear to be separated from his ancestor by an entire world. His "Three Graces" have nothing artless and primitive about them; we recognise that they are ladies by something stiff and patrician in their attitude and their appearance, and we vaguely feel that, in spite of being draped as goddesses, each of them possesses a carriage, a steward, and fifteen footmen in yellow stockings. His "Banished Lord" is a sentimental elegy, and after the manner of Young. His great noblemen are no longer easy-going and well-dressed cavaliers, who are equally ready for a combat or a ball, but are not good for anything else; such simplicity of pure and genuine painting does not satisfy him; he has set his wits to work, has sounded the depths of the inner man, has said to himself that "one never puts into another's head more than is contained in his own," and fortified by that reflection, he has pourtrayed reflecting souls. By degrees the moral element becomes subordinated to the physical; painting will be converted into a system of psychology; the sensation of the eyes will be treated as an accessory, and the painted canvas will be but the foreground, a curtain behind which the intelligence and the soul perceive in the distance ideas, purposes, lessons, studies of character and of manners.

Hogarth was the first who set forth this theory and put it in practice. According to him it is indispensable, in order to impart interest to a physical type, that it be the expression and the counterpart of a moral type. In fact, he treated painting as a moralising novelist, in the manner of Defoe and Richardson, and his pictures are sermons against vice. When we gaze upon them we forget the painting and become spectators of a tragedy or of a domestic comedy. Figures, costumes, attitudes, all the accessories, are summaries of characters, biographical abridgments. They form a concerted series, they compose a progressive history, they are the illustrations of a text half revealed; under the surface, chapter by chapter, we read the text itself. Note in the "Marriage à la Mode" the sorrowing gesture of the old steward, who foresees the ruin of the house, and deprecates with uplifted hands the gross and sensual folly of the bridegroom. The mind follows the precedents and the consequences, comprehends their necessity, and arrives at a conclusion as after hearing a sermon. Less conclusive but not less literary in character are the works of Wilkie—the "Village Festival," the "Blind Fiddler," the "Parish Beadle," "Blindman's Buff," "A Wedding." He is a painter of humble life, a Teniers, if you will, but a reflecting, observing, thinking Teniers, who is in quest of interesting types and moral maxims. His pictures abound in ingenious designs, happy satires, instructive points, like Scott's "Antiquary" and Eliot's "Adam Bede." He furnishes matter for thought and amusement; but outside the sphere of painting and around him many others are writers and poets, who have mistaken their vocation, as he has done.

Among the artists who have gone astray, Turner is one of the greatest and the most mistaken. Nowhere can we more clearly discern the error of a man of talent, who, being qualified for addressing the senses, undertakes to address himself to the intelligence and the soul. The collection of his works fills three rooms. There are some very beautiful, simple, and imposing landscapes by him, wherein may be found a profound and, I venture to add, an exalted, appreciation of living nature, such as "Knighton Bank," "Frosty Morning," "Bligh Sands," "Cattle in Water," "St. Mawes, Cornwall;" but these are in his earliest style. By degrees the sensation of the eye, the optical effect, appeared to him of secondary importance; the emotions and reveries of the speculative and reasoning brain obtained the empire over him; he felt a wish to paint gigantic, and philosophic, and humanitarian epics; he believed himself to be the first of painters, and I have been told that he died insane. In any case, his painting degenerated into lunacy, much in the same way as the prose and poetry of Victor Hugo. "Apollo killing the Python," "Snowstorm—Hannibal and his Army crossing the Alps," "The Deluge," "The Destruction of Sodom," "Light and Colour," "The Morning after the Deluge," "Rain, Steam, and Speed—the Great Western Railway," "A Snowstorm—Steamboat off a Harbour's Mouth," and thirty or forty others, carefully collected by himself, and arranged according to his instructions in a place apart, compose an extraordinary jumble, a sort of churned foam, a wonderful litter in which shapes of every kind are buried. Place a man in a fog, in the midst of a storm, the sun in his eyes, and his head swimming, and depict, if you can, his impressions upon canvas;—these are the gloomy visions, the vagueness, the delirium of an imagination which becomes deranged through overstraining.

At the present day the centre of gravity which kept art in position has been displaced by the growing exaggeration of mental and cerebral life. English painters have an affinity to the Dutch masters in some external particulars, by the small size of their canvases, by the choice of their subjects, by the taste for reality, by the exactness and minute treatment of details. But the spirit has changed, and their painting is no longer picturesque. Compare, for example, the animals of Potter with the carefully wrought and studied animals of Landseer, more particularly his deer and his dogs. The English painter does not love the animal for its own sake, as a living creature, nor yet on account of its form standing out in relief, or of its coloured shape harmonising with the surroundings; he looks deeper; he has meditated, and he refines. He humanises his animals; he has philosophic, moral, and sentimental ends in view. He desires to suggest a reflection; he acts the part of a fabulist. His painted scene is a species of enigma, of which the key is written below. For example, "Peace and War," "Dignity and Impudence," "Low Life and High Life," "Alexander and Diogenes," a "Dialogue at Waterloo," are all explained by types and attitudes of dogs. The procedure of the figure-painters is the same. In their opinion the essential thing is the anecdote, the little romance, the literary story, the aspect of manners they take for their subject; the charm, the harmony, the beauty of the outlines and the tones are ranked as accessories; this applies to Maclise, Leslie, Hunt, and to one of the most famous among them, Mulready. I have seen twenty pictures by him—"First Love," the "Wolf and the Lamb," "Open your mouth and shut your eyes," the "Battle Interrupted," the "Younger Brother," the "Vicar of Wakefield's Wife." Nothing could be more expressive, greater efforts have never been expended in addressing the mind through the medium of the senses, in giving a good illustration of an idea or of a truth, in collecting within the compass of twelve square inches a larger heap of psychological observations. What patient and penetrating critics! What judges of man! What a variety of skilful combinations! What aptitude for rendering the moral feeling by the physical appearance! What capital vignettes they would make for an edition of Sterne, Goldsmith, Crabbe, Thackeray, and George Eliot. Here and there I perceive masterpieces in this style; for instance, Johnson's "Lord and Lady Russell taking the Sacrament." Lord Russell is about to mount the scaffold, his wife looks him full in the face to see if he be reconciled with God. This ardent gaze of the wife and the Christian is admirable; she is now at ease, and assured of her husband's salvation. Yet what a pity that, instead of using the pen, they have determined to employ the pencil!

XXXII.

MODERN PAINTERS AND RUSKIN'S CRITICISMS.

OWING to the attention being wholly concentrated upon the moral element in man, the optical sensibility of English painters is blunted and unhinged. I do not think that paintings more displeasing to the eye have ever been produced. It is hard to imagine more crude effects, more exaggerated and violent colouring, more extreme and glaring dissonances, a falser and more abrupt commingling of tones. In Hunt's "Two Gentlemen of Verona," blue-tinted trees stand forth against the brown earth and scarlet clothes; "Christ, the Light of the World," is set in a greenish-yellow atmosphere, resembling that perceived on ascending to the surface of turbid water after a plunge. In Millais' "Daughters of Noah leaving the Ark," the violet of the dress, and the manner in which it is relieved by its surroundings, is a thing to be seen. In Crowe's "Pope presented to Dryden" are light blue waistcoats and red velvet coats, while the accessories are brought into full and harsh relief, apparently for a wager. Mulready's "Bathers" seem to be made of porcelain. In the "Eve of St. Agnes" of Millais, a lady in a low-bodied evening dress is represented through the medium of a studied effect of twilight, as having the appearance of a corpse-like green, and the chamber is of the same hue. On every hand there are landscapes in which blood-red poppies are set in grass of the tint of a green parrot; apple trees in blossom, whereof the staring white of the petals against the dark branches is painful to the sight; a green churchyard in the sunlight, where each blade of grass shows its brightness like the blade of a penknife; sunsets which might certainly be taken for displays of fireworks. Indeed, the condition of their retina is peculiar. In order to comprehend this, recourse must be had to analogies, and they may be found in twenty details of daily life, in the red and violet, the lees of wine, the raw-green, tints with which their children's books are coloured, in the flaunting and overdone dresses of their women, in the aspect of their meadows, their flowers, their landscapes beheld under a sudden gleam of sunshine. Perhaps it must be admitted that in every country the external appearances of things educate the eye, that its customs form its tastes, that there is a secret affinity between the arrangement of its artificial decorations and the colours of its natural sights. Here, in fact, the brilliancy, the freshness, the opulence of the style of dress recall the splendours, the youthfulness, the magnificence, the contrasts and appearances of the vegetation. Resemblances may be detected between their mauve and violet silks and the changing colours of the distances and the clouds, between their gauze scarfs, their fleecy lace shawls, and the pale or splendid haze of their horizons. Yet a number of effects which are harmonious in nature, are displeasing when painted; they are unfit for representation on canvas, at least they should not be reproduced in all their nakedness. In the latter state they produce discord, in default of the surroundings with which they harmonise. For nature has many resources at her disposal which are wanting in painting—among others, the full sun, real light, the sparkle of daylight on water, the scintillation of sunbeams upon a green leaf. These are the supreme values which dominate all the others, and relieve them of their excessive crudeness; deprived of this atmosphere, the others produce as unpleasant an effect as a chord from which the leading note is omitted. They must, therefore, be transposed in order to be expressed. No painter, no artist, is a pure copyist. He invents, even while he confines himself to translating; for that which Nature executes through the medium of one system of means and values, he is obliged to render by another system of values and means. Herein is the mistake of contemporary English painters. They are faithful, but literally so. After seeing their country, it is obvious that the majority of their effects are truthful. This picture really represents a piece of English turf vivified by a recent shower. This other one represents the white morning sky; the glittering sands at low water; the bright green or violet hue of undulating waves. This one represents the ears of corn against the pale-yellow hue of the sheaves, the ruddy purple heaths under the sun on a lonely common. On reflection the exactitude of all this cannot be denied; better still, we recall that the sight of the real landscape gave pleasure, and we experience surprise at feeling dissatisfied in presence of the painted landscape. This is because the translation is nothing but a transcription. It is because, desiring to be faithful in one thing, they have misrepresented the whole. With the patience of fastidious workmen, they have put on canvas one by one the unmodified sensations of their eyes. Meanwhile they meditated, moralised, following as poets the soft or sad emotions which the real landscape awakened in their souls. Between the workman and the poet the artist has had no place. Their patience commands applause. We feel that we should be touched in the presence of the original; their copy, however, is but a memorandum, and we gladly turn away from it because it is ugly.

A man has arisen among them to justify and elevate their practice into theory, namely John Ruskin; an admirer and a friend of Turner, an earnest, impassioned, and original writer, perfectly competent, very studious, very popular, and possessing a thoroughly English intellect. Nothing is more precious than personal, independent, and well-ordered impressions, especially when, like his, they are boldly expressed; they lead us to reconsider our own. There is no one to whom Ruskin's works, such as " Modern Painters," and the " Stones of Venice," fail to suggest topics for thought. His first principle is that the literal truth and the characteristic detail must be loved with enthusiasm : " Every class of rock, earth, and cloud must be known by the painter with geologic and meteorologic accuracy." " When there are things in the foreground of Salvator of which I cannot pronounce whether they be granite, or slate, or tufa, I affirm that there is in them neither harmonious union nor simple effect, but simple monstrosity." Titian worked with the most laborious botanical fidelity. " Witness his ' Bacchus and Ariadne,' in which the foreground is occupied by the common blue iris, the aquilegia, and the wild rose." " The foreground of Raffaelle's ' Miraculous Draught of Fishes ' is covered with plants of the common sea colewort." And all these plants are painted with scrupulous accuracy. But truth is only a means to produce beauty: art goes farther still; its proper object is to awaken lofty emotions. Nor is it satisfied with producing sensible pleasure. "This pleasure may well be the base of the impression, but it must also be combined with a feeling of joy, next with a feeling of love for the object painted, next with a perception of the bounty of a higher intelligence, and finally with an outburst of gratitude and veneration for this intelligence. No impression can in anywise be regarded as an impression of beauty unless it be composed of these emotions; in like manner we cannot say that we have an idea of a letter, if we only perceive its perfume without understanding its contents and its purport." This is, indeed, the æsthetic system of a man of the North, an idealist and a Protestant, and all his judgments are in the same vein. He cares little for picturesque painting; a sensation pleasing to the eye has no value for him. "The old landscape painters only exhibited mechanical and technical qualities. I refer only to Claude, Gaspar Poussin, Salvator Rosa, Cuyp, Berghem, Both, Ruysdael, Hobbima, Teniers (in his landscapes), P. Potter, Canaletti, and the various Van somethings and Bach somethings, more especially and malignantly those who have libelled the sea." "The object of the great body of the professed landscapists of the Dutch school is merely to display manual dexterities of one kind or another; and their effect on the public mind is so totally for evil, that though I do not deny the advantage an artist of real judgment may derive from the study of some of them, I conceive the best patronage that any monarch could possibly bestow upon the arts would be to collect the whole body of them into one gallery, and burn it to the ground." On this head many persons will hope that Mr Ruskin may never be appointed king under any pretext whatsoever. He is equally hard upon Italian painting, upon its spirit, upon its worship of the athletic and perfect human form. According to him, the mythological and nude subjects which compose one-half of it have been produced in order to gratify sensuality, and take rank with opera ballets. In early times, "art was employed in the display of religious facts;" in Raffaelle's time "religious facts were employed by him to give the display of art." "The crowned Queen-Virgin of Perugino sank into a simple Italian mother in Raffaelle's 'Madonna of the Chair.'" Was this, then, a healthy change? No. It would have been healthy if it had been effected "with a pure motive, and the new truths would have been precious if they had been sought for truth's sake. . . . . He could think of the Madonna as an available subject for the display of transparent shadows, skilful tints, and scientific foreshortenings—as a fair woman forming, if well painted, a pleasant piece of furniture for the corner of a boudoir, and best imagined by combination of the beauties of the prettiest contadinas. . . . . . It was thus that Raffaelle thought of the Madonna." Shortly afterwards Mr. Ruskin depicts with faith and awe the apparition of Jesus showing Himself to His disciples at the lake of Galilee; and he contrasts Raffaelle's cartoon of the "Charge to Peter" with the actual occurrence. "Note the handsomely-curled hair and neatly-tied sandals of the men who had been out all night in the sea-mists and on the slimy decks. Note their convenient dresses for going a-fishing, with trains that lie a yard along the ground, and goodly fringes, all made to match—an apostolic fishing costume. Note how Peter especially (whose chief glory was in his wet coat girt about him and naked limbs) is enveloped in folds and fringes, so as to kneel and hold the keys with grace. . . . . The whole group of the apostles, not round Christ, as they would have been naturally, but straggling away in a line, that they may all be shown." "Beyond is a pleasant Italian landscape, full of villas and churches." "The simple truth is that the moment we look at the picture, we feel our belief of the whole thing taken away. . . . It is all a mere mythic absurdity, and faded decoction of fringes, muscular arms, and curly heads of Greek philosophers. . . . . Whatever they could have fancied for themselves about the wild, strange, infinitely stern, infinitely tender, infinitely varied veracities of the life of Christ, was blotted out by the vapid fineries of Raffaelle." It is easy to condemn a painter, even a very great one, when something is required of him whereof he never dreamt. Raffaelle's design was to represent fine and serious men—well shaped, well posed, well grouped, well clad, and he never thought of doing anything else. Mr. Ruskin reproaches him for having represented St. Paul as a meditative Hercules, leaning upon a conqueror's sword, and he adds that no artist has yet painted the real St. Paul. Better is it that he has not been painted: "the ugly little Jew," to use M. Renan's phrase, was beautiful as to his mind only, and his mind is in his Epistles. Raffaelle was right; in contradistinction to literature, painting has the living body for its object, and does not depict the soul except indirectly and as an accessory. Mr. Ruskin calls upon the latter art to perform the functions of the former. "The principal object in the foreground of Turner's 'Building of Carthage,' is a group of children sailing toy boats." That, according to him, is one of the most elevated of thoughts, worthy of epic poetry, for these infants at play manifest the maritime aptitude and the future greatness of Carthage. On the contrary, "Claude, in subjects of the same kind, commonly introduces people carrying red trunks with iron locks about, and dwells with infantine delight on the lustre of the leather and the ornaments of the iron." What if the red suit and the burnish act as a set-off, as complements, as useful values for arresting, retaining, or preparing the vision, resembling the scale of a horn or hautboy in a symphony; he who omits the scale has no ear; can he who omits the burnish and the red have eyes?

Thus the fact, the actual thing, the material and physical object, is to be studied for its own sake, is to be placed intact and faithfully upon canvas, with its own physiognomy and all its detail, is to be so perfectly rendered and framed that a special scientific man, botanist or geologist, will find a trustworthy record in the picture; nothing being allowed for ornamentation, for the gratification of the senses, for the secret exigencies of the eye; beyond that, and as a contrast, are the impressions of the moral personality, the silent communing of the soul with Nature, the dull and prolonged re-echoing of a deep-seated ego, full of vibrating fibres, a great inner harp which responds with unlooked-for sounds to all exterior strokes; such is the object of art. To them, this powerful ego is the principal personage of the world. Unseen it dominates and encompasses the things which appear; their worth consisting in having a meaning for it, in corresponding in some respects to it, in drawing out from or completing in it some latent emotion. The spiritual being is the centre to which the rest gravitates. To secure this leading place, it was essential that it should be extremely strong and absorbent. It is so, in truth, and one perceives this upon considering the principal traits of the English character, the need of independence, the power of initiating, the energy and obstinacy of the will, the strength and ruggedness of the concentrated and controlled passions, the rough but unheard working of the interior machinery, the vast and tragic spectacle which a compact soul furnishes to itself, the habit of introspection, the seriousness with which they have always regarded human destiny, their moral and religious preoccupations, all the remains of faculties and instincts which were formerly displayed by the hand of Shakespeare and in the heart of the Puritans. Confining oneself to the moderns, one may say that in every Englishman there is a trace of Byron, Wordsworth, and Carlyle—three minds entirely dissimilar, and yet resembling each other in a point which is at once a strength and a weakness, and which for lack of other terms I shall venture to style the hypertrophy of the ego.

XXXIII.

ENGLISH POETRY AND RELIGION.

TO a mind thus attuned, the true medium of expression is poetry. In proportion as the English are inferior in the other arts, is their superiority in this one. To my thinking there is no poetry which equals theirs, which makes a stronger and sharper impression on the mind, of which the words are more charged with meaning, or which more faithfully reproduces the struggles and aims of the inner being, of which the grasp is more effective and firm, and which moves the individual and deep-seated fibres within us so as to draw forth from them such splendid and far-reaching harmonies. On this head it would occupy too much space were I to pass their literature in review; I content myself with citing only one recent poem, "Aurora Leigh," by Elizabeth Barrett Browning, an extraordinary work, which is also a masterpiece; I repeat that space fails me in order that I may state, after having perused it twenty times, how beautiful I consider it to be. It contains the confession of a generous, heroic, and impassioned spirit, one superabounding in genius, of which the culture has been complete, of a philosopher and a poet dwelling amid the loftiest ideas, and surpassing the elevation of her ideas by the nobility of her instincts, wholly modern by her education, by her high-mindedness, by her daring, by the perpetual vibration of her strained sensibility, wound up to such a pitch that the slightest touch awakens in her a vast orchestra and the most wonderful symphony of concords. It is all soul, and the inward monologue, the sublime song of a young girl's and artist's great heart, attracted and irritated by an enthusiasm and a pride as strong as her own; the sustained contrast of the masculine and feminine utterance, which, amid the outbursts and the variations on the same theme, continually become separated and opposed in greater measure, till at last, suddenly combining, they unite in a prolonged, mournful, and exquisite duo, of which the strain is so lofty and so penetrating as to be wholly unsurpassable. Formerly, an epic poem turned upon the foundation and destruction of cities, and the strife of gods; this one turns on the struggles of ideas and passions, on the transformations of characters; its author having drawn her materials, not from the outer, but from the inner life; and large though the epic framework is, the inner life is still ample enough to fill it. The vicissitudes of a soul so redundant and full of life are as important as the encounters of armies. In default of legends and divine apparitions, it has forecasts of the infinite, dreams and aspirations which comprise the world, a wild or luminous conception of beauty and of truth, its hell and its heaven, dazzling visions, ideal vistas which, unlike those of Homer, do not open upon a tradition, nor, like those of Dante, upon a dogma, but upon the highest peaks of modern ideas, in order to reunite at a still loftier eminence around a sanctuary and a God. There is nothing official in this God; he is the God of the soul, of a fervid and fruitful soul, in which poetry becomes piety, which develops its noble instincts all around, and diffuses over infinite nature its sentiment of holy beauty. The whole is set forth in a style almost unique, which is less a style than the most daring, most sincere, and most faithful notation, created at every moment and in every variety for the purpose, so that one never thinks about the words, beholding directly, and, as it were, face to face, the living thought leap forth with its quiverings, its surprises, its soarings suddenly checked, its unheard-of flights from sarcasm and familiarity up to ecstasy; a strange language, but true down to the minutest details, the only one fitted for translating the heights and depths of the inner life, the approach, the arrival, and the turmoil of inspiration, the sudden concentration of a crowd of ideas, the unexpected outburst of imagery, and the endless illuminations which, like the aurora borealis, successively flash forth in a lyrical imagination.

> "Never flinch,
> But still, unscrupulously epic, catch
> Upon the burning lava of a song,
> The full-veined, heaving, double-breasted age:
> That when the next shall come, the men of that
> May touch the impress with reverent hand, and say,
> 'Behold—behold the paps we all have sucked!
> This bosom seems to beat still, or at least
> It sets ours beating; this is living art,
> Which thus presents and thus records true life.'"

A style like that is the natural complement of such thoughts.

> "Let us think
> Of forms less, and the external. Trust the spirit,
> As sovran nature does, to make the form;
> For otherwise we only imprison spirit
> And not embody. Inward evermore
> To outward—so in life, and so in art,
> Which still is life"

Poetry, thus understood, has but one personage, the inner being, and but one style, the cry of a triumphant or broken heart.

The more I reflect upon this conformation of the English mind, on their habit of introspection, on the pre-eminence of the moral being, the necessity for regarding nature through the eyes of the moral being from first to last, the more clearly do I arrive at an understanding of the strong and innumerable roots of that serious poem which is here called religion. In order to comprehend with exactness its value and authority, it is essential to distinguish two things—on the one hand the wording of the editor, on the other the sentiment of the reader.

This wording varies according to the views of the different sects—Quakers, Presbyterians, Wesleyans, Unitarians, Anglicans; but that of the last is the most commonly accepted. And with reason, for the Church of England has on her side antiquity, her alliance with the State, her privileges, her endowments, her bishops seated in the House of Lords, her preponderance in the Universities, her mean position between two extremes, between the faith, the dogma, and the spirit of the Puritans, and the faith, the dogma, and the spirit of the Roman Catholics. In the first place, she is an old and legal compromise, and this suits the majority, which everywhere loves compromises, willingly follows tradition, and is obedient to the law. Moreover, she is rich, she is a power in the State, she has ties among the aristocracy, she has good connections, she is one of the organs of the Constitution, and, in virtue of all these titles, she finds favour among statesmen, among Conservatives, among men of the world, among all those who wish to be considered "respectable." To crown all, her Prayer-Book is very beautiful, her services are noble and impressive, her conduct is semi-tolerant, she permits some play to the free judgment of the individual. Thus accredited, she proposes and imposes her version, and it may be said that this version is generally admitted. There are three distinct parties in this State Church: one, which is the more aristocratic, leans more upon authority, has the greater fondness for ritual, is called the High Church; the other, which is more popular, more ardent, more eager to make conversions and renovate the heart, is called the Low Church party. Both of them, being rather narrow and inflexible, leave scope for the operations ot a Liberal party, the Broad Church, which includes the minds that are the most eminent and conciliatory, and the best qualified for reconciling science and faith. Thanks to the latter party, the gulf which separates lay thought from ecclesiastical tradition has ceased to be impassable.

Among several other polemic and dogmatic treatises, I have just read Alford's "Greek Testament," one of the most authorised commentaries on the Scriptures. He does not go so far as the German critics; his historical judgment is burdened by foregone conclusions, yet his concessions are sufficiently large to satisfy common sense. According to him the Evangelists are not in perfect accord; sometimes even, more especially as regards chronology, they contradict each other. "This is because they were not mere speaking-trumpets, channels of the Holy Ghost, but simple, holy men inspired by it." They had common materials from which to write, to wit, tradition and some imperfect texts, but these materials were "subject to all the varieties of diction, arrangement, omission, and addition which a narrative admits of when it is the offspring of several individual minds and several different places." Each narrator, according to the nature, the defects, and the compass of his information, his memory, his imagination, and his sentiment, left his mark upon it. The whole is true, but it is true as a whole only. Now, between the divine kernel and the human covering, the dividing point is not clear; each person may cut off more or less, and even in the Church itself many persons cut off a large portion. According to Dean Stanley, being a Christian does not consist in believing in particular events in the life of Jesus, in particular dogmas revealed by Jesus, but in Jesus Himself, in the moral and religious spirit with which the Gospels are inspired. He explains the gift of tongues in the same way as M. Renan. He admits, like the German theologians, that the Gospels, such as we have them, were composed long after the Epistles of St. Paul. His comments on these Epistles are in the style of modern criticism, being marked by the details, the judgment, the independent and piercing forecasts which now-a-days distinguish a commentary on Dante or Pascal. He depicts Corinth, with its sea and its temples, after Pausanias, after the reports of travellers, after the experience of his own travels. He exhibits St. Paul dictating to Sosthenes, a disciple who sits beside him, and who stops every now and then to remind him of an omission. "We can imagine that the letter to which St. Paul replied was unrolled before him in such a manner that he could see at a glance the difficulties suggested, raise objections in turn, sometimes citing them in the very words employed, and sometimes in his own language." He effectively describes and explains St. Paul's style, a style as powerful and wonderful as the matter itself; a style jerky and forced, owing to the interior emotion, wholly composed of outbursts or of rough fragments of burning thoughts leaping and clashing like pieces of lava amid flame and smoke; he likens it in some respects to that of Thucydides, better still to that of Cromwell. He shows the Hebraic temperament and the Oriental imagination of the Apostle, apropos of which he recalls the state of mind characteristic of the Prophets and the Psalmists, and he goes the length of pointing out the relics of a similar form of mental exaltation among the Mahometan dervishes. In short, according to him, in order to understand the era of the Evangelists it is necessary above all to form a conception of enthusiasts and of the scenes of enthusiasm such as formerly occurred among the Puritans, and may now be found in the "shoutings" of America. Mr. Jowett carries criticism farther still. When reading the New Testament he puts the common version on one side, and takes that of Lachmann, the first being to the second what the Sophocles and Thucydides of the Revival are to those of Dindorf and of Becker, or what the "Pensées" of Pascal, published by the Port-Royal, are to the same "Pensées" edited by M. Feugère. The faith of the early Christians did not exactly resemble ours. "They believed that the end of the world and the second coming of Christ were at hand;" transported with their conversion they lived in a species of "ecstasy;" their faith was simple and child-like, "it was the belief of men who did not try to penetrate the designs of Providence, and who had never dreamed about the perspectives of the future; it was the sentiment of men who thought about the coming of Christ as we think about the return of a lost friend, many of them having seen him upon earth, and being unable to believe that he had been taken away for ever." Regarding the outside only, and from the world's point of view, they left the impression which would now be made by a sect of Dissenters, poor dreamers whom the men of the world would consider fanatical, narrow-minded, eccentric, and even dangerous. Their language bears marks of their mental disposition. The words justice, faith, charity are much more vague as used .by St. Paul than by us; they correspond to a more excited frame of mind, to a less definite play of ideas. When he says that Adam's sin is imputed to us, he is moved by an outburst of passion, he writes in the style of the Hebrews; this merely means "that we are all as one man by the community of our evil nature," and by this community, and not otherwise, are we all united in Adam's transgression. The excitement and the imagination of the Apostle and the Oriental are manifested by his frequent use of "very nearly," and his figures of speech are not formulas. When he speaks of redemption and sin offering, he alludes to a Jewish custom. Between this stormy and inspired spirit, which comes out of the Synagogue, speaks in ejaculations, thinks in blocks, and the lucid, exact, discursive modern intellect, which separates and follows, one by one, the mass of precise ideas, the difference is enormous. It would be absurd, and horrible in addition, to elevate local metaphors into philosophical doctrines. The reader sees for himself the consequence of principles like these—to wit, the advent of philology, of criticism, of psychology, the renovation of theology, the transfiguration of dogma. The effect of this is visible already. Distinguished men, historians, clergymen, have resigned their positions in the University and in the Church because their consciences no longer assented to the Thirty-nine Articles. Bishop Colenso, of Natal, when questioned by converts about the Old Testament, and asked to pledge his word of honour that it was all true, fell into deep reflection, began to study the subject, read the German explanations, and ended by publishing a book which relegated the Biblical stories to the rank of myths. One of my friends, who is very well informed, estimates that out of twenty-four bishops there are four who favour the liberal criticisms emanating from Oxford; moreover, these find support among a large number of influential and respected laymen, who approve of them. The modern spirit filters through other fissures—by geology and natural history—for which the English have great aptitude, by the experimental psychology which they have always cultivated. In truth, an Englishman chiefly loves demonstrated facts, either external or internal—the incontestable and existing facts of which every one can at any moment gain experience either within him or without. This disposition may give birth to theories and even to a system of philosophy, to theories like those of Lyell, of Huxley, of Darwin, and of Tyndall, to a philosophy like that of J. S. Mill and Herbert Spencer. Where such a taste predominates, it leads the mind towards one of the forms of positivism, and indeed, under diverse forms, especially among men of science, positivism is no rarity here.

Among contemporary nations, among the French, for instance, these things, in different proportions, are very much alike. There, too, we find a symbol, a text accepted by the majority, comprehensive or narrow interpretations admitted by several small groups, a scientific scepticism to suit some free-thinkers and several men of science who devote themselves to a special pursuit. In all these things the points of resemblance are striking, but they are merely superficial. The inner emotion remains to be considered, the attitude of the reader in presence of the accepted symbol; it is in this particular that the two nations differ irreconcileably. An Englishman is naturally influenced by the sentiment of the far-beyond. For him, beyond human experience prolonged as far as it is possible to imagine, there is an abyss, a vast we know not what, whether blankness or brilliancy; and in this matter the most determined votaries of pure experience are at one with the believers. Beyond attainable things Herbert Spencer expressly places something unattainable, the "unknowable," the infinite basis, whereof we can touch but a portion and the surface. If J. S. Mill dare not affirm this infinity which oversteps all limits, he at least admits it as a possibility. An expanse of darkness, empty or peopled, enveloping the narrow circle wherein flickers our little lamp, such is the common impression made upon the sceptics as well as upon the faithful by the spectacle of things. Such an impression puts the mind in a solemn attitude; it does not proceed without a tincture of terror; the human being is in presence of an incommensurate and overwhelming spectacle; he is inclined to wonder and awe. As he is reflecting, prone to moralise, he has no difficulty in recognising the far-beyond in the moral, as in the material world. He speedily feels that his power is limited, his vaticination short, his undertakings uncertain, that he resembles a leaf carried away in a vast and angry current. During days of sorrow, at the funerals of his relations, in sickness or in peril, when his dependence and ignorance stand before him in sharp and dread outlines, this emotion becomes poignant. He turns his eyes towards the great universal movement, towards the obscure and imposing government of the whole. By dint of meditating, he tries to image it to himself, and, in default of another image, he pictures it as the government of some one, as the result of an intelligent and determinate guidance, as the work of a power and a mind to which nothing is wanting of those things in which he himself is deficient. Yet another step. If, amidst the imperfections he discovers in himself, the gravest in his eyes are his evil inclinations, if he is chiefly concerned with ideas about the just and the unjust, if his conscience is awake and active, the primitive emotion guided, rendered clear, and completed, terminates in the conception of a moral Deity. Thomas Arnold wrote to a person troubled with doubt, " Begin by regarding everything from the moral point of view, and you will end by believing in God." Upon the structure thus reared, at the summit of all these converging pillars, this belief comes of itself and takes its place there as the keystone of the arch. The mysterious, the infinite, the far-beyond, becomes the mysterious Providence, and the texts of Scripture and the Liturgy are simply mediums for expressing the inarticulate yearning of the heart.

Such is the soundless preparation, the inner ferment, whereby the conception of God is formed and developed. The child receives it from without like a graft. But, in order that this graft should take hold, and should not remain a piece of dead matter in the mind, it is necessary that the mind should adapt itself, and cling to it and impart its sap to it. This is not performed but after tedious, hidden, and unconscious labour. It ordinarily takes years for the junction to be made and the foreign cutting to become transformed into an acquired branch. As far as I can judge, this is done naturally and successfully in an English mind, according to the process I have described, by the conception of the infinite powers which overwhelm us, by the concentration of these shadowy powers in one person, and by the installation of this personage on the throne of the moral world. In this manner religion ceases to be an official formula which men repeat, and becomes a living sentiment which men feel. In order to be convinced of this the reader has but to study the details of daily life in the correspondence, in the biographies, in the poems, in the romances, in all the spontaneous evidences which cannot be suspected of hypocrisy. Some time ago the newspapers published a letter which a poor sergeant, slain at Petropaulowski, wrote to his wife Alice, on the eve of the engagement; nothing could be nobler, more touching, more profoundly earnest; it was the testament of a soul. Among three novels taken at random there are two in which at a momentous crisis we perceive the intervention if not of prayer at least of the solemn emotion of the human being who feels that above his own head and every head reigns infinite Justice. The doctrine may be discussed; in presence of the sentiment itself we can but bow the head; it is sublime.

XXXIV.

A TRIP THROUGH SCOTLAND.

I LEFT Manchester for Glasgow at two in the morning. At daybreak I saw the unvaried English landscape, composed of a meadow and a hedge-row on a soil not naturally rich and fertile, as in Flanders, but laboriously tilled, and forced by human industry to yield its increase. Beyond Carlisle the ground is undulating, with long and high slopes which serve for grazing ground; it is a solitude, neither trees nor cultivated fields being visible; here and there is a house; sheep dot with white points the huge green eminences. This everlasting green, always moist and always pale, produces a curious impression.

Nearing Glasgow there are innumerable chimneys, flaming blast-furnaces; I counted as many as sixteen in a heap. Glasgow, like Manchester, is a city of iron and coal. It, too, is situated in the district which is coloured black in the maps, and the Clyde makes of it a port, connecting it with the ocean. One is inclined to see in the physical characteristics of the locality the forecast of its history: the green land, the flocks, the dairy produce, the damp and cold climate, the barren soil, engender a carnivorous, an energetic, a stubborn, and an industrious creature; the coal, the iron, the

A TRIP THROUGH SCOTLAND. 357

proximity to the sea, the rivers adapted for ports, tempt him to become a manufacturer and a merchant. The population numbers nearly half a million. But the sight of these vast hives is always painful; barefooted children crawl in the mud; women in rags, and whose torn gowns expose their persons, sit at street corners suckling their infants. The climate is worse than at Manchester. It is now the end of July, and the sun is shining, still I do not find my overcoat too heavy. Happily, the human frame can adapt itself to its surroundings. Grown-up girls, lolling upon the grass, have neither stockings nor shoes; little boys are bathing in the river. Besides, particular traits of moral character yield a compensation. I am staying in a hotel frequented by commercial travellers, and during the twenty-four hours, especially at table, I see scores of them. Their physiognomy is a combination of landed proprietor, professor, and shoemaker, that of our commercial travellers being a mixture of the wag and the soldier. Now, in matters of business and commerce the former character succeeds much better than the latter; and this distinction is not met with among the commercial travellers of the two countries alone.

In the luminous morning mist, amid a line of masts and rigging, the steamboat sailed down the Clyde to the sea. We proceeded along the indented and rugged coast from one bay to another. These bays, being almost entirely closed in, resemble lakes, and the large sheets of water mirror an amphitheatre of green hills. All the corners and windings of the shore are strewn with white villas; the water is crowded with ships; a height was pointed out to me whence three hundred sail may often be counted at a time; a three-decker floats in the distance like a swan among sea-mews. This vast space spread forth and full of life, dilates the mind, one's chest expands more freely, one joyfully inhales the fresh and keen breeze. But the effect upon the nerves and the heart does not resemble that of the Mediterranean; this air and country, instead of predisposing to pleasure, dispose to action.

We enter a small vessel drawn by three horses, which transports us along the Crinan canal, between two banks of green turf. On the one side are rocks covered with brushwood; on the other, steep declivities of a grey or reddish tinge; this, indeed, is colour at last, a pleasure for the eye, well mingled, matched, and blended tints. On the bank and amid the bushes are wild roses, and fragile plants with white tufts smile with a delicate and charming grace.

At the outlet from the canal we go on board a large steamer, and the sea opens out wider than ever. The sky is exceedingly clear and brilliant, and the waves break in the sunlight, quivering with reflections of molten tin. The vessel continues her course, leaving in her track a bubbling and boiling path; sea gulls follow unweariedly behind her. On both sides, islands, rocks, boldly-cut promontories stand in sharp relief in the pale azure; the scene changes every quarter of an hour. But on rounding every point the infinite ocean reappears, mingling its almost flat line with the curve of the white sky.

The sun sets, we pass by Glencoe, and Ben Nevis appears sprinkled with snow; the bay becomes narrower, and the mass of water, confined amid barren mountains, assumes a tragic appearance. Human beings have come hither to little purpose; Nature remains indomitable and wild; one feels oneself upon a planet.

We disembark near Fort William; the dying twilight, the fading red rays on the horizon, enable us to get a glimpse of a desolate country; acres of peat-bog, eminences rising from the valley between two ranges of huge mountains. A bird of prey screams amid the stillness. Here and there we see some wretched hovels; I am told that those on the heights are dens without windows, and from which the smoke escapes through a hole in the roof. Many of the old men are blind. What an unpropitious abode for man!

On the morrow we voyaged during four hours on the Caledonian canal amidst solitudes, a monotonous row of tree-less mountains, enormous green eminences, dotted here and there with fallen stones. A few sheep of a dwarf breed crop the scanty herbage on the slopes; sometimes the winter is so severe that they die; in the distance we perceive a shaggy ox, with savage eyes, the size of a small ass. Both plants and animals perish, or are stunted. In order to make such a land yield anything it must first be replanted with trees, as has been done in Sutherlandshire; a tree renews the soil, it also shelters crops, flocks and herds, and human beings.

The canal terminates in a series of lakes. Nothing is more noble than their aspect, nothing more touching. The water, embrowned by the peat, forms a vast shining plain, surrounded by a circle of mountains. In proportion as we advance each mountain slowly grows upon us, becomes more conspicuous, stands forth with its form and physiognomy; the farther blue peaks melt the one behind the other, diminishing towards the horizon, which they enclose. Thus they stand in position like an assemblage of huge, mournful beings around the black water wherein they are mirrored, while above them and the lake, from time to time, the sun flashes through the shroud of clouds.

At last the solitude becomes less marked. The mountains are half-wooded at first, and then wholly so; they dwindle down, the widening valleys are covered with harvest; the fresh and green verdure of the herbage which supplies forage begins to clothe the hollows and the slopes. We enter Inverness, and we are surprised to find at almost the extreme north of Scotland, on the border of the Highlands, a pretty and lively modern town. It stretches along the two banks of a clear and rapid river. Many houses are newly-built; we note a church, a castle, an iron bridge. In every part are marks of cleanliness, forethought, and special care. The window-panes shine, the frames have been painted; the bell-handles are of copper; there are flowers in the windows; the poorest houses are freshly white-washed. Well dressed ladies and carefully-dressed gentlemen walk along the streets. Even a desire to possess works of art is shown by Ionian pillars, specimens of pure Gothic, and other architectural gimcrackery, and these prove at least the search after improvement. The land itself is clearly of inferior quality; industry, order, economy, and labour have done everything. How great the contrast between all this and the aspect of a small town on the shores of the Mediterranean, so neglected and filthy, where the lower middle-class exist like worms in a worm-eaten beam!

I spent eight days in the neighbourhood with a friend. Nearly all the cottages are well-kept, or renovated. The small farms and the labourers' huts are surrounded with honeysuckle, and have gardens attached, filled with blooming roses. It is true these too low-built dwellings have often only a ground floor, and are narrow, because the cost of building materials is so high. It is also true that the ill-ventilated bed occupies an enclosed space in the wall because of the extreme cold in winter. Yet these drawbacks of soil and climate have been a spur to man. Everywhere, in the lowliest cottages, there are books—the Bible in the first place, in addition a few biographical works, books of travel, guides to health, hand-books of fishing, agricultural treatises, from eight to twenty volumes in all. Nearly all the Scotch peasants can read and write. Our entertainers shook hands with all the honest women and young girls, telling us to do likewise; the latter showed no signs of embarrassment. Each peasant considers himself master in his home, independent in spiritual as in temporal things, charged with his salvation, and this imparts to him a natural dignity. The rich and the gentry do not keep themselves to themselves, nor remain apart out of distrust, dislike, selfishness, as in France; they deliver public lectures, they expend some of their income on public works. A church built by one of them was pointed out to me; another, who has erected a suspension bridge, requests the passengers in a notice to walk their horses across it. The wall round his park is but two feet in height; every one may enter, to injure anything being alone forbidden.

Between Keith and Aberdeen I met an excursion train, in which all the carriages were crowded. Their occupants were going to a religious meeting, a gathering for edification, and the expression of Protestant emotion; a Revival which many celebrated preachers were to address. The crowd is so great that it is necessary to telegraph for more carriages, and yet in many carriages young girls may be seen sitting upon men's knees. My neighbour says that twenty thousand persons will be present; some of them come from great distances, from fifty to sixty miles. During the stoppage of the train, the women began to sing a psalm with an air of sincerity and conviction; the sacred music here is always grave and sweet, and never fails to afford me pleasure. The carriages are third-class, and their occupants are shopkeepers, workmen, agricultural labourers, all of them dressed like our lower middle class; their clothes, made of grey or brown cloth, are clean and often new; their physiognomies are lively and intelligent; the race appears more active, more astute than in England. These are the common people, but they are clearly better cultured than our villagers.

On arriving at the hotel, which was a temperance one, I found on the landlady's table, amid many moral romances and books of devotion, a tract containing an apology for Revivals. In it the exclamations, the faintings, and the impassioned manifestations are justified. "In the highest circles, a mother, a father, are beside themselves for joy when a son returns whom they had given up for lost, and no one condemns their conduct as irrational; how much more natural is it to act likewise when the soul suddenly feels that it is saved, being redeemed by grace?" A clergyman censures Sir Walter Scott in a newspaper for having brought the Covenanters into disfavour by his novels. To me it seems that the Presbyterian form of Protestantism is the appropriate poem here, sad, grandiose, limited in range, excellently fitted for leading man to look inwards, for rendering him inclined to labour, and for making him endure the burden of life.

At service, on Sunday, there are no paintings, statues, or instrumental music. The church is a plain meeting-house, supplied with seats, furnished with a gallery on the first-floor, very well adapted for public lectures; in truth, divine service here is nothing but a moral lecture. The minister takes for his text, "We must work out our own salvation," must not wait for help from others, must make an effort, must act by ourselves; God will help us, grant us His grace, not because of our exertions (it being given gratuitously), but in proportion to our exertions. The sermon was well delivered, soberly and judiciously, being devoid of set phrases or ejaculations. Though rather abstract, the precept is practical and may awaken reflections and individual reasoning in some heads, more especially in winter or when rain falls. To follow continuously such argumentation with the help of the Old or New Testament text is an occupation elevating to the mind and provocative of work for the conscience. Besides the sermon, the service consisted of reading certain passages of Scripture, especially from St. Paul; of prayers in prose spoken aloud, psalms and hymns sung by the congregation. The prayers and the hymns were correctly insipid and wholly modern; no one has really known how to address God since the great literary age of Shakespeare and Milton. But the psalms, though feebly rendered, are sustained by the strength of their sentiment and spirit; even at this day a soul in trouble, conscious of its responsibility, can enter into their meaning; they are the dialogue of the human heart and the Eternal Judge alone and face to face. By means of them, amidst controversial theology, dry preaching, and monotonous labour, the moral sentiment expands into a poetical flower. It is not too much to have one flower, one only, in a religion of which the usages and the dogmas resemble a thicket of briars. The congregation was very attentive; I am told that Scotland is even more religious than England; the most rigid Presbyterianism has not been considered in Scotland to be sufficiently rigid. In 1843, many persons thought that the presentation of ministers by a patron was contrary to the law of God; hence was formed the Free Church, which is maintained by the voluntary subscriptions of its members. She became the equal of the Established Church within the space of a few years. At present she has an income of £300,000 sterling; she has founded 700 schools; she has adherents in every village. From the trifling importance of the point in dispute, from the thoroughness of the separation that was effected, from the promptitude, the vastness, and the cost of the work which was accomplished, may be estimated the theological susceptibility and the zeal of the contributors. The like remark applies to Sunday observance; compared with that of Edinburgh, a London Sunday is pleasant.

The surrounding landscape is very neat and very pretty; the soil appears to be mediocre; but the tillage is less regular than in England. A ruder Nature lends herself more reluctantly to discipline; the surface is undulating and would please a painter. Flowers abound, they are delicate and dainty, more particularly the wild roses, which bloom along all the road-sides. Small, clear, and murmuring streams meander through the meadows. On the slopes the violet heaths are spread like a silken carpet under the scanty firs. Higher still are large patches of evergreen wood, and, as soon as the mountain is approached, a brown circle of barren eminences may be discerned towards the horizon. At the end of an hour the desert begins; the climate is inimical to life, even to that of plants. A tarn, the tint of burnt topaz, lies coldly and sadly between stony slopes whereon a few tufts of fern and heather grow here and there. Half a league higher is a second tarn, which appears still more dismal in the rising mist. Around, patches of snow are sprinkled on the peaks, and these descending in rivulets produce morasses. The small country ponies, with a sure instinct, surmount the bog, and we arrive at an elevation whence the eye, as far as it can reach, embraces nothing but an amphitheatre of desolate, yet green summits; owing to the destruction of the timber, everything else has perished; a scene of ruined nature is far more melancholy a spectacle than any human ruins. On our return across the lake, a bag-piper played on his instrument. The music is strange and wild, its effects harmonising with the aspect of the bubbling streams, veined with striking or sombre reflections. The same simple note, a kind of dance music, runs through the whole piece in an incorrect and odd manner, and continually recurs, but it is always harsh and rough; it might be likened to an orange shrivelled with the cold and rendered bitter.

These are the Highlands. From Braemar to Perth we journey through them for many long miles. It is always a solitude; sometimes five or six valleys in succession are wholly bare, and one may travel for an hour without seeing a tree; then for another hour it is rare merely to see in the distance a wretched twisted birchen-tree, which is dying or is dead. It would be some compensation if the rock were naked, and exhibited its mineral structure in all its fulness and ruggedness. But these mountains, of no great elevation, are but bosses with flabby outlines, they have fallen to pieces, and are stone heaps, resembling the remains of a quarry. In winter, torrents of water uproot the heather, leaving on the slopes a leprous, whitened scar, badly tinted by the too feeble sun. The summits are truncated, and want boldness. Patches of miserable verdure seam their sides and mark the oozing of springs; the remainder is covered with brownish heather. Below, at the very bottom, a torrent obstructed by stones, struggles along its channel, or lingers in stagnant pools. One sometimes discerns a hovel, with a stunted cow. The grey, low-lying sky, completes the impression of lugubrious monotony.

Our conveyance ascends the last mountain. At length we see a steep declivity, a great rocky wall, but it is unique. We descend again, and enter a habitable tract. Cultivation occurs first on the lower parts, then on the slopes; the declivities are wooded, and then entire mountains; forests of firs spread their sombre mantle over the crests; fields of oats and barley extend on all sides; we perceive pretty clumps of trees, houses surrounded by gardens and flowers, and then culture of all descriptions upon the lessening hills, here and there a park and a modern mansion. The sun bursts forth and shines merrily, but without heat; the fertile plain expands, abounding in promises of convenience and pleasure, and we enter Perth thinking about the historical narrations of Sir Walter Scott, and the contrast between the mountain and the plain, the revilings and scornings interchanged between the inhabitants of the Highlands and the Lowlands. From Perth to Edinburgh the landscape continues attractive and varied. More undulating, more fragmentary, poorer than England, Scotland is more picturesque; Nature, less uniform and less tractable, is not there a mere manufactory of milk and meat.

So is Edinburgh compared with London. Instead of a regular, modern, and flat city, the centre of business, of comfort, and of luxury, we find an old city rich in contrasts, extending over three valleys and several eminences, where steep streets, tall houses, the multiplied imprints of the past, afford unexpected views. A feudal castle crowns one of the heights. Thence, in descending towards Holyrood, along the sides of the street, old-fashioned alleys plunge abruptly towards the bottom; these are the wynds and closes, genuine dens of the middle ages, whereof the walls blackened by rain and smoke have retained their leprosy during four hundred years. Round or square towers cling together and hang over. Narrow, odd-looking and ill-shapen windows are barred like the air holes of a prison. Stone stairs, with low and slimy steps, wind in the obscurity of the interior, amidst creeping shadows of which a ray of light makes us feel the depth. On the steps are crowds of infants, with bare feet, white skulls, and crouching men taking food, recalling the fantastic figures, the semi-glooms, the strange guests which people the cellars of Rembrandt.

Quantities of statues, of Gothic and chiefly Grecian monuments, and two picture galleries. The Calton Hill, with its colonnade and two or three temples, aspires to be an Acropolis, and the erudite, lettered, and philosophical city styles itself the Northern Athens. But how greatly out of place is antique architecture here! The pale haze, scourged by the wind, floats and spreads itself in all directions. A vapoury veil lingers on the declivity of the Calton Hill and winds around its columns. The climate is at variance with these forms of a dry and warm country, and the wants, the tastes, the habits of the people here are more at variance still. For example, in this place the prevailing temptation is to give way to drunkenness; and temperance societies oppose it by a mixture of Biblical maxims and utilitarian arguments. Concerning this subject, I saw placards on which two expressive figures are pourtrayed, the one representing "a man," the worker, the other "a thing," the drunkard; while appropriate precepts are written underneath. Sixpence a day for ale and tobacco make so much at the year's end, and it is proved by statistics that with this sum so many articles of bedding or of furniture, so many pairs of shoes, so many shirts may be purchased along with the indispensable Family Bible. This calculation and this mention of the Bible are traits of character. On entering the picture gallery afterwards, and looking at the three or four great works by Vandyck, one by Garafolo, one by Veronese, and especially two sketches of women by Tintoret, I felt as if transported to the opposite side of the globe.

XXXV.

RETURN HOME. FRENCHMEN AND ENGLISHMEN.

LEAVING Edinburgh on the left, one beholds the sea, surrounded by distant mountains, which gradually diminish in height, and form a delicate and carefully-wrought border to the great shining deep. Berwick is passed, looking lively and picturesque, with its red-tiled houses and tranquil harbour, in which lie a few vessels. Farther on comes Newcastle, where the coal descends directly into ships for the supply of the coast towns of the North Sea, a city of coal and manufactories, black, smoky, and gloomy as a prison. Along the whole route the country is flat, and almost entirely destitute of trees or hedges; at intervals, however, a small wooded cove shelters a hamlet. But from one end to the other of this journey the sea is in sight, and the train skirts the coast, now being encompassed by, and now overhanging, a belt of rocks. The heart dilates before this vast shimmering sheet of water; the indistinct, even line, merges into the lower edge of the sky; tiny hillocks of foam fleck its azure with white spots. Two or three ships flit like birds in the distance; overhead, the great pale sky curves its vault, and we forget the troubled spectacle of the human ant-heap in reflecting afresh upon the calmness, the simplicity, and the divine immutability of things.

At York in the morning. A graceful and clear river shines softly between rows of Gothic towers; farther off is a bridge, a heap of black boats; we cross the water in a ferry-boat; there is nobody in the streets; the air reaches our cheeks as fresh as in the country. We pass by old-fashioned houses, of which each story overlaps the one below it; we see low archways, curved doors studded with large nails. Grass grows in the interstices of the pavement; in a square near the cathedral, trees, centuries old, spread their leafy domes. All is green, clean, peaceful, savouring of olden times, as in a Flemish city. The vast and venerable cathedral forms an addition to the resemblance. Intact without, this Gothic colossus rears itself higher and more spacious than Notre-Dame, with massive power, under the three towers which crown it. Within, the iconoclasts of the Reformation have stripped it; it is whitewashed, naked, and dismal. The only remnant of the old ornamentation is the enclosure of the choir, a labyrinth of carving, of statuettes, of hangings, of small sculptured pulpits, which commingle their forms with delicate and endless fantasy. How charming are these quiet old cities! But in the hurry of the journey such spectacles flit before the mind like so many pieces of scenery.

From York to London.—As my duty must be performed to the end, I remain in a third-class carriage for nine hours, in order to have a good view of the commonalty. The two most striking types are those I have previously met with — the sturdy individual and the worn-out individual, the one having the figure and broad shoulders of an athlete, ruddy complexion, red whiskers, eyes of a bull, rough gestures, a gruff or threatening expression, yet turning at times to kindliness when a smile lights it up or he is spoken to politely; the other having twinkling eyes, compressed features, his neckcloth tightened to the verge of strangulation, at once worn out and starched. Looking at the country people, I note that none have the form and mien of our peasants—that shrewd, defiant, yet astonished look which proclaims another species, a descendant of the labourers under compulsion, an ancient fellah, an intelligent yet uncultured race, still bound to the soil on which his heart is set, and which is the limit of all his thoughts. The villagers who enter at the intermediate stations have more the appearance of workmen or of small tradespeople; in truth an English farm is as much a manufactory as any other, giving employment to day labourers and bailiffs. From York to London the landscape confirms this idea. A square of verdure enclosed by a hedge, then another, and so on in succession, always of large extent, of monotonous regularity, without any of the varieties which denote small properties and peasant culture. In the same carriage with me is a Newcastle family, the husband, the wife, and her mother, small tradespeople, pretty well dressed and in new clothes. They are going to Venice for pleasure, and yet they are not rich, seeing that they travel third-class. Journeying so far in so uncomfortable a way, and at a cost necessarily considerable, manifests a very strong passion for travel. Families by no means well-to-do, with which I am acquainted, expend all their surplus in the same fashion; with their forty or fifty pounds of savings they go to the Continent every year—to Holland, to Norway. They put nothing aside; each year has to provide for its wants and suffice for its labour. My three fellow-passengers prepare themselves conscientiously; they have their Murray, a manual of Italian phrases, a special guide-book filled with figures for the passage over the Alps. The mother wearing spectacles, respectable, silent, resigned, sits bolt upright with the patience of a stoic upon the hard wooden seat. The wife cons Italian phrases, and looks up the words in a pocket dictionary. Her husband is qualified to fight the battle of modern existence; active, energetic, a face pitted with small-pox, earnest and ardent eyes. What strange visitors to Venice! Nevertheless, they are sensible folks, capable of learning, and who, if they do not appreciate painting, will bring back with them all kinds of information and useful notions. Since leaving Glasgow I have conversed with numbers of my fellow-passengers of the middle or lower class, a commercial traveller, a house-painter, shopkeepers, tavern-keepers. They never indulge in empty chatter; they have not too absurd ideas about foreigners; they are by no means hasty in speech; they are never boasters; I have always found that they possess a fund of upright and rational ideas.

London, Dover, and the Steamer in the rain.—From London to Dover in the first-class, a would-be gentleman proposed a game of cards to his neighbours, at which bets were made, every stake being five pounds. At first they refused, then they suffered themselves to be persuaded, and naturally they lost. I calculate that in an hour the card-player gained one hundred and fifty pounds. What struck me were the players' faces; not one wrinkle, not one gesture, not a single exclamation; concentrated and suppressed pride; but I divined the attraction, the dull and strong passion, the obstinacy, the determination to conquer. One of them, a stout and big man with the face of an immovable ox, constantly doubled his stake, drawing out his banknotes with the air of a combatant in a boxing-match. The risk pleases them, and produces the same effect on their minds that spirits do upon their palates.

One of my friends returned at the same time as myself, and we compared the result of our observations. Which of the two forms of civilisation is the more valuable, that of England or that of France? That is too vague; we must divide and distinguish. Three things are superior in England.

The Political Constitution.—It is stable, and is in no danger, like ours, of being forcibly overturned and remodelled every twenty years. It is liberal, and permits individuals to take part as actors or assistants in public affairs, instead of regarding them with mere curiosity; it confides their guidance to the upper class, which is best qualified to direct them satisfactorily, and which finds in so doing their natural occupation, in place of withering or being corrupted for want of something to do, as with us. It lends itself without perturbations to continued improvements, and tends in practice to good government, that which pays the most respect to individual initiative, and confides power to the most worthy. The English Three per Cents. are at 94; the citizens speak and form associations at pleasure: no Press in the world is equally well informed, nor are any assemblies equally competent.

Religion.—It subordinates rites and dogmas to morality. It inculcates self-government, the supremacy of conscience, the cultivation of the will. It leaves a sufficiently large space to interpretation and to individual sentiment. It is not actually hostile to the spirit of modern science, nor to the tendencies of modern times.

Its ministers are married; it founds schools; it approves of action; it does not counsel asceticism. Thus associated with the laity, it has authority over them; a young man entering life, the adult providing for his career, are restrained and guided up to a certain point by a collection of ancient, popular, and fortifying beliefs, which furnish them with rules of conduct and an exalted idea of the world. Among us a young man of twenty, being obliged to frame this rule by and for himself, does not succeed in doing so till late, sometimes does so imperfectly, or never does it at all.

The Greatness of the Acquired Wealth, combined with the Increased Power of Producing and Amassing.— Every useful work executed centuries ago, is transmitted and accumulated without loss; England has not been invaded for eight hundred years, and has had no civil war for two centuries. At the present day her capital is several times larger than that of France. The tokens of comfort and opulence are more numerous there than in any other country of the world. Examine the statistics, the calculations of her commerce, of her industry, of her agriculture, of her annual profits. This is true of moral as well as of physical matters; not only does England understand better than France how to manage her public and private affairs, enrich her soil, improve her cattle, superintend a manufacture, clear, colonize, and turn to account distant countries; but she knows still better how to cultivate herself. If we consider but the select few, we shall find, it appears, minds in France of equal calibre, except where politics are concerned, to the most notable minds of England, perhaps even a few superior minds, of wider and more philosophic range, at once more comprehensive and of finer mould. But the majority of those with an average intellect, a country gentleman, an ordinary clergyman, is endowed here with more extensive and more solid knowledge. Assuredly, his head is better furnished, his intellectual furniture being less old-fashioned and less incomplete. Above all, the number of persons adequately informed and capable of forming an opinion in political matters is much greater. Compare one of our English clergymen and English gentlemen with the *bourgeois* and *curés* of France; or, better still, examine in turn the daily food of their intellects, the English newspaper and the French newspaper, especially a French gazette of a small town and an English gazette of a small town; the distance is prodigious. Now, it is not the select few, it is the average majority which gives the tone, inspires opinion, conducts affairs. On the other hand, three things are better in France.

The Climate.—This is self-evident; yet without personal experience and prolonged reflection it is hard to imagine the effect of six or eight degrees of latitude at the least, in warding off bodily suffering and mental sadness.

The Distribution of Wealth.—There are four or five millions of landed proprietors in France, and properties after death are divided in equal portions among the children. On the whole, then, our institutions, our instincts, our habits combine to provide that no one has too large a slice, and that every one has a small one. Many live poorly, but nearly all can exist without too great difficulty. The wretched are less wretched; the labourer, entirely dependent upon the work of his hands, does not feel that beneath him yawns a dreadful abyss, a black and bottomless pit, in which, owing to an accident, a strike, an attack of sickness, he and his family will be engulfed; having fewer wants and fewer children he bears a lighter burden; besides, want debases him less, and he is less drunken.

Domestic and Social Life.—Several circumstances render it more easy and more enjoyable. In the first place, the natural temperament is gay, more open, and more neighbourly. Then the absolute, or nearly absolute, equality established by law or by custom between parents and children, between the eldest son and his younger brothers, between husband and wife, between the noble and the commoner, between the rich and the poor, suppresses much constraint, represses much tyranny, prevents much superciliousness, smoothes many asperities. In France, in the narrow domestic circle, the members open their hearts, enter into the spirit of the moment, combine to live together freely and affectionately; in the large social circle, they chat, display a half-confidence, meet together in order to pass an hour freely and pleasantly. There is less constraint at home and in society; kindliness and politeness supplant subordination with advantage. To my mind a human being among us feels less frequently and less heavily the pressure of another rough and despotic human being's hand upon his head. Final cause of expansion: one may say everything in conversation, tell a story and uphold a theory to the end. Romances, criticism, art, philosophy, violent curiosity, have not to submit to the trammels which religion, morality, and official propriety impose upon them across the Channel. At Paris we think with more independence, with a more entire disinterestedness, in a wholly abstract style, without pre-occupying ourselves about the consequences, without standing in dread of the thunders of public reprobation.

In fine, all these differences contribute to render the

Englishman more powerful and the Frenchman happier. The costume of the former is more substantial, that of the latter more comfortable. The former has reason for enlarging his garment which cramps him at the corners, the latter would act wisely in avoiding those hasty movements which may rend his flimsy material. But it appears to me that each of them has the style of dress which he prefers.

THE END.

BOOKS ABOUT FRANCE

TAINE'S JOURNEYS THROUGH FRANCE

Being Impressions of the Provinces. IlId. Large 12mo, $2.50.
"One who has never visited France will be able to learn from these brilliant notes of travel more of the peculiarities of the people who inhabit the various towns and cities, and of the cities themselves, than from any other work with which we are acquainted."—*Boston Transcript*.

TAINE'S NOTES ON PARIS

The Life and Opinions of M. Frédéric Graindorge. Translated, with Notes, by JOHN AUSTIN STEVENS. Large 12mo, $2.50.

TAINE'S ANCIENT RÉGIME

Translated by JOHN DURAND. Large 12mo, $2.50.

TAINE'S FRENCH REVOLUTION

Translated by JOHN DURAND. 3 vols., $7.50.

TAINE'S MODERN RÉGIME

Vol. I. Large 12mo, $2.50.

TAINE'S MODERN RÉGIME

Vol. II. Large 12mo, $2.50.

LADY JACKSON'S OLD PARIS: ITS COURTS AND LITERARY SALONS 12mo, $1.50.

"We claim for it picturesqueness, discrimination, much piquancy of detail, and a fine healthy tone of rebuke and protest which is refreshing. It is an admirable *résumé* of the period."—*Literary World*.

LADY JACKSON'S OLD RÉGIME, COURT, SALONS, AND THEATRES 12mo, $1.50.

ADOLPHUS'S SOME MEMORIES OF PARIS

Describes the Streets Forty Years Ago, Two Balls at the Hôtel de Ville, The Last Day of the Empire, Entry of the Germans, The Commune, The Opera, Indoor Life, etc. 12mo, $1.50.
"The most noteworthy chapters deal with the agony of the great city in 1870-71. A vivid description is given."—*Nation*.

DABNEY'S CAUSES OF THE FRENCH REVOLUTION

12mo, $1.25.

YONGE'S HISTORY OF FRANCE

A compact and reliable history (to 1879) by the popular novelist, with Twelve Maps. 16mo, 80c. *net*.

LACOMBE'S GROWTH OF A PEOPLE

Translated by LEWIS A. STIMSON. 16mo, 80c. *net*.

HENRY HOLT & CO., 29 West 23d Street New York

If you want to know
> Who wrote it,
> Who painted it,
> Who modelled it,
> Who built it,
> Who composed it,
> And what it was like,

Consult

The New Volume of Champlin's

Young Folks' Cyclopædia
Literature and Art

With 270 Illustrations
604 pp. 8vo. $2.50

As the author covers so many subjects, he of course is obliged to confine himself to the more important books, poems, plays, tales, pictures, statues, buildings, operas (grand and comic), symphonies and songs. And yet he might almost say of his book as a popular playwright said of his drama, that it was not only up to date but up to the day after to-morrow, for he includes such headings as "Sherlock Holmes," "David Harum," "Hugh Wynne," "To Have and to Hold," "The Man with the Hoe," and "Richard Carvel."

The scope of the book is remarkable, for though there are synopses of the plots of the leading operas (giving nearly half a page to Lohengrin, for instance), such half-forgotten ones as "Cortez" and "L'Elisire d'Amore" are not omitted. The index contains some 8700 references, covering all the principal characters in mythology and literature, while several of the characters have devoted to them articles additional to those on the books in which the characters appear.

Though written for the young, this book is in no way childish, and may serve equally well for adults, for whom it selects and arranges material from many large volumes.

∗∗∗ *12-page circular with sample pages of Champlin's four Young Folks' Cyclopædias and of his War for the Union, free.*

HENRY HOLT & CO. 29 West 23d Street, New York
378 Wabash Avenue, Chicago

New and cheaper edition

"One of the most important books on Music that has ever been published."—W. J. HENDERSON, *Musical Critic of* N. Y. TIMES.

LAVIGNAC'S MUSIC AND MUSICIANS

Translated by WILLIAM MARCHANT. Edited by H. E. KREHBIEL. With 94 illustrations and 510 examples in musical notation. 3d Impression. 504 pp. 12mo. $1.75 *net*. (Postage 18c.)

Dial: "If one had to restrict his musical library to a single volume, we doubt whether he could do better than select the work called 'Music and Musicians'... We find in this new volume the same lucidity of exposition, the same economy of arrangement, and the same comprehensiveness ... in fact, although not in form, a veritable encyclopædia of music and will be found equally satisfactory as a work of reference and as a text-book for the actual study of counterpoint, the structure of instruments, the history of music, and the physical basis of musical production. A few supplementary pages, by Mr. H. E. Krehbiel, add American composers to M. Lavignac's list, and put the finishing touch of usefulness upon a work which we cordially recommend to both students and general readers."

"It is impossible to speak too highly of this volume" (*Literary Review*, Boston)—"The most comprehensive reference-work on music published in a single volume and accessible to readers of English" (*Review of Reviews*)—"An encyclopædia from which all manner of curious facts may be drawn" (*Literary World*)—"A musical library in itself" (*Chicago Tribune*)—"A cyclopædia of knowledge concerning his art" (*Christian Register*)—"It adds a great deal that the student of music is not likely to get elsewhere" (*Springfield Republican*).—"The most complete and perfect work of its kind" (*The Home Journal*, New York)—"For the musical student and music teacher invaluable if not indispensable" (*Buffalo Commercial*)—"He has apportioned his pages with rare good judgment" (*Churchman*)—"It is of all things thorough" (*Brooklyn Eagle*)—"There is nothing superficial about it" (*Hartford Courant*)—"It has a reliability and authority which give it the highest value" (*Chicago Tribune*).—"Distinctly scientific" (*Providence Journal*)—"It seems to have been his desire to let no interesting topic escape . . . The wonder is that those parts of the book which ought to be dry are so readable . . . A style which can fairly be described as fascinating" (*N. Y. Times*)—"Free from superfluous technicalities" (*Providence Journal*)—"He has covered the field with French clarity and German thoroughness" (*Springfield Republican*). —"Not too technical to be exceedingly useful and enjoyable to every intelligent reader" (*Hartford Courant*)—"Lightened with interesting anecdotes" (*Brooklyn Eagle*).—"He writes brilliantly: even the laziest or most indifferent will find that he chains the attention and makes a perusal of the history of music a delightful recreation" (*N. Y Home Journal*)

"Capitally indexed. . . Mr. Marchant has done his hard task of translating exceedingly well" (*Transcript*).—". The pictures of the instruments are clear and helpful" (*N Y Times*).—"An unusually handsome book" (*Musical Record*)—"This superb volume" (*The Watchman*)—"This handsome volume, . . elegantly printed on the best of paper, and the illustrations are numerous" (*Christian Register*)—"An excellent translator" (*Providence Journal*).—"Well translated" (*School and Home Education*)—"The translation is excellent; . . . handsomely bound." *Home Journal*).

HENRY HOLT & CO., 29 West 23d St., New York
378 Wabash Ave., Chicago

ROWAN & RAMSEY'S ISLAND OF CUBA

A descriptive and historical account of the "Great Antilla." With bibliography, colored maps, points of international law bearing on the Cuban question, index, etc. 279 pp. 16mo. $1.25.

This authoritative book has passed through five impressions.

"It answers clearly and concisely just the questions which a thoughtful reader mentally asks. . . . The style is so graphic, at times picturesque, that reading for information is an intellectual delight."—*Boston Advertiser.*

"A clear and judicial account of Cuba and its history, evidently the result of careful and impartial investigation."—*Dial.*

"The authors' opinions on the Cuban question are of interest and value."—*Philadelphia Times.*

BAZIN'S ITALIANS OF TO-DAY

Translated by WILLIAM MARCHANT. 247 pp. 12mo. $1.25.

Treats of Elections, Excessive Taxation, Building Speculations, the Unification of Italy, Currency, Brigands, Universities, Literature, Music, etc.

"The translator has done the English-speaking world a valuable service. . . . A most readable book, not only because of its first-hand information, . . . but also because of its fair, free, and lucid manner of relating what the author has seen. . . . He touches upon everything."—*Boston Transcript.*

"It is quite an ideal book for cultivated readers whose tastes are not particularly specialized. . . . There is not a dull page in the whole book."—*Nation.*

CHEVRILLON'S IN INDIA

Translated by WILLIAM MARCHANT. 265 pp. 12mo. $1.50.

"No other than a poet with sensibilities quickly responsive to every impression of nature, and the mystery of life dominated by the profoundly impressive religions of the Orient, could have written such a book."—*Book Buyer.*

"It is never dull."—*Nation.*

"Few volumes of travel are so completely impregnated with the spirit of the country they describe."—*Atlantic.*

"Full of air and color, vivid, tense, and delicate in style."—*Dial.*

"A masterpiece."—*Critic.*

HENRY HOLT & CO. 29 West 23d Street, New York.

"More entertaining than any fiction."
—*Literary World.*

3d Impression of a remarkable book that is attracting attention in the United States, Great Britain, and Germany.

THE COURTOT MEMOIRS

The Memoirs of the Baroness Cecile de Courtot, Lady-in-Waiting to the Princess de Lamballe. Edited by MORITZ VON KAISENBERG. Translated by Miss JESSIE HAYNES. 298 pp. 8vo. $2.00.

This notable narrative of the love and adventures of the Baroness includes remarkably vivid descriptions of France during the Terror, Prussia under Frederick William III. and the beautiful Queen Louise, and France under the all-powerful First Consul.

N. Y. Times Saturday Review: "It has all the charm of a good historical novel. . . . The entire volume will be found of much interest, mainly through the great human interest centring around the friendship of these two devoted women, Cecile and Annaliebe, as well as through the historical details introduced, which are all graphically and fully treated."

Outlook: "This delightful Memoir. . . . Some of the most interesting impressions of the great ruler [Napoleon] which have yet appeared. The Memoir reads like a novel."

N. Y. Tribune: "The book is one of the strangest and most amusing ever produced in the department of revolutionary literature. . . . The Baroness is charming, and has much to say about many interesting personalities and events."

Pall Mall Gazette (London): "We are admitted behind the scenes and mingle with the actors in perhaps the most powerful drama the world has ever witnessed. . . . A most fascinating book. Here is a period that we have read about from our youth up . . . and we might almost say that we see it now for the first time."

Home Journal: "The pages are certainly of unusual interest, showing intimacy with personages and places, and throwing such light on them that we seem to see them almost as if we were eye-witnesses. . . . Filled with tragedy and romance."

HENRY HOLT & CO.   29 West 28d Street
New York

"A remarkable romance . . . told with wonderful skill."—*N. Y. Times' Saturday Review*

THE WINDING ROAD

By ELIZABETH GODFREY. 12mo. $1.50

Referring to the "best selling novels," *The Literary World* says: "A list of the best novels without reference to their 'selling' would be very much more to the purpose." Then it gives a list of nine of what it considers "the best novels" recently published. Among them are THE WINDING ROAD and THE WOOING OF SHEILA. In a "buying list of recent books recommended by the library commissions of Iowa, Minnesota, Wisconsin, Idaho, Nebraska, and Delaware," books of unusual merit are marked †, and those recommended for first purchase with an asterisk. The only book receiving both marks is THE WINDING ROAD.

"A winningly fantastic story of a gypsy wanderer, a gypsy fiddle, and a girl who was not a gypsy. . . . Miss Godfrey has contrived to combine and expand her materials in a fresh and original way, and has made a new and pretty tale."—*Nation*.

"As wild a story as ever was thought of, and in its conception undoubted talent has been shown. . . . It shows that Elizabeth Godfrey has brilliant literary capabilities. . . . Will surely leave an impress on the memory of the reader."—*N. Y. Times' Saturday Review*.

"This charming story. . . . A prose poem."—*Philadelphia Times*.

"A welcome relief from the current trend of fiction "—*Book-Buyer*.

"Miss Godfrey has written nothing but what was good, but 'The Winding Road' is her best. . . . A true romance of the road, the road that runs at nightfall straight into the enchanted land which, willy nilly, must be explored to-morrow. . . . By those to whom its speech is the vernacular and whose taste it hits, it will be counted a beautiful book—a handful of well water to one athirst in the desert."—*Chicago Post*.

"Seen with poetic vision and touched with delicate skill."—*Outlook*.

"Remarkable for its artistic truth. . . . The character of Jasper is a real human document. . . . The fascination of the story resides to a considerable extent in the mystery of the man's origin . . . The travels of the pair in France, Greece, and elsewhere seem, like the character drawing, to be based on actual experience. It is a story of unusual attraction."—*Brooklyn Eagle*

"One of the few notable books of the season."—*Era*.

Two Earlier Novels by Miss Godfrey

POOR HUMAN NATURE. $1.50

A STORY OF OPERA SINGERS.

"It is curiously convincing. . . . It is well written, it is nobly felt, it is altogether an admirable work."—*Bookman*.

THE HARP OF LIFE. $1.50

A STORY OF AN ENGLISH VIOLINIST.

"She has literary skill, grace, delicacy. . . . Her artistic sense is very keen. The characterization is effective throughout . . . This masterly tale."—*Boston Transcript*.

HENRY HOLT & CO.   29 West 23d Street, New York

vii '02

Lightning Source UK Ltd.
Milton Keynes UK
UKHW050858070422
401177UK00015B/378